The End of God-Talk

The End of God-Talk

An African American Humanist Theology

ANTHONY B. PINN

OXFORD
UNIVERSITY PRESS

OXFORD
UNIVERSITY PRESS

Oxford University Press, Inc., publishes works that further
Oxford University's objective of excellence
in research, scholarship, and education.

Oxford   New York
Auckland   Cape Town   Dar es Salaam   Hong Kong   Karachi
Kuala Lumpur   Madrid   Melbourne   Mexico City   Nairobi
New Delhi   Shanghai   Taipei   Toronto

With offices in
Argentina   Austria   Brazil   Chile   Czech Republic   France   Greece
Guatemala   Hungary   Italy   Japan   Poland   Portugal   Singapore
South Korea   Switzerland   Thailand   Turkey   Ukraine   Vietnam

Published by Oxford University Press, Inc.
198 Madison Avenue, New York, New York 10016

www.oup.com

Oxford is a registered trademark of Oxford University Press

Library of Congress Cataloging-in-Publication Data
Pinn, Anthony B.
The end of God-talk: an African American humanist theology / Anthony B. Pinn.
p.   cm.
Includes bibliographical references (p.).
ISBN 978-0-19-534083-9 (pbk. : alk. paper)—ISBN 978-0-19-534082-2 (hardcover : alk. paper)
1. African Americans—Religion.   2. Humanism—United States.   I. Title.
BL2525.P56   2012
211'.608996073—dc23   2011019519

1 3 5 7 9 8 6 4 2

Printed in the United States of America
on acid-free paper

Dedicated
to
Justin Anthony Valentin
and
Raymond W. Pinn, Jr. (1950–2011)

CONTENTS

ACKNOWLEDGMENTS

This book has been almost twenty years in the making, with bits and pieces of its argument developed and presented in various forms. However, the full expression of the ideas and claims that constitute this book is recent, and it is a result of a great deal of assistance and encouragement. I must begin by thanking my editor, Theo Calderara, for his encouragement, good humor, and patience. I would also like to thank the external readers who provide important questions and comments that helped me shape the manuscript. In addition, a host of colleagues provided important insights and critique along the way. Thank you to Stacey Floyd-Thomas, Juan Floyd-Thomas, James H. Cone, Katie G. Cannon, Peter Paris, Charles Long, James Evans, Gordon Lynch, and Miguel De La Torre. My graduate students (current and former)—over the course of classroom conversation, in African American Religious Studies Forum meetings, and within the context of other venues—provided insights that sharpened my work. Thank you. The embrace of my definition of religion and the resulting conversations initiated by Monica Miller, Terrence Johnson, and others were very helpful along the way. I must also thank the students who took my "African American Nontheistic Humanist Theology" course at Meadville Lombard Theological School. Their questions and comments during our week together helped me to clarify my thinking in significant ways. I would also like to thank Sharon Welch for the invitation to teach the course. Thank you all.

Much of the work on this book was completed during time away from teaching granted by the Religious Studies Department and Dean of Humanities at Rice University. I must also thank Maya Reine, the HERE Project coordinator, for taking on additional responsibilities and, in that way, helping me carve out writing time. I appreciate greatly the space and freedom that constitute my work environment at Rice. A good number of friends at Rice helped with this project in a variety of ways. They include Alexander Byrd, Edward Cox, and Michael Emerson. In particular, Caroline Levander took time from her own projects to read the full manuscript and offer comments that improved greatly the ideas in this book.

I want to thank my family and friends outside of Rice for their good wishes, good humor, care, and comfort—Linda, Joyce, Terry, Craig, Ashley, Morgan, Sidney, Sha-Nikka, Shelly, Richard, Raea, Reese, Ben, Eli, Ramon, Stacey, Juan, Janet, and Mother Floyd. Thank you all. Finally, this volume is dedicated to my godson, Justin Anthony Valentin, and to my brother, Raymond W. Pinn, Jr. In this way, the book is dedicated to new life and the memory of the ancestors: In both life and death, we find and recognize ourselves.

NOTE ON TERMINOLOGY

The full name of the theology presented here is African American nontheistic humanist theology. I understand the phrase is bulky, but it is necessary as a way to distinguish its various elements over against traditional black and womanist theologies, or liberation theologies in more general terms. To account for this bulkiness and to lessen its impact, I fluctuate between the full name and shorter versions such as nontheistic humanist theology or humanist theology. The same is the case for African American nontheistic humanism, which is reduced at times to nontheistic humanism, African American humanism, and so on. Readers should understand that the shortened designations do not entail a change in meaning or context. Rather, the aim is to adjust the name to foster flow and smooth out the prose to the extent possible.

The End of God-Talk

Introduction

The New Atheism has generated a great deal of conversation and debate. Its raw disregard for religion has received applause from some atheists and humanists, a corrective from some other humanists who do not find blanket condemnations of religion justifiable particularly in light of the scientism often embedded in the New Atheism, and apologetics for religion from those who embrace one tradition or another. This pattern of response is to be expected, but less common is discussion concerning the nature and meaning of theology resulting from the a/theist culture wars.

Some have denounced theology as religion's voice of un/reason—the effort to give systematic justification to the superstition that is religion. Others promote theological inquiry as a viable mode of human thinking on the most significant existential and ontological issues facing humans, in part because it works through the cultural wor(l)ds of human existence in ways the natural sciences cannot. What seems tacit within both of these perspectives is the assumption that atheists need not read theological texts, and, what is more, they should not (or, more forcefully, cannot) *do* theology. And this assumption is based on an often unchallenged and a literal defining of theology as "god-talk." No God, no theology. Figures in both of these groups of thought will find this book odd at best and, at worst, a dangerous mutation of atheism and theism. They might take this stance in that I am a humanist, one without belief in God, yet, I am one who takes seriously theology as a method by which to analyze human experience. In other words, theology need not revolve around attempts to prove the existence of God or to articulate the ramifications of this existence; such is only one mode of theological inquiry.

I not only read theology *as* a humanist but also have for almost two decades taught and written theological materials. What might confuse some within the a/theism culture wars even more is that I am an African American, a member of a community assumed to be deeply religious and dependent on god-based theological argumentation for the forging of geography of freedom over against racism and other modalities of oppression. After all, as some are quick to point out, recent studies highlight the widespread religiosity (e.g., belief in god and prayer) marking African American communities in the United States.[1] Over objections and perhaps dismissal by many atheists and theists, I think there are ways in which the conceptualization and practice of humanism, in this case African American nontheistic humanism, might benefit from theological analysis. That is to say, while much of theological grammar and vocabulary has run its course and offers nothing of value (e.g., the empty notion of god[s] or a god/human savior), there are ways in which the basic structural arrangements and moral/ethical markers within theological discourse still have some utility. Yet, certain questions are asked with great persistence.

Does theology really have any value within the contemporary world? Does it offer humankind valuable modes of thinking and living? At the conclusion of one of the components of a conversation with atheists, including Richard Dawkins, I was asked a version of these questions. While not having time to discuss the questions in full within that context, I begin this book with a response: There are certain modalities of theological discourse that lack the perspective and grounding necessary to offer balanced and reasonable answers to pressing moral and ethical questions, within the context of the democratically arranged public arena. However, this is not a good reason for condemnation of all theological platforms. In the same way phrenology and other pseudo-sciences (e.g., the Tuskegee Experiment) did not taint all scientific investigation, the full enterprise of theological discourse is not brought into question because of numerous flawed approaches. As with the distinctions one would make concerning various scientific legacies, one must also distinguish types of theology. There are ways in which theology—certain types of theology—raise the epistemological and ontological questions and highlight the cultural worlds underexplored in other quarters. For example, the "We are all Africans" T-shirts popular in atheist quarters speak a certain scientific truth. Based on the findings, who can argue with the science behind this statement? However, taken alone, the scientific "truth" of this proclamation does not wrestle with its cultural implications in light of colonial processes and structures that still affect the continent of Africa and people of African descent across the globe. Again, while scientifically accurate, it requires the humanities in general and the special abilities of theology in particular to interrogate the cultural implications and cultural pitfalls of this scientifically reasonable statement: "We are all Africans." In other words, the humanities in general and in this case theology in particular allow for interrogation of the cultural underpinning found within all human endeavors. It does so by surfacing the cultural assumptions and cultural beliefs embedded in our activities and interactions. This is all to say that yes, theology has a purpose; it addresses important needs that should be recognized even by atheists. That is the case, of course, when the more damning trappings of theological legacy and assumptions are stripped away. What follows in these pages is an effort to provide such a theology, one for and from my particular community of concern—the humanist community, in particular the nontheistic humanist community.

The End of God-Talk, as a nontheistic humanist theology, asserts God has never been anything more than a symbol—an organizing framework for viewing and living life in "relationship to...." This symbol has run its course, and it is no longer capable of doing the heavy lifting required for the contemporary world.[2] God is a matter of human need and desire, a schizophrenia of a theological kind. However, this need not remain the case. God is unnecessary, even for theologians – both humanist and "Christian." Concerning the latter, for example, "The Death of God radical theologians," writes William Hamilton, "are men without God who do not anticipate his return. But it is not a simply not-having, for there is an experience of loss. Painful for some, not so for others, it is loss nonetheless. The loss is not of the idols, or of the God of theism, but of the God of the Christian tradition...."[3] Death of God theology is a eulogy. It is a eulogy because the discourse involves both a passing and a call/celebration of life left behind. Hamilton and Thomas Altizer, along with their supporters, promoted recognition of new life without the same boundaries of expression. The eulogy points to something deceptively immanent, marked out in the context of otherness. It involves attention to paradox as the hallmark of Christianity. Regarding this stance, the appeal to Dietrich Bonhoeffer is explicit with Hamilton, who writes:

> My Protestant has no God, has no faith in God, and affirms both the death of God and the death of all the forms of theism. Even so, he is not primarily a man of negation, for if there is a movement away from God and religion, there is the more important movement into, for, toward the world, worldly life, and the neighbor as the bearer of the worldly Jesus.[4]

And Hamilton continues:

> Not only our waiting but our worldly work is Christian too, for our way to our neighbor is not only mapped out by the secular social and psychological and literary disciplines, it is mapped out as well by Jesus Christ and his way to his neighbor. Our ethical existence is partly a time of waiting for God and partly an actual Christology.[5]

Altizer makes a similar claim when saying, "'God is Dead' are words that may only truly be spoken by the Christian, not by the religious Christian who is bound to an eternal and unmoving Word, but by the radical Christian who speaks in response to an Incarnate Word that empties itself of Spirit so as to appear and exist as flesh."[6]

Those within the Death of God movement (a movement that by its negation of God still pointed to the presence of God) faced a firestorm of resentment because they refused to think of themselves as anything other than Christians who replaced God with a robust Christology. But what I suggest in the following pages does not claim the Christian label—it is not an attempt to reformulate black Christian theology in more acceptable terms. Instead, it is concerned with African American nontheistic humanism as a robust system of life meaning. Consequently, it is a theology meant to unpack—to explore and explain—the religious reality of humanism. But to accomplish robust work regarding life meaning, and to do so within the context of theological discourse, actually requires the end of *God*-talk. This is the end of usage but not the "death" of God. African American nontheistic humanist theology understands that symbols such as God don't die; they lose their function and are replaced—like any piece of intellectual machinery. The question has been asked by Mary Daly and others: Do verbs die, or do they fade away? The language of God has been invested with too much responsibility and required to carry too large a conceptual load as it carried the weight of all other religious symbols and signs. Yet, this need not be the case in that the very idea that something exists behind the symbol God is a human safeguard, a mechanism for protecting signs and symbols because of the ontological burden they bear. To lose this illusion, by extension, would necessitate a religious maturity—recognition that we have constructed the conceptual arrangements of this world and we must alone bear responsibility for this framing of life.

This nontheistic theology holds to geography of life with a vocabulary and grammar found within the context of the stuff of human embodied existence. Furthermore, what I suggest here is sensitive to postmodern formulations of life, and it entails theologizing in a way that does and does not resemble the dominant theological traditions of the West. In this regard, it theologizes without theology (i.e., *God*-talk), and in the process leaves the Black Church behind.[7] Ultimately, it, and the end of *God*-talk, is premised on an alternate definition of theology: *Theology is a method for critically engaging, articulating, and discussing the deep existential and ontological issues endemic to human life. So defined, African American nontheistic humanist theology is a way for African American humanists to speak and critique their collective life stories as these stories are guided by the structures and practices of nontheistic humanism as a quest for complex subjectivity.*, This reformulation of theology hinges on embodied aesthetics as opposed to *imago Dei*.[8] Accordingly, African American nontheistic humanist theology begins not with the proclamation of God's good health and efforts on our behalf, but rather with the end of the symbol God and the presentation of an alternate means of centering. It begins with an embrace of God's (already always) absence and continues by rethinking various dimensions of embodied life once assumed dependent on God(s). Herein is a sticking point: an atheistic turn to a new theology? In response, nontheistic theology is the logical outgrowth of African American nontheistic humanist life; it is the next step in theologizing when the lack of utility in traditional God-talk is acknowledged. The remainder of this book is an unpacking and explanation of this claim.

Presentation of a New Plan

The End of God-Talk, after the introduction, turns to a fundamental question: out of what material is this theological discourse built? While acknowledging the importance of sources traditionally used to develop black and womanist theologies, chapter 1 alters the doing (and consequently the findings) of theology by privileging nonwritten "texts"—the most significant being the body. In short, this chapter begins where other forms of African American theology end—with the implications of embodiment for the doing of theology. This sense of embodiment as theological resource is worked out here in two ways: photography and architecture. I turn to these two because they highlight the great potential offered by nonwritten materials, and they are ordinary items accessible in a variety of ways.

In chapter 2, the nature and meaning of nontheistic humanist religion is outlined as the subject matter for nontheistic humanist theologizing. It is argued that religious experience is *religious* in that it addresses the search for meaning in its most significant form(s), also called complex subjectivity. It is humanistic in that meaning does not entail transcendence *beyond* this world, and it is African American because it is shaped by and within the context of African American historical realities and cultural creations. The organizing principle of humanist religion is defined as "community." Community here is not a collective composed of various modalities of life—humans and other animals, for example. It is a more expansive framework. In part, the scope of this sense of community is worked out over against the sense of God as restraint found in the biblical story of Nimrod and the Tower of Babel.

In chapter 3, attention is given to the theological anthropology—the nature and meaning of the human as subject—guiding African American nontheistic humanist theology. In developing it, traditional appeals to *imago Dei* are stripped away, and biological and cultural embodiment is suggested as the centering reality of the human as subject. This form of humanism buttresses the worth of African American humanity through a rejection of standard theological anthropology and Christology found in African American Christian churches— denial of disciplining the body or keeping it in line as the method of transformation. Working through figures such as Foucault, Stephen Jay Gould, and Edward O. Wilson, the chapter argues for the body (both material and cultural creation) as the focus of theological anthropology. And finally, this is worked out through critical attention to the artwork of Jean-Michel Basquiat.

Based on theological anthropology noted in chapter 3, as well as the focus on community in chapter 2, chapter 4 argues for African American nontheistic humanism as a religious orientation that rethinks the typical African American Christian discomfort with the body, or disciplining of the body, as a required act for salvation. In place of suspicion concerning the body, African American nontheistic humanism proposes a radical embrace of the body. Rather than the sense of salvation marking much black and womanist theology (either personal engagement with the divine or salvation as new social arrangements), African American nontheistic humanist theology draws from the work of physicists and speaks in terms of the desired outcome of activity and thought as symmetry.

Chapter 5 outlines humanist ethics. The measured realism of African American humanism and nontheistic humanist theology pushes for a system of ethics that acknowledges the plausibility of human failure in its quest for meaning. Drawing on figures such as Henry David Thoreau, Harriet Tubman, and Frederick Douglass, nontheistic humanist ethics as outlined here gives primary attention to the implications of deliberation, attention to the particularities of life, and a sense of proper ethics as revolving around the fostering of good people whose shortcomings and failures much be acknowledged.

How does the humanist ritualize or celebrate the push toward complex subjectivity? The sixth and final chapter offers an answer to this question by first arguing that the significance given to humanity—the value placed on life within the existential contexts of human history, without appeal to transcendence—invests with deep meaning what theists might consider mundane and inconsequential activities such as eating a meal with loved ones or walking through one's neighborhood. These ordinary events, in a sense, become sacramental activities of a sort—activities that celebrate our efforts toward complex subjectivity. So conceived, this chapter offers a perspective on the sacramental nature of ordinary life—the depth of meaning found in the uneventful events of life. In addition, it argues for the possibility of group ritual processes based on the deep appreciation for the human body noted in earlier chapters. Finally, to develop some sense of these ritual processes and the location(s) for these processes, the chapter turns to an analysis of the nature and dynamics of the sacralization of life as body-based found in the work of Richard Wright and Lorraine Hansberry.

The conclusion following chapter 6 seeks to bring the project full circle by highlighting some of the book's basic claims and providing context for its argument and findings. It, in certain respects, is a clarifying statement and invitation to engagement in critical discourse and innovation.

In the end, within these six chapters and conclusion, I present an earthy theology, an embodied theology—a historically grounded and dependent articulation of humanity's big concerns. It is my hope this project will spark debate and additional development. Communities of African American humanists and the enterprise of religious studies deserve that much.

1

The Ordinary as Theological Source Material

African American nontheistic humanist theology has no sacred texts in a traditional sense because it pays no allegiance to the idea of revealed materials that link the transcendent and human history.[1] The Hebrew Bible and the Christian scriptures have some metaphorical or symbolic value through their teaching of both positive and negative life lessons, and to the extent this is the case, nontheistic theology understands them to offer source material for theologizing humanism. However, these books are read devoid of any sense that they contain some form of revelation from cosmic forces, and highlighted (as will be evident elsewhere in this book) instead is the appeal to humanistic frameworks lodged in these storybooks. Furthermore, these texts and their insights are no more significant and hold no greater meaning than what one gathers, for example, from the literary imaginings of figures such as Richard Wright and Toni Morrison. Nontheistic theology, then, makes use of African American literature, for example, with as much vigor as texts considered sacred within theistic theological discourses. They—African American literature and biblical stories—are simply part of cultural production, the cultural matrix of human expression. Nontheistic theology also draws from the visual arts and other modalities of expressive and material culture for insights regarding the quest for complex subjectivity.

While the theology outlined in this volume gives no special attention to the Christian tradition, unlike black and womanist theologies, it does share their concern with African American experience and history as theological source materials. Yet, it does not read these through the Christ Event as pointing toward the outcome of salvation history. Rather, African American experience and history are mined for what they say about humanist sensibilities and practices. In a word, these materials are all viewed for how they explicate the humanist tradition.

Although appreciating and making use of written texts, African American nontheistic humanist theology suggests an alternate perspective on source materials through the centrality of the body and the embodied self's presentation in time and space as marker of the religious. Through this focus on embodiment (e.g., what bodies do and where they are when in/active as text), strict privileging of the written text is brought into question.[2] Thereby this humanist theology seeks to interrogate more fully the ways in which the how and why of embodied selves occupying time and space get articulated. In a word, like other modalities of theologizing, it is a "secondary order enterprise," to borrow a phrase from Gordon Kaufman, because it follows on the heels of experience and serves to articulate through a particular lens the nature and meaning of that experience.[3] It is only through the investigation of a wide range of cultural markers of life that this brand of theology is able to articulate the rich and layered nature of humanism.

Some sense of this commitment is expressed through my mention of the visual arts, for example, yet more should be said. And notwithstanding the numerous possibilities, this chapter gives attention to two: photography and architecture.[4] These two modalities of storytelling provide graphic examples of how the structuring of religious space and meaning is framed and articulated within ordinary life episodes and contexts.[5] For instance, thought behind the taking of the photographic image—the arrangement of the body (e.g., the pose) and the dressing of the body, as well as how the actual photograph is handled and shared—says something about the nature and meaning of the embodied self stretching toward complex subjectivity, and it does so in ways begging for theological attention. Architecture offers a way to understand how time and space are consciously reconfigured to provide a *p(l)ace* for ritualization of mundane happenings of so much importance to nontheistic humanists.

Photographs as Theological Resource

So as to suggest the theological value of both individual and collective experiences and framings of life, this discussion of the photographic image begins on a personal note. Furthermore, this turn toward the personal—appeal to a particular embodied self—avoids the tendency in black theology to speak in terms of and theologize from the vantage point of a generic or ideal black person. In this regard, and concerning particular dimensions of the engagement of embodied selves, capturing moments of an individual life in photographs has significant import. In the words of Susan Sontag:

> Not to take pictures of one's children, particularly when they are small, is a sign of parental indifference.... Through photographs, each family constructs a portrait-chronicle of itself....[6]

Consistent with Sontag's comment, many of the more significant moments of my life have been captured in photographic form. Early childhood years dressed in Easter outfits, school activities, roughhousing with neighborhood friends, and those church functions marking my early religious identity are all fixed in film and shelved away. Whether staged or spontaneous placements in time and space, and lodged within the fabric of my social existence, these photographs tell a story. They capture beyond words the shape and texture of life experienced.[7] Some forty years after many of those photographs were taken, they continue to help *re*-member and contextualize patterns of self-expression, patterns of just ... *be-ing*. Taken by friends and family, they serve to humanize and present my inclusion in the social body—my relationship to (my)self and to others. They speak with a texture and richness that is impossible through speech or the written word with the same intensity and focus.

During the years I was involved in church ministry, people who "read" the photographs often remarked—although there were not clear signs of this, such as a robe or Bible in hand—that I looked like a preacher. They read my body vis-à-vis photographic images and concluded that I *looked* like a preacher? By this comment, they meant to sum up through the arrangement of my physical body an ethical, epistemological, and existential calling. From their perspective, through the photographs was present a way of gauging an overall posture toward the world, and suggested by this reading is a porous discursive body and a supple material body. The former is porous in that the perspectives and inclinations of the reader easily infiltrate the discursive body, and the latter is supple in that it accommodates these inclinations and the accompanying reworked discursive body. Regardless of the expressive culture engulfing the material body and informing the discursive body—that is, clothing, hairstyle, and so on—readers noted a preacher. The reading was not simply a social depiction of my space, but rather it was a depiction of religiosity, an exploration of my ontology vis-à-vis the aesthetics of vocation.[8] Viewing the photographs in this way held in tension the discursive body (framework of worn vocation) and the physical body (the materiality of vocation). The overlap between these two, the degree to which they produce a creative tension accounted for the strength of the statement: "You look like a preacher!" It is possible that this reading was informed and influenced by their knowledge of my vocational interests and in this way served as communal affirmation. However, the same is said at times now although my vocational inclinations have changed radically. (Would exposure of my tattoos and the exchange of my modest earring for more "bling" alter this perception, if the photos were updated vis-à-vis figure 1.1?).

These anecdotal remarks point to an important dimension of embodiment: the manner in which the material body serves as an archive of sorts. It stores the workings of the discursive body. It preserves elements of the social body, while

Figure 1.1

opening them for examination and review at any time. Photography, hence, provides what Shawn Michelle Smith calls "visual narrative" by which knowledge is made and stored.[9] When assembled with intentionality, or archived, photographs outline, critique, or confirm particular discourses.[10] The photograph diagrams embodied meaning in ways that can be rather compelling. Reading photographs, by extension, means more than sensory perception as biological. Deciphering photographs entails this and much more in that it involves, as Kathryn Geurts remarks, sensing "bodily ways of gathering information" that affect "cultural identity" and also "forms of being-in-the-world."[11] That which is perceived, then, in this case photographs, involves more than moments of monitored time because they pull the subject into herself and the reader out of herself. Or as bell hooks remarks regarding a photograph of her father, "such is the power of the photography, of the image, that it can give back and take away, that it can bind."[12] In this sense, the presentation of images through photography is a force of multiple and fluidlike determinations. Photography offers a graphic language, one that seeks to position the embodied self.[13]

Images are powerful, and this power has been both appreciated and met with some discomfort over the course of time. Consistent with the nature of human experience, they present the senses with information that can both enlighten and confuse.[14]

A simple definition of the photograph is "light-writing," a type of "communication through images."[15] It represents in content and form effort to frame the world, to capture moments of experience for consumption and expansion. Although one can make distinctions concerning the use of the photograph as means of communication (expert or amateur), and one can make distinctions concerning equipment used and the mode of presentation, I am less concerned with debate over photography as art or the dynamics of its development. And I am more concerned with how this light-writing is read and what it says about the nature and meaning of nontheistic humanism as the quest for complex subjectivity read through bodies in time and space.[16] In the photographic image, bodies and their surroundings—the signs and symbols associated with them—are held in place but not rendered stable, in that they are open to investigation and review.[17] What photographs, some more so than others, entail can either support existing structures—racism, sexism, classism, homophobia, and so on—or resist and challenge the dominance of these structures. Bodies depicted, then, could represent the docile and acceptable, or bodies could depict resistance to those standards.[18] It is also possible that bodies could both confirm and deny these standards. For example, early photographs commissioned by African Americans that displayed their families as orderly, aesthetically sound, and situated within comfortable surroundings signified discourses on black inferiority represented by poor family structure, general antisocial tendencies, and the physical scars of punishment.[19] But these images also can further normalize these same notions of the proper role and postures related to the aesthetics of masculinity and femininity for men and women, respectively, because images are thought, presented, and read within the larger framework of our cultural world(s). Even more to the point, "we wear our identities on our bodies and our bodies are used by religions to virtually communicate world views."[20] The photographic image speaks twice: the material captured and also the question of that which the image does not contain. It is this openness, the porous nature of the photographic image, that nontheistic humanist theology invites readers to explore religiously.

There is more than meets the eye in that the language(s) used in the construction of the photographic text invests "every aspect of the photographic space" with a "potential meaning beyond its literal presence in the picture."[21] The public is privatized, and the private is made public and tied to the religious by nurturing unanswered questions: what more is here? And who/what am I that I pick from this image/text these certain things? Answering these questions informs structures of the self, the self in relationship to others, and both in relationship to objects.[22] Even if in another context, unnoticed by the camera, a similar moment is indistinguishable based on significance, once captured in a photo, viewers assume it must have some type of value even if this value is not immediately apparent.[23] Theological usefulness and importance are not premised on how well photographs correspond to standard signs and symbols. Clearly, interpreting or reading photographs poses a challenge, but it is no greater than the challenge present in the reading of any source material in that all such items are marked by the dilemma of shifting contexts and the fragile nature of historical-cultural memory. For example, as I have noted elsewhere, oral and recorded folktales function in this manner. The story of Brer Rabbit and the long tail can be read as a critique of white supremacy and a signifying of the God associated with white supremacy. In this story, the Rabbit goes to God in search of a long tail for purposes of function (e.g., it keeps flies away) and fashion. After completing a series of tasks, Brer Rabbit is disappointed in that God chases him away, pronouncing, "You are so smart get your own long tail." Those who read this as protest against injustice understand the story to suggest God has provided the oppressed with all they need to fight injustice.[24] Or as I have interpreted it, the story speaks to a sense of humanism critical of all metaphysical claims regarding God and God's involvement in human history and instead pushes humans to take full accountability and responsibility for human life.[25] Such complications—the difficulties of reading source materials—are unavoidable and should be recognized as an inherent risk of theologizing.

Architecture as "P(l)ace"

Having talked about the significance of photographs for nontheistic humanist theologizing, one might think the next logical step would be to suggest the religious significance of the spaces holding photographs beyond personal collections in homes: the gallery or museum as real space and as symbol—representing "a place of making as well as showing."[26] The gallery or museum in this regard can be considered a site of embodiment, where bodies come into contact for the purpose of engaging other worlds. In these spaces, the past and the present collude in the presentation of meaning making through the manipulation of materiality. What Alan Trachtenberg says about Mathew Brady's 1861 gallery in New York might be applied to such spaces in more general terms. "An enshrinement of national icons analogous to that of roman household gods," writes Trachtenberg, "the gallery performed a quasi-religious function...."[27] This structuring of meaning in the form of museums and galleries is, as Arthur Danto remarks, the shaping of the museum as a type "of secular church, where the congregation affirmed and reaffirmed its identity."[28] Danto's comment brings to light from the perspective of art criticism a synergy between space and purpose whereby hallowed ground is established in unlikely ways.

Danto's insight is a widely shared formulation, having generated a type of interdisciplinary approach to the nature and meaning of religious space drawing into its orb historians, theologians, philosophers, sociologists, and others. Church architecture and aesthetics has certainly been analyzed in this manner.[29] However, *genealogies of church aesthetics (a Rothko Chapel, for example) and discussion of the sociohistorical development/use and philosophical meaning of sacred space do not constitute the realm of architectural concern probed in nontheistic theology.* While I think there is something to such approaches, in that their findings are of value to the extent they give some sense of how many shape the context of religious encounter in fixed ways, this alone is insufficient in that it involves too narrow a range of considerations. In reference to formal structures (e.g., ritual sites and buildings), readers might think of architecture as the combining of aesthetics and construction.[30] However, nontheistic theology's sense of architecture has an archaeological (determined work but also uncertain work) quality to it in that it involves digging through constructions or building projects (both physical and metaphorical) in search of the underlying dynamics that finally give substance to the arrangement of encapsulated or embodied time and space. Or one might think of this process as a mode of forensic investigation. Yet, this cannot be pushed too far in that the materials nontheistic theologians mine are not all static and not unmoving. Therefore, the archaeological quality as understood here is not meant in a strict sense but instead as a way of describing the posture (or organizing trope) of the theologian in confronting her or his work with source materials of both great possibility and great failure. It is this posture in part that moves nontheistic theology to push beyond the obvious.[31]

For example, although traditional geographies such as churches can play a significant role for some humanists (particularly those referencing themselves as religious humanists), nontheistic humanism actually can be expressed in the very living of life within the broad plans and hidden corners of mundane existence. Dedicated buildings and isolated locations are unnecessary. Consequently, the markers or signs of nontheistic humanism are not as reified as one might find with respect to African American Christianity or African American Islam. Instead, the primary marker is the manner in which embodied selves occupy time and space (and what they make of and think about this occupation)—and the residue of that active occupation. The whole of our engagement with ourselves, with others, and in/with world becomes, then, the material out of which theology takes shape. Accordingly, nontheistic theology tracks and articulates the quest for complex subjectivity as this quest is embedded in mundane occurrences in a variety of restricted and unrestricted geographies.[32] Put another way, privileging embodiment/bodies as the primary arena for humanist theological thinking must involve attention to the spaces with/in the structuring of religious thought and engagement. Hence, African American nontheistic humanism and its theology require a less rigid understanding of place, as readers are encouraged to understand it as any of the various and multiple settings "of the events of human life."[33] Thinking along these lines gets closer to what is meant by architecture within nontheistic theology. *Simply put, architecture is the conscious and dedicated arrangement of "p(l)ace" (physical or mental) so as to give time and space deep significance as recognized location where embodied bodies engage in the quest for complex subjectivity within the context of the ordinariness of life.*[34] Architecture, then, has to do with a conscious entering into, through refocusing or altering time and space. And thereby certain obligations and formulations of the individual (even in relationship to others) give way to questions of complex subjectivity in their unspectacular and rather mundane forms.

Arranging P(l)ace

While **place** is used to connote general locations of a physical nature, *p(l)ace* should be understood as a step way from this generic use. The latter entails the setting of parameters and boundaries of focus around time and space so as to mark off opportunities to wrestle with fundamental questions of life. It is a closing off in order to open up opportunities for deep wrestling with the challenges of life meaning within the context of the quest for complex subjectivity. P(l)ace is not fixed and not every instance of time/space will generate for everyone this same yearning for more life meaning. (It is not Mircea Eliade's "sacred space.") In this regard, as Mary MacDonald notes, "Place is not only a particular physical location, but also an idea, a mental construction which captures and directs the human relationship to the world.... Places are human constructions that come into being when people act on space"[35] Mindful of MacDonald's words, p(l)ace is understood as an intentional locale for embodied meaning making; it is experiential in nature, and it is special only because someone or some group marks it for attention to this quest for complex subjectivity. In short, the quest for complex subjectivity is in p(l)ace. But unlike sacred space in African American theistic orientations, p(l)ace, according to African American humanism, does not draw individuals or groups out of themselves through projected connection to something transhistorical in nature. P(l)ace is embodied, arranged in and through, and by means of relationship to bodies (culturally constructed and physical).[36]

If p(l)ace equals "space plus 'something' "[37] (and I do not see this as problematic), that "something" in this instance is an embodied intentionality regarding large-scale life meaning. In this regard, *architecture involves the construction of particular cartographies of life meaning that give the parameters of time and space significance not always present.* That is to say, the arrangement of p(l)ace requires bodies for its construction, but it also constructs bodies; bodies experience p(l)ace as the context for the quest for complex subjectivity, and bodies also are experienced in/through p(l)aces. And these p(l)aces are un/familiar as a result of this layered involvement.[38] This arrangement of p(l)ace calls the individual to a sense of himself or herself but does so in ways that seek to enliven an awareness of, but not necessary a capturing of, the individual in context. There is nothing nostalgic about this. It does not hark back to some idealized moment, some *Leave It to Beaver* or *Cosby* sense of the collective. It, p(l)ace, is much less certain than either of these models—*Leave It to Beaver* and *Cosby*—and we know it (or come to know it) in large part through negative logic: we know what it is not. Efforts toward this elusive something collapse and end all too quickly. Again, one misses the point if the assumption is architecture constructs fixed places. Instead, think in terms of what some have labeled *place identity*: "the inter-relation between the physical attributes, the activities and our conceptions of who, how, what and where. This means: who we are going to meet in the place, how it is going to look, what is going to happen there and where the different activities are going to take place."[39] P(l)ace entails effort to increase life meaning, and it is connected to things social and historical. Although particular material items may be present prior to this process, p(l)ace has everything to do with human activity and intent, and nothing to do with supernatural claims and expectations.

P(l)ace need not last for long periods of time, and it need not incorporate any particular range of individuals or groups. Measuring its quality or authenticity in that way is useless. Life outside the context of this "p(l)ace" teaches early and often that this process of building is fragile and ongoing. It is not the successful attainment of something that marks the importance of a p(l)ace. Rather, it is simply the conscious push toward *more*[40] that matters. Furthermore, the framing of the quest for complex subjectivity as historical opens to a variety of mappings of p(l)ace. In fact, it is found in what many would consider the most unlikely of locations. For example, Starbucks offers an interesting example worth at least brief consideration.

Lattes and Life Meaning

Through attention to the following, the theologian of African American nontheistic humanism is able to decipher the p(l)ace of Starbucks (and a similar set of methodological markers will work in deciphering other p(l)aces as well):

1. Theo-ethnographic study of customers at particular Starbuck locations
2. Religio-theological analysis of Starbuck literature (e.g., the employee handbook available from various online sources)[41]
3. Theological interrogation of Starbucks in light of sensory history models for evaluation of the interplay of senses and religious awareness and need[42]
4. Interrogation of the meaning of the visual in Starbucks through intellectual synergy between theology, philosophy of art, and art criticism[43]

5. Theologically formulated presentation of the significance of furnishings and space through attention to elements of design and architecture theory and models[44]

6. Theological analysis of the geography of space through attention to the work of geographers who have become increasingly concerned with the spatial nature of the body[45]

Through these methodological considerations, it becomes apparent quickly that it is not necessarily the coffee that brings people into Starbucks. As one patron remarks concerning his own experience:

> This is the true, surprising story of an old white man who was kicked out of the top of the American Establishment, by chance met a young African-American woman from a completely different background, and came to learn what is important in life. He was born into privilege on the affluent Upper East Side of Manhattan, she into poverty in the projects in Brooklyn. He once had a high-powered advertising job and now had nothing; she came from the streets and now had succeeded—so much so that she was able to offer a stranger a chance to save himself.[46]

This encounter is drawn from the opening paragraph of *How Starbucks Saved My Life: A Son of Privilege Learns to Live Like Everyone Else* (yet more to interrogate).[47] In it, Michael Gates Gill describes the ways in which working in the Starbucks environment opened new possibilities of self-understanding. The few lines presented here point out problems: There is so much wrong with Gill's statement. The angst of the haves (the fragile nature of privilege!), gender construction and gender bias tied to race, class, notions of women's surrogacy, as theologian Delores Williams puts it, are just a few of the ways the proclamation can and should be interrogated.[48] However, for the purposes of this chapter, I want to focus on the location—the context—for this transformation, over against its more problem-prone content. And while work was transformative for this particular individual, I am more mindful of how Starbucks affects the larger grouping of "customers" who consciously and intentionally make that space/time a modality of p(l)ace.[49]

According to some, one can get an almost comparable cup of coffee (although there is some difference noted with respect to specialty beverages) for less at places like McDonalds: "Coffee drinks prepared by Starbucks and McCafe [McDonalds] failed to impress coffee experts at *The Coffee Review*, an online publication that rates and reviews coffees. In a recent taste test, the Starbucks' coffees scored higher than their McCafe equivalents, though neither company's offerings earned gold stars."[50] But would the Starbucks faithful take this information and trade in the former for McDonalds, or even Dunkin' Donuts? Doubtful. There is something more to Starbucks than tall, grande, and venti options and the seemingly limitless combination of coffee drinks. So much that takes place in Starbucks shops has little to do with the beverages (and food items) available. Rather, those beverages and foodstuffs become the grammar or the invitation for various modalities of individual and group engagement. This invitation, so to speak, was first conceptualized and offered to the public in 1971, in Seattle, Washington. Named after the first mate in *Moby Dick*—Starbuck— the coffee shop was initially devoted to a deep regard for coffee on the part of all three founders (Gordon Bowker, Jerry Baldwin, Zev Siegl). The name, Starbuck, writes Taylor Clark, "manages to evoke the vaguely mystical, hint at an antique tradition, and subtly remind customers what they're there to spend."[51] This claim marks the space in a particular way and announces a shift in reality initiated with a push of the door and the welcome from the barista. However, this atmosphere took shape over time, from a place in Seattle primarily concerned with selling coffee for home use to what we currently see on so many street corners in so many neighborhoods.[52] Through economic logic offered by "Magic" Johnson, for example, Starbucks recognized the value of diversification—sprinkling in cautious and limited ways of offering p(l)ace throughout a range of communities.[53]

While Starbucks still frames from the perspective of many (and somewhat validated by the high cost of the items)[54] a particularly middle-class ethos, the diversity of those present in that ethos has increased. Nonetheless, what turns time and space into p(l)ace is dependent on the conscious intent of those who walk into Starbucks. And there is something deeply sensual about this process in that it can be triggered through any of the senses because they are all capable of pulling us into particular moments of the quest for complex subjectivity. This is true in the same way the presentation of the church building and even the orchestration of the experience by the ministerial staff cannot force a spiritual experience. Instead, this experience is dependent on the interest, openness, and desire of each congregant. One might consider the physical arrangement of time as suspended and broken within any Starbucks. The layout of physical space is meant to encourage ease and thought and thereby promote opportunity for a modality of p(l)ace that is not religious in a traditional sense, but is set up to facilitate personal and communal reflection—some of which could easily entail the large questions of life meaning. Accordingly, "when we are fully engaged," the Starbucks Web site notes, "we connect with, laugh with, and uplift the lives of our customers—even if just for a few moments. Sure, it starts with the promise of a perfectly made beverage, but our work goes far beyond that. It's really about human connection."[55] The suggestion here is not that everyone who enters Starbucks engages it as p(l)ace. For many, it is simply a space for the purchase of coffee before moving onto something else, and for some others, its appeal even in this regard is in decline.[56]

Again, the arrangement of time and space into p(l)ace requires a conscious decision; it is an act, an intentional shift. In the case of Starbucks as a corporate culture: this was facilitated through two parallel moves. First, the management had to reorient it as not a place people came to get coffee to brew at home (i.e., Starbucks is just about coffee), but rather a p(l)ace of the moment and for the moment.[57] Second, this reorientation had to also entail an invitation, an opportunity, for people to linger and arrange their time and that space in ways extending beyond the actual coffee drink. Through these two shifts, Starbucks changed from the initial model (based on the philosophy and aesthetics of Peet's Coffee and Tea of Berkeley, California) and became more than a shop.[58] Turning again to Clark: "...how excited can people really get about coffee and milk? Starbucks's worldwide explosion was about more than coffee; it was about the way the company was selling it...coffeehouses provided something society needed: a place to just *be*."[59] The space of Starbucks shifted to allow for the altered needs of the embodied selves making their way to the counter. At a 2006 meeting, Taylor Clark notes that Howard Schultz thought of Starbucks in this very manner and privileged this larger role in a spiritualized way: "he spoke earnestly of Starbucks as a balm for our 'secular existence'...."[60] The point is not whether everyone hearing that proclamation believed it. What is more vital is the manner in which this claim is suggestive of a shift from mere coffee distribution to a recognized sense of the importance of "p(l)ace"—the location for work on life meaning. In fact, without the same religio-theological charge in mind, Starbucks leadership began to call Starbucks a "third-place," beyond home and work. [61] As its mission makes clear, Starbucks is concerned with inspiring and nurturing "the human spirit—one person, one cup, and one neighborhood at a time."[62] Work on the physical and cultural self and the self in relationship to other embodied realities is free to take p(l)ace in these coffee shops.

In a shift from its early years, and coming out of its period of extreme growth, Starbucks offered itself as available for conscious and intentional arrangement of time and space, and embodied bodies entered and affirmed this arrangement. Indicators of time are hidden or removed, and patrons are able to suspend the traditional demands of time in that, for example, Starbucks policy does not allow employees to rush customers. One is free to stay as long as one likes.[63] The fact that it is hard to avoid Starbucks in that shops seem to be everywhere may indeed point to the desperate need for p(l)ace.[64] Albeit overstated in certain respects in light of the framing of p(l)ace offered, there is still something telling about the following statement: "The coffeehouse," writes Clark, "gave a harried and disjointed nation a place to hang out and recharge. This, every bit as much as the addictive and alluring main product, was what made Starbucks into a new cultural institution: we went there because we had nowhere else to go."[65] Even if transformation into p(l)ace had not been of concern—not necessarily with the full range of implications I suggest—it would not have mattered. Architecture as p(l)ace does not require the approval of those in charge. Instead, it simply needs the conscious (re)arrangement of time and space by those who seek religious (i.e., quest for complex subjectivity) engagement in its many and usually unspectacular forms.[66] P(l)ace affords a location for altered focus, a shift in perspective, and an opportunity for reflection. Such is the meaning of the church altar or meditation room for some, and the corner table at Starbucks for others: The religious and encounter with the religious are not confined to spaces constructed and fixed simply for that use. Connection to the religious happens wherever the quest for complex subjectivity is the focus. This can be in a church…or a Starbucks.

There have been issues related to Starbucks business dealings, but such corporate concerns do not of necessity detract from this other function on the local level in the same way churches and other theistic organizations of p(l)ace survive their moral and ethical challenges. Nonetheless, not all encounters in Starbucks, or other locations as p(l)ace, can be labeled as "good" in a traditional sense. Yet, this is not a problem in that it does not damage the concept of religion proposed in this book, nor does it damage the value of theological discourse related to this sense of the religious in the nontheistic humanist context. There is no determined need to even think of humanist religiosity in terms of good and bad—with good being liberative and bad meaning oppressive. (When nontheistic humanists struggle against atheists and theists who find it difficult to think of this "tradition" as religion at all, the fine distinction between good and bad becomes a moot point anyway.) While I would still posit a meaning-making (but marked by plasticity) function as central to nontheistic humanist religion, I would agree with much of what Robert Orsi argues by noting that this meaning making is not something one can easily categorize.[67] The very yearning for complex subjectivity itself and the various responses to this yearning are more complex than that and cannot be so easily lodged within the conceptual frameworks suggested by qualifiers such as "good" and "bad." Mindful of this, the words offered by Starbucks's corporate office must be engaged based on a measured realism:[68] "When our customers feel this sense of belonging, our stores become a haven, a break from the worries outside, a place where you can meet with friends. It's about enjoyment at the speed of life—sometimes slow and savored, sometimes faster. Always full of humanity." Yes, at times "full of humanity," but at other times this p(l)ace lends itself to what those with a norm of liberation or freedom, or justice, or peace might label destructive in that it is a warped individualism or a radical egoism in the guise of egalitarianism. In either case, and every case in between, it remains a p(l)ace abundant with struggles over and for life meaning. In a sense, it is not nontheistic humanist religion (or any religion) as the quest for complex subjectivity that is good or bad, but rather our subjective (and sociopolitical) interpretation of that human experience gets filtered through what we need or want to understand as useful or harmful. This judging of quality is a matter of our moralizing brought to the p(l)ace of religious encounter.[69]

Starbucks offers the theologian of nontheistic humanism a familiar but typically downplayed source material for theologizing. P(l)ace, then, as some attention to Starbucks suggests, is momentarily dedicated space but not sacred in the old sense. Location is not a problem to be solved or overcome. Whether theologians get or miss the point, Starbucks tries to provide a space for the exploration of life meaning by embodied selves that respects the individual but allows the individual self to engage relationship to other selves. And it does this in a manner similar to that offered in other contexts.[70]

P(l)aceing the Local Barbershop

In addition to Starbucks, nontheistic humanist theology recognizes the vitality of source material housed in a variety of mundane locations: concrete halls, community centers, wilderness, one's comfortable rocking chair placed near a window, a favorite walking path tackled with headphones and Tupac's *The Don Killuminati: The 7 Day Theory* blasting, a location selected for "Krumping,"[71] or a barbershop. Traditional religious vocabulary does not necessarily appear in the name or description of these p(l)aces. The consciously arranged p(l)ace could be marked by a simple announcement: "Hair cuts $20."[72]

I am not the first to note the multilayered impact of barbershops on African American cultural community; however, what the remainder of this chapter adds to this conversation is a clear attention to the religio-theological wealth of this "something more" and the manner in which attention to it can inform and enrich nontheistic theologizing. The importance of the black barber—called "a waiting man" during the period of slavery—is not a twentieth-century development, notes Douglas Bristol Jr. To the contrary, the specialized skills and role of this figure began to emerge with some clarity during the period of chattel slavery, as black barbers provided a highly desired service to the slaveholding class of means within the various colonies. The desire on the part of the planter class to mirror the markers of gentility associated with Europeans was in particular ways satisfied through the skills of enslaved Africans, whose labor allowed for the maintenance of the aesthetics and other trappings of sought-after social refinement. There was perceived to be an abiding connection between the existential and the ontological—the outward and the nature of the inner person—and the styling of the hair was a testament to this relationship.[73] These barbers, in addition to maintaining the "look" of slavery, also functioned in a variety of other capacities—anything from running errands as needed to managing plantation functions. In this way, they had exposure to the mechanics of antebellum society in ways unavailable to other enslaved Africans. Their care for the appearance of slaveholders was tied intimately to navigation of the geography of society.[74]

African American barbers held a keen perspective on collective life as a result of their position and had a range of motion and opportunity that set them apart from those around them. All this stemmed from their mastery of the tools of a trade providing, through artful application, great social appearance. While war—the Revolutionary War and then the Civil War—would alter perceptions of connection between aesthetic display and sociopolitical identity and standing, African American barbers maintained a presence in everyday life, although their social status was at times marginal. This in part was because, regardless of opinions on excesses of fashion and the look of an "American" man, the sensual nature of life still imposed itself through the presentation of the body, including the hair and beard. During the early period of African American barbers, their physical work provided support for the social arrangements of life by tying aesthetics to the embedded logic supporting discriminatory patterns of life. Using their skills to address the sociopolitical and economic inequality marking enslavement and freedom during the nineteenth-century, African American barbers point out the creative means by which some sought advancement and security in an absurd society. While white society was hostile toward African Americans in general terms, there were cracks in this posture with respect to black barbers. "They," Bristol writes, "worked in pleasant indoor environments at a time when most black men could find only sporadic employment in physically demanding, outdoor jobs. In spite of restrictive laws and white discrimination, they operated increasingly lavish barbershops on Main Streets throughout the nation...." African American barbers are key to the establishment of high-quality barbershops known for rich décor and great care to the aesthetic needs of their clientele.[75]

While their attention during the antebellum period focused on a white clientele, as the sociopolitical dynamics of the nation changed, African American barbers, many who had earlier refused African American customers, began rendering their services more systematically to the African American population. Yet, this usually presented itself in coded and restricted forms due to the persistence of discrimination and the threat of racialized violence.[76] Challenging on a variety of fronts and often receiving mixed reviews from scholars interested in heroic imaginaries of African American resistance, the environment of the barber—the barbershop—entailed a space and time with notable placidity. White men served might use these barbershops (that is, until an influx of Europeans provided substantive alternatives) as the location for envisioning the maintenance of their domination of others, the revitalization of their self-understanding in the social hierarchy. African Americans often made use of the barbershop to rethink and reimage what it might mean to be African American within the context of a troubled world and to be able to think as well as discuss these life-meaning frameworks within a context somewhat removed from the primary markers of inferiority. From the early years on, African American barbers developed the codes of conversation, the ways in which to foster a particularized type of space and time so as to allow for an interaction that extended well beyond the securing of a haircut.

The look and "feel" of the twentieth- and twenty-first-century barbershop takes form in the north during the nineteenth century and is marked by shifting sociopolitical sensibilities.[77] Although often misunderstood and questioned regarding connection to the "race," barbers and barbershops in African American communities became something of a matrix (perhaps reluctantly at times) for thick information: politics, cultural developments, social relations, and so on. Bristol, from whom I have drawn historical markings of the black barber and barbershop, concerns himself with barbers and barbershops for what they say—as a matter of history—concerning the struggle over issues of race within the sociopolitical life of the country. And while I have some concern for this, my interest is more directly related to the configuration of time and space taking shape within barbershops and to think about this as a matter of theological construction.[78] Yet, with this said, Bristol and I share a sense of the barbershop as a something of note, a location where the ordinary takes on charged meaning. The look and feel of the barbershop, the intentional and determined arrangement of its elements, encourages exchange and comfort.

During my youth, one of the early markers of increasing maturity and responsibility was the freedom to go alone to the barbershop—to walk from my home, down Delavan Avenue, to Woody's (now "Woody & Manuel's Afro Styles"). It was a special time composed of conversation about a variety of topics within a comfortable environment marked by attention to the individual's personal aesthetic and within the context of large group concerns and commonalities. While many showed up on Saturday in preparation for Sunday, waiting for what seemed hours, time at the barbershop concerned more than haircuts and shaves. Of course, people wanted to look good as they left and as a result had a favorite barber for whom they would wait—even if other barber chairs were available. The shop tended to be loud and bright. Conversation usually drowned out the music (unless an especially appealing song came on the radio), and the television shown in the background at times was a type of shifting insignificant backdrop unless there was just something highly fantastic taking place—like the O. J. Simpson trial or the Clarence Thomas congressional events. The same scenario was acted out in various other barbershops I frequented before I started cutting my own hair as a graduate student (and even now, although there is much less to cut). These shops, more or less, all have a similar aesthetic—the same images (including a chart of various hairstyles), reading material (a host of magazines), chairs strategically positioned, the barber chairs as central, a large mirror for viewing the barbers' handiwork, and the shelf with tools of the trade. And from opening until closing, the shop welcomes a variety of figures all looking for a good haircut, but entertaining something more. By this, I mean the haircut was important in the same way coffee at Starbucks is the point of initial contact, the pretext, but like Starbucks, the barbershop also offered a p(l)ace for conversation, self-examination, reflection, and communal engagement. Issues of sociopolitical, economic, and cultural importance are debated and at times worked out. This expansive role held by the barbershop is long-standing, and examination might yield significant insight into the nature and meaning (the scope and shape) of the quest for complex subjectivity as a humanistic enterprise.

Through the work of Melissa Harris-Lacewell, one is able to connect a political science perspective to the phenomenon of the African American barbershop as site of communicative exchange to Bristol's presentation of barbershops as alternate history of business success challenging race-based discrimination. Harris-Lacewell, by means of an ethnographic study, points out the multiple levels of meaning functioning within the context of the barbershop—the manner in which it is about aesthetic transformation of the individual (i.e., the cut or shave, for example) within the framework of soft cultural norms of care and style. But it is also the location for orienting conversation and exchange that pull at deeper levels of life meaning and ontological intent. "To make any assertion about everyday black talk," writes Lacewell, "you must eventually enter the barbershop. The barbershops and beauty parlors, more than the churches, the schools, or the radio, exist as spaces where black people engage each other as peers, where nothing is out of bounds for conversation, and where the serious work of 'figuring it out' goes on."[79] Who can deny the validity of this statement, unlike the mixed opinions one might anticipate regarding the claims made for Starbucks earlier in this chapter? I have no argument with her assertion, but I simply want to more narrowly focus this conversation away from what Harris-Lacewell labels "political information and ideas" to the conscious arrangement of time and space that constitutes the barbershop as a p(l)ace.

The workings of the barbershop, the conscious suspension of time and space—setting it off over against the demands and struggles outside that geography—allow for communicative placidity and dynamic exchange. Individuals work on themselves in a variety of ways and within the context of the group.[80] Thereby, the body is tended to (the aesthetic shifts to the physical body), and the embodied self is also addressed through more fundamental attention to the challenges of complex subjectivity. Intriguing is the manner in which the function of barbershops as a place for exchange and organizing overlaps with a similar conversation concerning black churches. The difference is the assumed secularity of the former and the sacred nature of the latter. However, for the African American nontheistic humanist, these tags are meaningless. What is more, for nontheistic humanist theology, the manner in which the exchanges within the barbershop are already and always embodied—fully dependent on the material nature of the body—says something intriguing about the material content of our most charged and pressing thoughts and exchanges. As was the case with Starbucks, I am not arguing that all who go to barbershops seek or have this experience of p(l)ace. This is not a precondition. Rather, I am suggesting the configuration of the barbershop, the fluidity of its environment, and context allow for the type of intentional and conscious arrangement of time and space that make available to those interested an experience of p(l)ace. The ontological and existential dimensions of embodied life are free to collide in this p(l)ace, and in the process, alternate epistemologies are forged and new framing of life meaning may be sparked...at least for the time the person is in the shop. And that is enough. Even if not long-term, if not resulting in sustained transformation of the individual in relationship to all else, this momentary entanglement with and shift toward *be*-ing with regard to the large questions of life (question of religious import) tells the theologian something and, as a consequence, constitutes vital source material.

Through ethnographic work, attention to online and other written materials related to the barbershop as p(l)ace, theologians stand to gain a great deal of information concerning the nature and meaning of religious questions "on the ground." Starting with Starbucks because it is perhaps the more difficult to embrace (and a somewhat unlikely topic within the context of theological work) and moving to barbershops, the resource materials available for African American nontheistic humanist theology cover all the locations of life—the spots and structures in which and through which embodied life happens. In this way, the ordinary is given its proper and more central place as vital source material for nontheistic humanist theologizing.

Community as Centering Category

"You believe in God, don't you?" African American humanists are asked this in both explicit and implicit ways.[1] This question has impact because it points to *the* common denominator, the primary category of meaning—the litmus test of moral belonging. Other elements of belief can be altered, shifted, or ignored to some extent without tremendous difficulty, as long as the questioned person maintains a basic belief in God as the organizing principle and shaper of life. The extension of this question revolves around the ethical connotations of belief: "If you do not believe in God, what do you believe in? What keeps you focused in acceptable and productive ways?" The implication here is that one must have a grand, preferably transhistorical reality holding one responsible or chaos will reign.

It has often been the case that African American nontheistic humanists have been shy to respond to these questions because of the sociocultural and at times economic implications (e.g., loss of community, cultural isolation, threat to livelihood, charges of antipatriotism and anti-Americanism). Yet, recent studies suggest a growing number of African Americans ("nones") who clearly articulate disbelief in the basic premises of theism, including the notion of God.[2] At times, in response to theistic challenges, "nones" can be dismissive in aggressive ways that suggest a form of fundamentalism different from theistic modalities but just as dialogically damning.

The God question is an oddly worthwhile question as a step in constructing and configuring the relationship between the basic elements of a nontheistic theological system. However, the question requires some nuance: It is the start of an important process of interrogation, but one should not assume it is a matter of nontheists attempting to make themselves theologically acceptable to their theistic counterparts. It is important to begin by first providing context in the form of a statement on why African American nontheistic humanists move away from talk of God, away from the concept of God as organizing principle, as "ultimate concern." This is accomplished by turning attention to typically despised lessons found in the very book endorsed by African American

Christians as a viable commentary on doctrine of God—the Bible. Yet, in this case, African American nontheistic humanist theology offers an alternate read of this mythology and thereby suggests a different perspective on the God idea— one that finds it of no substantive value.

Nimrod: The Despised One

African American religious life and thought have been dominated by assumptions concerning the proper posture toward God premised in part on subtle reference to the "crime" of human self-importance and growth chronicled in the Book of Genesis: the Garden of Eden and the story of Nimrod.[3] In both cases—expulsion from the Garden and Nimrod's Tower of Babel—the behavior of the divine is premised on a felt impingement on divine authority that threatens the epistemological and ontological distinction between transcendent reality and humanity. (It is this very distinction the concept of God is meant to safeguard.) Of these two defining moments in the development of theological anthropology, perhaps the most fantastic is the story of Nimrod—the great hunter who is famous (or infamous) for the construction of the Tower of Babel—in that it suggests an extremely graphic signification of divine presence and authority, with cracks apparent in the structuring of the divine's dominance.[4]

Some might argue the Nimrod account promotes the proper and favorable view of God entailing divinity as a necessary restriction on human self-importance and activity awry. Others might suggest the Nimrod event points to the very nature of religious devotion.[5] This much—anthropological confinement as biblical concern—black and womanist theologies have learned from the Western theological tradition. African American Christians have traditionally understood this limitation on human creativity and imagination as a fundamental good because it is a way of protecting us from ourselves. Through a traditional reading of the text, we are to believe Nimrod's action is an attempt to be god—to assume the shape and posture of the biblical god—and to promote a form of imperialism. Yet, one can reasonably argue that, through the building of the Tower, Nimrod rebels against a certain type of metaphysically imposed limitation on human creativity and action. Mindful of this alternative read, African American nontheistic humanist theology highlights the story of Nimrod for its anthropological merits by positing God as the metasymbol of restraint.[6] Restraint is God.[7]

In the story of Nimrod, African American nontheistic humanism sees a battle between the logic and workings of the conception of God and the human desire for fullness of being.[8] Restraint as God has been the source of fear and dread in that the pervasiveness of Restraint meant humanity could not escape a sense of burden—something pressing on them, restricting them, determining them, owning them—in a world that is monitored ultimately by divinely imposed parameters of life. The freedom suggested by Nimrod's action is not best described as a freedom *from*, but a freedom *to* develop meaning within a context larger than the self. It is a freedom *in* responsibility as opposed to a freedom *from* responsibility. Nimrod's actions suggest a sense of interdependence, of mutuality—but one that allows humans to build their world, no matter how compromised and fragile those structures may be. But this posture works against Restraint as God. Isn't it for this reason—the attempt to confine humans through destruction of community because humans have exercised creativity by building a new structure of meaning—that the dispersal and the confusing of language take place? By destroying a unified language as symbolic act, Restraint as God seeks to accomplish the demise of human creativity as a communal endeavor by imposing isolation, loneliness.[9] Exercise of human ingenuity and creativity is projected as an offense against the status quo, against God—*a symbol that always involves a form of negative restraint.*

Human maturation entails the absorption of restraint, the recognition that restraint must issue from the inner self in the form of measured realism. It must be promoted by and for the self in relationship, and it does not rightly issue from some external force. The story of Nimrod involved an attempt to cover this process through acts of aggression and denouncement, talk of a divine and overarching will, giving shape to human interactions. The nontheistic humanist read of Nimrod epistemologically and existentially breaks open this deception. Damage is done to the metaphysical groundings of Restraint. Nimrod's activities entail the saturation of life with responsible freedom and accountability in a world in which human creativity and ingenuity can trump the divine. Through Nimrod's action, a new epistemology is introduced: Restraint is not the ultimate response to questions of meaningful be-*ing*. And the Tower symbolizes the effort to make meaning, to confront existence. However, this act vis-à-vis the Tower fails because Nimrod's exercise of human will involves the tragic, a push for human betterment that celebrates achievement while recognizing its shortcomings. The process of construction contains both a promise and a pitfall: It reflects human creativity and human limitation. This is a cautionary tale, one that promotes intentionality: Will and creativity are what we have, but they accomplish only so much. In an existential turn, Nimrod establishes new human-centered values. The conceptualization of God was never the same after the events in the first eleven chapters of Genesis. Nimrod compromises it by raising a question of ontological and epistemological import: Is it possible to live without God, without an externally erected sense of collective responsibility and cooperation that seeks to pull humans out of themselves?

For the African American nontheistic humanist and consistent with the underside of the Nimrod story, the notion of God is empty of redeeming value.

It has run its course as a conceptual framework. But even with this said, African American nontheistic humanist theology seeks to be more than a theology by negation—such a negative theology is not the intent dictated by the title of this volume, nor is it the general posture of this work. Rather, it desires to be a positive discourse but one that appreciates the merits of negative discourse as a starting point—a way to foster space for alternative arrangements of theological thinking.[10] Yet, nontheistic humanist thought and activity must have a centering "something," a means by which to frame the nature and meaning of lived life in ways that allow for a balanced perspective. This something must relate to and fill out the nature and meaning of the quest for complex subjectivity (i.e., religion), as well as human involvement in this quest (i.e., religious experience). *This organizing principle is community.*

Community is the foundational symbol—the proper centering point for African American nontheistic humanism and, by extension, African American nontheistic humanist theological analysis of religion's claims. Perhaps most notable about this humanist formulation of community is the disconnect between it and the Beloved Community promoted by Dr. Martin L. King Jr. and used by King to portray the nature of sociopolitical and "spiritual" togetherness desired as marking civil rights gains within a redeemed nation. Beyond this example, however, the notion of community promoted here differs from the general sense of community both explicitly and implicitly discussed in African American religious circles. As context for these claims, and prior to outlining community in the tradition of nontheistic humanist theology, this chapter offers attention to notions of community within community studies.

Community: Contextual Considerations and Definitions

While there are numerous uses of community terminology and various formulations of the content of community, for much of the twentieth century, work within the area of community studies involved attention to the intersections of "social transformation and social cohesion." This framing also involved concern with deciphering the impact of modernity on notions of the social—particularly the dynamics and articulation of "social solidarity," primarily within the urban context—combined with attention to the physical geographies of community.[11] For some, this entailed efforts to decode the matrix of relationships within a particular geography defined by relative agreement on a life work/map.[12] And this was connected to interrogation of the meaning and expression of individual (through a turn to ethnographies) and group identity within the context of this geography. All this work had something to do with social relations based on, at times, shifting social identities and patterns of solidarity, guided as they were by a desire for "rootedness, cohesion and belonging."[13] In this sense, much of the available literature at least implies the normativity of community constructed as a solidifying and organizational medium of multidimensional individual and/or collective purpose. And for some the safeguarding of values, virtues, and ideologies accomplished by the formation and maintenance of communities so defined makes them worthy of "protection."

Contained in this is a sense that communities are under siege and threatened on a variety of sociopolitical and economic fronts. Whether confronted by modern life (including political developments and economic mechanisms associated with the contemporary nation-state) or by the destabilizing consequences of postmodern critiques of fixed identity and clear structuring of meaning, community as a signifier of an agreed-to organizational framework is often projected as being on the cusp of destabilization. And because of what can be accomplished through communities—at least this is the hope— strategies are necessary to preserve and enhance them. Of course, all this assumes that the vague defining of community that dominates discussion really identifies a discrete structuring of collective life. That is to say, there is something of an "I know you," or at least "I should know you" because we have "something in common," quality to most structuring of community. Hence, to be "strangers" is to work against a basic premise of this configuration of relationships. While sparking interest, this presentation of the human predicament is not an essential interpretation. Instead, such an interpretation fails to recognize the give-and-take marking communal exchange and fails to account for the dynamic nature of difference.[14] When conceived over against fear of the stranger, community can be understood as providing a space from which to touch and respond to the world—a space of the familiar for embodied beings within a larger environment prone to fits and shifts. There is also the sneaking suspicion that community may not involve a physical location at all and may not require physical arrangement of bodies. To the contrary, "communities...may be 'without place.'"[15] All this—the geographically real assumption of community over against community as idea—is to suggest that notions of community are far from static.

Whichever of these formulations of community, or something in between, one embraces, there is still a sense in which relationships—felt or thought— are of fundamental concern.[16] Or as Anthony Cohen remarks, "'Community,' then, has become a way of designating that *something* is shared among a group of people at a time when we no longer assume that *anything* is necessarily shared."[17] People remain paramount even in this somewhat sober description in that, if David Studdert is correct, community requires "action and sociality."[18] Furthermore, Andrew Mason seeks to clarify the framing of community through a process of negation: Community is not "a mere society or association," in that these two collective realities do not override individual want or desire. Connection between people within either societies or associations is premised on the ability to achieve personal ends.[19] Mason would have us believe that, to the extent community can be defined, it is premised on a level of shared outlook and the overwhelming of individual want and desire by collective vision, loyalty, and group recognition of its members. In addition, when these criteria are met *and* intentional justice and solidarity between members mark the collective, the community so described is not simply a "community in the ordinary sense," but instead it functions consistent with a "moralized concept" of community.[20]

For some scholars of community studies, one begins to distinguish communities from other arrangements of value by noting families, friendship groups, and neighborhoods as examples of community lived; yet, these arrangements are vulnerable to larger systemic shifts within human life.[21] What remains essential for study of community is human interaction governed by a range of somewhat agreed-on principles, platforms, and so on. What Thomas Bender notes in the late 1970s, when reviewing the literature on community, is echoed in much more recent work. "Community," he remarks, "is not a specific space or a mere base line for historical change; it is a fundamental and enduring form of social interaction."[22] To the degree one can name and distinguish types of community, relationship and intentional interaction as more than private consideration persists as both the paradigmatic generalization and nagging detail. Relationships and interaction in this context, although not necessarily face-to-face, assume time and space as a proper container.[23] Furthermore, the shared values and life strategies marking community mean that wherever physically located, members of the community think and act as embodied beings in ways primarily consistent with the aims of the collective.[24] So conceived, one must note the tangled nature of community as geography of life organization and meaning. More than this, however, critical attention to the nature and meaning of community seeks to provide not only the macroanalysis but also the microanalysis of community as signifier and as signified.

As with any area of study, there are internal tensions and disagreements of a theoretical, methodological, and data nature. In this particular area, community studies, some argue the critical attention on community misses the mark and says little that really captures what is taking place in the world external to scholarship. As David Studdert laments,

> While the academic community generates a vast array of books osten- sibly about community, the language of the social sciences, like political language itself, seems lifeless, irrelevant and outmoded; the communities

they speak of seem enfeebled, still born, hardly worth fighting for, bearing little resemblance to the communal life taking place—albeit in a reduced form—outside, in our truncated social world....[25]

Studdert is concerned with the manner in which humans have lost the ability to understand and direct their lives outside the workings of the "state." As a result, we have lost use of a rich range of mechanisms for judging life and tend to limit a concern with our "human and social being-ness" to the private. Consequently, public be-*ing* can be somewhat truncated, and our sense of our social self is confined to private spaces.[26] Efforts have been made to counter this, including the argument that this depiction is inevitably true. Derek Edyvane, for example, claims we should focus on shared life as the meaning of community and think about this shared life as encompassing agreement and disagreement, conflict and cooperation. Thinking about community as shared life, from Edyvane's perspective, frees us to think beyond the myopic and rigid notions that have passed for signifiers of community.[27]

Even this more flexible theorizing of community maintains a static sense that the logic and integrity of community revolve around human relationships that are sociopolitical, economic, and cultural in nature. Whether these relationships are evident to us, whether they are a matter of imaginaries carved out of signs and symbols, or whether they are expansive or geographically fixed, they exist and define a vital grid of meaning. They may be thought or "felt," but in either case, they have importance. And it is generally assumed a problem not to be able to view community in this fashion—either as a negative statement against modern life (including political, cultural, and economic misalignments) or a shortcoming of scholarly insight.

Despite this backdrop and contextual sense of the debate over notions of community, the concern shaping the rest of this chapter is much more confined to the extent it reflects on the nature of community within the African American context. And one of the dominant framings of community within the larger African American geography of theologizing—of which African American nontheistic humanist thought is a part and which it must accept or reject for cause—entails some version of the Beloved Community. Whereas other notions of community, some briefly noted previously, entail a more flexible perspective—for example, community can be a problem or a solution; it can be stifling and freeing, as well as both open and closed[28]—the beloved community is only understandable as the final resolution to social problems. It is a signifier of ultimate, collective harmony and purpose. The task at this point entails testing Beloved Community as a theological category of meaning capable of serving both a theistic and a nontheistic humanist purpose.

Narrowing In: Beloved Community
and Community as "Unity"

The concept of the Beloved Community, although widely associated with Martin Luther King Jr. and the civil rights movement, originates in the thought of Josiah Royce.[29] In his later work, one gains a sense of the "Absolute" operating through and on the geography of our layered concerns and frameworks of life. Royce sought to demonstrate that "the will of the Absolute is sovereign, it is manifest in the democracy of the Beloved Community, and expresses itself also in the individual life since reality is but the fulfillment of individual purpose."[30] Individuals, then, need involvement in and relationship to the larger community as Royce defines it. This form of community is to be desired, but our ability to achieve it is not so certain. This sociotheological and ethical framework, part of the intellectual world King absorbed as a student, provides a way to conceptually capture the collective hopes *and fears* of the civil rights struggle. King seeks, through the cultural world of black churches and the intellectual schematics of the academy, to fill in some of the gaps and to outline, in light of mid-twentieth-century angst and tragedy, the scope of community. And King purports to do so in relationship to the more demonic dimensions of our collective existence.[31]

This notion of the Beloved Community framed by the love of God serves as the dominant conceptual reality and imaginary for King's approach to religious life and social protest.[32] The manner in which the love of God operates in human history demands a sense of one's welfare and is deeply dependent on the welfare of others. Through attention to the love of God in light of his theological anthropology, there is established for King effort to express in our own activities a profound mutuality. The idea and reality of substantive connection is presented by the Beloved Community, through which markers of difference are not denied but instead put in perspective in light of the unifying nature of uncompromised love and regard.

While Beloved Community is central for King, he, like Royce, has difficulty with a full framing of its content and historical achievability. Scholars go back and forth on this issue, but primary materials such as *Stride toward Freedom* leave the Beloved Community less than fully articulated, in large part because it requires the participation of humans. "Human progress," writes King, "is neither automatic nor inevitable." Yet the need is urgent in that "we can choose either to walk the high road of human brotherhood or to tread the low road of man's inhumanity to man."[33] Furthermore, his last book—*Where Do We Go from Here: Chaos or Community?*—promotes the "not yet" status of this communal arrangement of human life.[34] Whether fully realized at any particular historical moment or not, the Beloved Community for King meant the most significant arrangement possible of the individual within the context of meaningful relationship. As his thinking on the United States as empire and the consequences of its global reach became more developed, this framing of community served as cartography of interaction extending beyond the borders of a particular nation-state and beyond racial or ethnic similarity. But even this expansive geography of collective life remains framed by the example of Christ and the ongoing sense of divine (but embodied) involvement. Hence, tied to his liberal Christology and doctrine of God was a sense of theological anthropology guided by the *imago Dei* whose ontological link between humans and God promoted possibilities that could not otherwise exist. Shaped by this synergy between human nature and God, King promoted a radical mutuality that wiped out the negative connotations of the other in that one must be ever mindful "of the sacredness of human personality. Deeply rooted in our political and religious heritage is the conviction that every man is an heir to a legacy of dignity and worth."[35] As James Cone notes, King "believed deeply that all 'life is interrelated.' No person or nation can be free or at peace without everyone being free and at peace."[36] King referred to this arrangement as being constituted by the "recognition of the solidarity of the human family."[37] The draw of community and the necessity of community are tied, therefore, to the very meaning of life in that "he who works against community is working against the whole of creation . . . creation is so designed that my personality," writes King, "can only be fulfilled in the context of community."[38] Urgency is undeniable in that there is no way to think of life as fulfilling and robust outside the construction of this Beloved Community. "Somehow, and in some way," King proclaims, "we have got to do this. We must all learn to live together as brothers. Or we will all perish together. . . . We are tied together in the single garment of destiny, caught in an inescapable network of mutuality."[39]

Although the Beloved Community is not synonymous with the church, the latter has a role to play in its actualization: "Another thing that the church can do to make the principle of brotherhood a reality is to keep men's minds and visions centered on God."[40] This link tends to soften the blow of human frailty and provide a way of seeing the potential for success within dire situations. The framing of life in relationship to this concept of community involves attention to the ontological merits and substance of the person.[41] King urges recognition that evil acts do not define a person but instead constitute difficulties overcome through a repositioning of intent in light of recognition of the importance of others.[42] "In the final analysis," King says, "God does not judge us by the separate incidents or the separate mistakes that we make, but by the total bent of our lives. In the final analysis, God knows that his children are weak and they are frail. In the final analysis, what God requires is that your heart is right."[43]

A similar linking of faith with community formation and its content is present in much African American theistic theology, although it is seldom interrogated beyond points of omission, such as issues of gender discrimination, sexism, homophobia, and classism. In this regard, drawing from King's formulation as well as earlier notions of "togetherness" and relationship found in African American sermonic traditions, musical traditions, and so on, African American theistic theologies have promoted a sense of community that privileges the wide application of a rather narrow range of life possibilities. The result is an envisioning of community as constituted by an embrace of various shades of the same—same ideological leanings, same religious (theistic) sensibilities, same political involvements, same sense of the future and how it is framed.

Theologizing of African American nontheistic humanism's centering dimension is troubled by King's sense of the Beloved Community (as borrowed and refined from Royce's work) not simply because it is grounded in the love of God: "Agape is love seeking to preserve and create community. It is insistence on community even when one seeks to break it. Agape is a willingness to sacrifice in the interest of mutuality. Agape is a willingness to go to any length to restore community."[44] In addition, missing here is creative (and strong) tension between the individual and the group, the type of synergy between the two—individual and group—one finds, for instance, in the writing of Howard Thurman. As Thurman scholar Luther Smith recounts, for Thurman, "Whatever one seeks to discover about the meaning of life in general must take into consideration how such meaning is found in one's own life."[45] The centrality of community for King is similar to the place it holds in the thought of Thurman. However, for Thurman, community is not simply an arrangement of sociopolitical, cultural, and economic relationships made possible through synergy of humanity and the divine. Community is not external to the divine in this manner. Instead, it, community, seems to account for the very presence of God in the world with humanity. Community is the unity of all.[46]

There is for Thurman a teleological quality to this shaping of community: To the extent it is the unity of all, it is the final purpose of all. So conceived, community entails fullness, the recognition of life's capacity in more expansive ecological and biological terms than one finds with King. Religious experience recounts and pushes toward community through the eventual embrace of connection with all. In this sense, community is synonymous with communion. While Thurman makes an effort to extend this sense of unity beyond human relationships and thereby to encompass all life, he equates community with a fuller sense of embodiment. Hence, from the perspective of nontheistic humanist theology, his depiction promotes a "something" too certain, too measurable. Such a framing is too confining, too small. While more robust than King's vision in certain ways, Thurman's formulation simply equates community with an expansive array of interconnections and relationships. Even if one wants to maintain this sense of community as a series of interconnected and mutually dependent interactions and relationships, is it possible in our current context?

In addition to the necessity of grounding community in the resources of a god concept, King's sense of community, as well as Thurman's, involves a limited number of "parts"—all revolving around a teleological sense of exchange and framed in terms of a limited sense of the geography of lived life. All this is tied to a sense of outcome based on the involvement of God.[47] At points, King argues involvement of humans in the development of the Beloved Community means progress is not as sure as liberal thought would suggest, in that it "never rolls in on the wheels of inevitability."[48] Yet, theologically firm and epistemologically confident statements concerning the involvement of God in this process (as an immutable force) follow quickly more measured statements. In this way, human frailty is mitigated by the persistent capacity for involvement offered by his doctrine of God—in the form of the Trinity. Thereby the fundamental meaning and importance of community is never lost, even when it seems most threatened. King's concern with the welfare of a complex assortment of human beings beyond national boundaries suggests that what he means by community is reducible to relationships and interactions between mutually dependent beings.

King and Thurman are not alone in making such assumptions. Figures in community studies, whose interests are to extend beyond the structures of concern known to King and Thurman, still argue for defining relationship as the fundamental dynamic. Take, for instance, Andrew Mason who laments the loose use of the term but still frames it in this way:

> There is a range of disputes over what kind of social relationships can be communities. Some argue that communities have to be face to face, whilst others allow that they may unite those who do not know each other. Some maintain that members of a community must inhabit the same locale, whilst others allow that they may be geographically dispersed. Some argue that communities must involve relationships of a certain moral quality, e.g., where exploitation is absent, whilst others allow that feelings of solidarity may be sufficient, even if these feelings rest upon illusions or misconceptions about the moral character of the relationship.[49]

My point here is not simply to promote a sense of belonging that ecologically extends beyond humans to include all other modalities of life. This is important, and such a framing of life is worthy of attention by African American nontheistic humanists, but the concern is larger than this. Required here is a way to theologically move beyond the community frameworks offered by theistic thinkers such as King and Thurman.

Not King, Not Thurman … a Bridge Concept

Reworking the nature and meaning of community is difficult, but such difficulty may just point to its importance and shape. Related to this, and while not offering the sense of community I mean, there are ways in which Benedict Anderson's pushing of modern community beyond biology serves as a bridge (his assumptions of modernity and biological geography of meaning notwithstanding) between the framing offered by King and Thurman and the concept of community associated with African American nontheistic humanist theology.[50] Mindful of this possibility, my goal is to briefly distill the significance of nonbiological meanings or framings of community as a prolegomenon to rethinking or signifying community in nontheistic humanist terms, as opposed to giving attention explicitly to Anderson's application of these meanings directly to nationalism. In this regard, I am less concerned with the implications (and critiques) of his thought related to the practices and structures of nation-states. And I am more concerned with how his work might prove useful—through the fostering of a certain type of epistemic dissonance—in helping articulate a sense of community as a centering nontheistic humanist theological category. His presentation of community does not answer all questions of importance to African American nontheistic humanist theology, nor does it take into consideration all the existential concerns of undeniable meaning to African American nontheistic humanism. Yet, it provides, again, intellectual grounding for a shift away from Beloved Community formulations.

In an effort to interrogate notions of the nation and nationality, Anderson suggests one might think of the nation as "an imagined political community," and by this, he means its members will never know each other outside what they think to be the case about the members of this grouping. Membership is fixed and limited along the lines of what is thought or imagined to be the configuration of belonging. It has none of the certainties of religious community in that "belonging" is an imaginary without the boundaries offered through, say, the cultural world of religious ritual. Communities, as Anderson discusses them, are differentiated based on how they are imagined as opposed to any concrete "realness." In a somewhat related vein, one could argue that communities are not only a matter of imagined connections but also constituted by the more negative notations the imaginary might also imply. That is to say, they are both actual, as a process of real thinking about connections, and false, in that scoping out the accompanying territory can be without the lines of an actual referent. Thomas Bender's comments, made better than thirty years ago, point to this possibility of paradox but resolve it by framing community in terms of experience over against a particular geographical arrangement of boundaries around a designated space. "As simply as possible," Bender writes, "community is where community happens" because "a definition of community must, therefore, be independent of particular structures."[51] Such a stance, made earlier than Anderson's argument, provides a step away from more rigid notions of community. And while Bender's appeal to experience as the foundation of community steps away from the more determined models of economic and political factors, it does not go quite as far as Anderson in that it does assume a type of felt interaction and recognizable relationships between embodied bodies.

Anderson's rethinking of community depends on expanding and shifting ways of engaging and perceiving the world in both local and grand terms.[52] Accordingly, there remains a longing—perhaps not always physically achievable beyond the local—for connection to others that means community. He provides, in this regard, a somewhat dated (in light of the decline in use of physical newspapers; Internet community members are no more certain) but still useful example of imagined community so perceived as it revolves around reading a newspaper:

> It is performed in silent privacy, in the lair of the skull. Yet each communicant is well aware that the ceremony he performs is being replicated simultaneously by thousands (or millions) of others of whose existence he is confident, yet of whose identity he has not the slightest notion.... At the same time, the newspaper reader, observing exact replicas of his own paper being consumed by his subway barbershop, or residential neighbours, is continually reassured that the imagined world is visibly rooted in everyday life.

The conceptualization of community offered here says something concerning humanity's effort to address losses during the modern period revolving around the nature of connections, the frameworks of power, and the scope of time as mediating factors in life. And, the written word—as language housed and spread (carried along and expanded in part as a "capitalist enterprise")—orchestrated this process of reconstructing life meaning as tangled multiplicities enabling the porous imagined community.[53] Economics, politics, and technologies of communication, one gathers from Anderson, are of vital importance in the origin and maintenance of imagined communities.

The telling element here is the shift of community to imaginaries over against known biological realities and relationships, and this is done without concern for the frameworks of the traditionally religious (although the decline in certain framings of religion and sacred language provides in part the context for community). It is a matter of representations and of assumptions detached from anything physically verifiable. Even so, it is an imagining of relationship between biological realities assumed real, and it is guided through political and economic developments, while articulated through language and the written word. Community does not take shape as a result of actual exchange between biological beings. Rather, it is premised on the orchestrated thinking of these interactions and relationships, or "the inventions of [people's] imaginations."[54] Like some within community studies, Anderson suggests community, rather than being geographically definable as distinguishing different presentations of physicality, involves configuration of an "idea or quality of sociality" with no material presence.[55] Nonetheless, community still revolves around the stuff of human interaction and exchange, albeit in this case, these are ghost interactions and exchanges because they are "felt" but not physically experienced across time and space.

African American nontheistic humanist theology appreciates Anderson's efforts to detangle community from moorings in actual human relationships. His theory of community as discursively arranged and imagined connections offers a way of thinking about the cartography of meaning in a context in which fixed assumptions are brought into question and the sacralized—often through the logic of divine demand and human need—framing of life is fractured. The sense that community has no reality beyond this imagining is useful.[56] Theories of community tend toward discussion of the (dis)embodied content of community and the ideological structures supporting this content. However, African American nontheistic humanist theology seeks to frame community differently, noting the irresolvable tension between the content of what is typically labeled community juxtaposed to the feeling that there is great absence in this very framing. *African American nontheistic humanist theology wants to go further and frame community in terms of the profound awareness of the "presence" of absence.* This statement begs a question that merits some attention before moving on: Why continue the use of the signifier "community"? This is a reasonable question to ask, and my response is straightforward: I think there are ways in which community still serves a purpose within humanist vocabulary and grammar. When altered as I suggest, it still provides a useful way of framing a certain formation of ontological and existential concerns. It, unlike the concept of God, is marked by sufficient plasticity to allow its framing in ways off-line with common usage. The key is contextual application. I mean this in the same way "freedom" and "democracy" still have meaning and still motivate certain responses to life conditions.

Community as Nontheistic Humanist Theological Category

Ultimately, the sense of community promoted in this chapter is not reducible to relationships, whether embodied or matters of imaginaries, to interactions definable by an array of sociopolitical, economical, and cultural patterns.[57]

This approach is much too clear-cut and much too firmly expressed through a teleological take on the outcome of activity. Although both African American nontheistic humanist theology and African American nontheistic humanism are concerned with and framed by embodiment, community as centering is not captured adequately by a matrix of complex and thick relationships between various forms of life. Embodiment and the historical arrangement of embodied life remain key.

Community is not outdone through the forging of particular types of relationships in that, like nontheistic humanist religion, there are no fixed assumptions concerning notions of good and bad. In this regard, community involves recognition of the integrity of the quest for complex subjectivity. It is the acknowledgment and expression of the dynamic nature of this quest. One would be accurate to say that *community pulls at embodiment and its consequences and exposes it for what it is and what it is not—laying bare the limits and importance of the empty spots in its geography.* One can include in this conceptualization all living things, and this would still be insufficient for capturing the meaning of community, in that community has more to do with what is not achieved, what is not captured, than the manner in which we arrange and display relationships, no matter how complex they are. Community involves the "yes" to the "always beyond" nature of this quest for complex subjectivity. Unlike notions of the divine within other modalities of African American orientation, community here is not responsible for providing motivation and certainty. Nontheistic humanist theology wants to avoid any tendency to essentialize community, while still retaining a sense that it means something akin to the substance of the uncertain, a misty recognition of "*and....*"

King and those who embrace the theory of the Beloved Community—and this is the case for much in community studies as well—assume community can be fostered, nudged, and created and that it can be understood. And they are frustrated and disappointed to the extent this does not occur.

Community as a nontheistic humanist theological category cannot be molded and shaped, nudged. It is not constituted in that way. And to think community can be developed—confined to some formulation of opinion agreed upon within a certain embodied mapping of time and space—is to mistake political relationships, economic relationships, and so on for community. Human relationships and interactions must remain important for African American nontheistic humanism. This much seems obvious. Yet, these relationships and interactions do not define community but rather speak to ethics and celebration and, in this way, say something about a limited sphere of meaning. Community, again, pulls at embodied life, enveloping it—including it but extending beyond it, leaving behind awareness and a feeling of "*and....*"

It, community, is not the equivalent of creativity writ large, although human creativity and ingenuity are appreciated within the workings of African American nontheistic humanism in that they are vital for ethics and the ritualization of mundane happenings. Nonetheless, community is acknowledged through a radical openness that cannot be properly articulated—a sense of "and..." that is not satisfied simply through other humans or other embodied and known modes of life. Recognition of this "and..." does not entail a singular response or outcome but rather involves a quality of unsettledness. Community has something to do with a shared restlessness that encompasses various geographies of embodied life but that is not defined by the presence of these embodied forms of life. This does not prevent ethical action, nor does it discourage intentional movement through the world. Rather, community defined in this manner allows for activity (i.e., relationships) full with ambiguity and uncertainty of targets and outcomes. It involves suspicion that our embodied existence points beyond itself to more *and* less—to clarity and greater confusion. Community signifies the sum of this (un)certainty, this glimpse into something and nothing all at once. Unlike the Beloved Community, what is meant by community in this nontheistic humanist theology does not constitute a cipher through which and by which life meaning based on static presuppositions is better understood and lived. The Beloved Community is premised on the difference of race viewed through a particular historical moment, and, while effort has been made to extend this vision, it continues to premise community on rather static models of identity and embodied context.

There are ways in which and places in which humanists share together or engage the quest for complex subjectivity individually, and this constitutes defined humanistic relationships. And again, as important as these relationships are as a platform for ethics and celebration, they do not constitute community. (The quest for complex subjectivity involves a sense of subjectivity not fully consumed by a more robust humanity developed.) In this sense, African American nontheistic humanism—although in earlier work I have played off this notion— is not simply the "human as the measure of all things," at least not fully. Community provides a way of confronting this statement without denying the vital importance of embodiment and without assuming humans can be anything other than human.

While the spillover regarding the nature and meaning of community might bring humanists together in a variety of ways, this coming together does not constitute community. In addition, while the nature and meaning of community might encourage thick relationships sensitive to all embodied life, these relationships do not constitute community. And although the "awareness" constituted by the signifier community pulls at our embodiment in ways that expose the need to celebrate the mundane occurrences of life, community is not worshipped. It does not replace the empty symbol of God in that manner. Rather, the "and..." it signifies—the awareness of more *and* nothing it constitutes—actually serves to prick us in ways that instigate the value of the ordinary and encourage greater attention to the often belittled or theologically ignored dimensions of our existence.

These are the dimensions of life—the heartache, the restlessness, the sharing of affection, the purchase and possession of goods, and so on—that line the imagination and content of the blues and hip-hop. Nonspectacular events mark out the nature and meaning of life within the context of these profound forms of musical life lessons. Such events are given priority as the significant markers of life movement. And as the artist indicates, he's writing a letter delivered through the air:

> Because the March wind blows
> it blows news every where.[58]

Or as another artist indicates, movement between mundane spaces can have an important effect:

> I want somewhere to go
> to satisfy my mind.[59]

Finally, from within the world of hip-hop, Outkast chronicles appearance, giving it a special significance and importance. Whether an expensive pair of crocodile shoes, or a fur coat, clothing speaks to the arrangement of life meaning. In fact, these rather mundane markers map out the naming of one's occupation of time and space:

> That's why they call me the gangsta mack
> In the Cadillac!! Yeah!![60]

Taking its cues from these and other lessons on the ordinary, nontheistic humanist theology recognizes these belittled and ignored realities as prime. They constitute the realities of human life, and, consequently, for the humanist they are also the context for theologizing. In this way, community as theological category centers and rescues from theistic neglect and abuse the ordinary and thereby recognizes the ordinariness of existence for what it is—the religious.[61] Keeping in mind the sense of community operative in this chapter—*community pulls at embodiment and its consequences, and exposes it for what it is and what it is not, and in the process it lays bare the limits and importance of the empty spots in its geography*—the arrangement of bodies in time and space displayed in and by source materials such as photography and architecture points in the direction of this organizing notion of community. In so doing, something of a particular cartography of the quest for complex subjectivity as humanist endeavor is uncovered. And furthermore, embedded in all this is a statement concerning the nature and meaning of the human.

3

The Humanist Human

Self, Subject, Subjectivity

Black and womanist theologies have used divine connection as a way to rescue and then safeguard African American humanity: African Americans are fully human and deserve all the accompanying rights and responsibilities—such as an end to oppression—because they, like all humans, are created in the image of God.[1] By extension, blackness is given an ontological significance, and in its most extreme form, this is because God is black.[2] In other instances, the deep meaning and significance of human existence weaves through all communities. The body (as framing of the embodied self) is representational, a symbol of both the divine and the despised, and it is this tension that liberation theologies seek to work out and articulate through theological anthropology. Oddly enough, the earthy experience of oppression and resistance these theologies claim to address is at times disembodied and spiritualized through doctrines of God and Christology that often overwhelm anthropology. Resulting from this dominance of the invisible has been a prioritizing of thought/belief over practice/experience.[3] Yet, there are ways in which the Christ Event, for example, can be troubled so as to promote a greater sense of human presence. While not firmly lodged in the cultural expression of African Americans, Hayes Carll's country tune—a "cousin" of the blues—"She Left Me for Jesus" provides an irreverent take on this possibility done with great irony. In this song, a former girlfriend who has left him because she has taken up with Jesus, so to speak, encourages him to also embrace Jesus in that by doing so:

> I'll know peace at last.

Yet, he remarks:

> but if I ever find Jesus I'm kickin' his ass.[4]

The problem to be solved is a failure to recognize and relate to embodiment (the embodied self)—on the level of the individual and within the context of groups—and the culprit in part is nonphysical discursive arrangements of meaning and physical confinement. The dilemma for those possessing bodies so formed is that there is little space for a diverse range of opinions and perspectives related to the nature and meaning of these bodies (embodied selves). Hence the embodied self fought by black and womanist theologies is a mutation, a matter of warped reality by which the discursive body represents a piece of meaning that has lost its integrity and relationship to a more robust depiction of humanity.[5] Furthermore, and this is the primary point here, the theological anthropology undergirding African American nontheistic humanist theology promotes a sense of the human as embodied self known not through stories found in sacred texts (e.g., *imago Dei*). To the extent it can be known, it is through the workings of science and through the development of culturally bound discourse.[6]

Humans, as embodied selves with will, are flawed, but this does not constitute the grounds for a basic need for ontological reconstruction. It is just the nature of the human who has the wiring necessary to do great good and great harm, as relative as these concepts are. In certain contexts, it would be appropriate to echo the sentiment of Monica L. Miller, who states something we have known for some time: "The spiritual has always had a sartorial dimension for black people in America...."[7] In this nontheistic humanist context, the language (and certain metaphysical implications associated with the notion of the spiritual) is toned down to simply say humans are capable of "doing," and identity is defined in these terms and "dressed" both literally and figuratively to announce this rich presence in the world. One might describe this situation as "play"—the manipulation of time and space to have them reflect on one's importance in ways that directly speak to this importance while also signifying counterarguments.[8] And this give-and-take stems from the intersections of our biological and our cultural world(s), with significance extending beyond economics and party politics. The goal of this theological anthropology is to speak of humans in ways that not only affirm perceptions of experience but also change the ways in which particular categories of embodied selves (e.g., African American embodied selves) are viewed and processed. *Theological anthropology in certain ways, then, is the articulation of the embodied self as aware—the chronicling of the embodied self's engagement with the world as related to the quest for complex subjectivity.*

Shifting the Theological Anthropology Terrain

To further explicate this theological anthropology, I turn to "death of God," but I do so in light of the epistemological twist offered by postmodern theologian Mark C. Taylor, whose *Deconstructing Theology* contains a foreword written by Thomas Altizer.[9] According to Altizer, Taylor's book arrives at a critical moment corresponding to "the breakdown of the theoretical traditions of the West, at least insofar as those traditions have been grounded in human or trans-natural meaning and identity."[10] By this statement, Altizer intends to point out Taylor's revival of theology as a mode of analysis devoid of the "primal ground" of the Western theological tradition. In short, what Taylor offers is something of a "secular" theology in that it emerges after, while being comfortable with, the death of God as a postmodern necessity. As a related matter of context and content, Taylor's atheology exists outside the tomb of church-based assumptions. One can, as Altizer does, trace the signs of this theological transformation through a variety of figures. Yet, according to the historiography of secular theology offered in Altizer's foreword, Taylor is uniquely positioned to undertake this task in that he "is the first American post-ecclesiastical systematic or philosophic theologian, the first theologian free of the scars or perhaps even the memory of Church theology, and the first theologian to address himself solely to the purely theoretical or cognitive problems of theology."[11] Hence, Taylor did not kill the transcendent God and was not the first to announce the death of God, but he, according to Altizer, is the first to theologize experience fully aware of and in full embrace of this emptiness or absence.

Taylor's deconstructive theology (his a/theology) and the basic concerns of African American nontheistic humanist theology (once the more focused interests of both are bracketed) have some overlap and several shared postures.[12] For example, each is marked by effort to reformulate theological thinking outside the strictures of the old Western tradition (including the confinements of the God concept), while still finding useful some of the vocabulary and grammar associated with that theological tradition. Yet, African American nontheistic humanist theology reads "death of God" in a different way. The imaginary of God's death yields too much ground to old formulations of the nature and meaning of divinity and transcendence. Deconstructive theology and earlier modalities of death of God theology maintain the shadow of the transcendent God (which is precisely what Taylor suggests we must destroy). The basic framing of theology as reflection on God is maintained but simply presented as mirror image (or opposite) of the Western, positive standard. The theological tradition suggests a direct relationship between God and reflection; in soft ways, so does Taylor. While the Western theological tradition typically presents a positive depiction of God in relationship, Taylor offers the equivalent of the photographic negative of that depiction. Nonetheless, the central symbol remains God—either as a positive or as a negative (i.e., death of God). Positioned thusly, Taylor's early theological extension of death of God theological thinking is not as great a departure from the Western tradition of theological reflection as one might think (perhaps still having something of what he calls "modernist post-modernism" embedded deep in it).

African American nontheistic humanist theology seeks to present something less dramatic and instead simply notes that the symbol God, as organizing principle, has never contained any "real" substance and does not serve a purpose. That is to say, God does not "die" in that God never lived. God, in other *words*, is simply an age-worn bit of theological vocabulary. God must be replaced with a symbol capable of generating a different and more productive response and organizational pattern to life. It, God, is simply a part of our mechanisms of articulation for shaping the world that has run its course and should be retired without a great deal of ceremony. This is the retiring of a symbol in the same way that the notion of *be*-ing hip has been replaced on numerous occasions—fresh, funky, dope, and so on. (Perhaps this example shows my age.) Or it is akin to the ongoing shifts in naming associated with the identity transformations for people of African descent in the United States—Negro, black, Afro-American, and African American.

More challenging than the death of God is the assumed implication of this death. For Taylor, death of God also accounts for the end of the subject. In other words, the death of God makes impossible the establishment of the human as the *imago Dei*. The *theo* loses its traditional meaning in theology, as the Author of Truth is gone, and the self as an "empirical referent," as source of discourse, is recognized as a product of discourse.[13] "Thus the self-estrangement and the self-alienation of self-consciousness," writes Altizer, "is the site of the death of God."[14] In a word, the subject disappears when God died in that it marks the rejection of any hopes for a robust self. "This line of reasoning," Taylor states, "rejects the common belief that the death of God entails the liberation and actualization of the individual self...if theology is to have a future, we must learn to speak of God godlessly and of self selflessly."[15] What does this proclamation mean for African American nontheistic theological anthropology? Does this form of theological anthropology have anything to say, and does it have a place from which to say it? Without hesitation, African American nontheistic humanist theology denounced the category of God so precious to black and womanist theologies, but can it also surrender the African American as subject? Better yet, does it need to do so?

This chapter addresses these questions not in light of liberation theology because its framework provides little to someone who acknowledges the futility of the god symbol, and, more to the point, the politics of identity embedded within liberation theologies does not address necessarily the postmodern posture assumed by Taylor. (Related to this posture: I move away from liberation theology because I agree with Taylor's critique of the liberated self as possible, fully.)[16] Rather, the goal is to offer a brief prolegomenon on the subject and on subjectivity from the perspective of nontheistic theological anthropology—drawing on a dual understanding of the subject as cultural construct but also as materially embodied "something" (that lives and dies). To put it a different way, the embodied self is not simply "a manifestation of theology." Theology is not a privileged discourse or action. Instead, the embodied self is the source *and* outcome of a theological map, but also the process of mapping.[17] Theology not only maps the embodied self. The embodied self also maps theology. Nontheistic humanist theological anthropology is really an acknowledgment of this complex relationship within the context of embodied life and for the purpose of the quest for complex subjectivity.[18]

One might argue over the form and content of this subjectivity, but it has real impact, felt meaning, when one contextualizes it in terms of human experience. Yet, it is wise to think of various ways to critique modernity—not all involving the destruction of the self. Identities are far from stable—national identities, for example, troubled through borders as solid markers of difference—and other markers of subjectivity are damaged.[19] The subject becomes a problem—no metanarrative of meaning to depend on—yet the self remains vital and remains embodied. It is the outline of the "scenarios" that "focus the mind" and direct the body's engagement "in particular courses of action." In this regard, the self as subject is already always tied to the body, dependent on the body, and the body, in turn, needs the self to maintain itself. And all this has something to do with "conscious experience" as a "physical and not a supernatural phenomenon."[20]

The death of God, from the perspective of African American nontheistic humanist theology, did not alter the nature of the human—other than to remove illusions—but instead brought into clearer focus how humans are to live out their fragile and shifting subjectivity as constructed and embodied selves. In the long run, this understanding provides the basis for the perspective on the nature and meaning of the human—theological anthropology—advocated by nontheistic humanist theology. It does not look through the embodied self for the "soul," but rather it is concerned with a sustained focus on the embodied self and the nature and meaning of its occupation of time and space. Theological anthropology is a matter of attention to earthy existence marked by struggles and developments for individuals and collectives determined through felt life and the unstable workings of human activity and intent—as uncertain as the former might be and as troubling (if not fictitious) for some as the latter might be.[21] Traditional notions of faith (confidence in outcomes based on metaphysical assumptions) undergirding black and womanist theologies (and related to their theological anthropologies) are replaced with the uncertainty of "fleshy" selves at work through word and deed. Key to this approach is the way in which the embodied self is decorated, presented, as well as what it constructs, what it fears and loves—all the postures and things that form and trail these *be-ings* speak to the fostering of life stories and meaning(s). One need not look beyond the active embodied self—as sociocultural construct and as physical reality— for the expression and presentation of those things labeled the religious.

If the death of God—the negation of a concept—can be the basis for theological discourse, cannot the troubling of the subject serve as the starting point for a theological anthropology? From my vantage point, theology does not have much more to offer than a struggle to figure out the nature and meaning of the subject and to direct (to some extent) and measure the possibilities and consequences of struggle. The rest is built on this platform. If liberation theologies could be understood as entailing an extended Christology, African American nontheistic humanist theology takes as its foundation the delicate nature and meaning of the human—the "subject." There is no god whose existence safeguards human life, and evolution is not the same type of personified force. Instead, African American humanist theology promotes a sense of the human—anthropology—as revolving around a rather earthy and earthbound sense of human-generated structures and discourses. In this way, it is less about salvation history in a traditional sense but is concerned with the uncertainty of human life—the ups and downs of human endeavors and relationships as having significance in and of themselves.

Theological anthropology is first and foremost *anthro*pology. The origin, nature, and destiny of humanity constitute a rather mundane and *earthy* story. The nature and meaning of the human cannot be described in extrahistorical ways, through a modeling of humanity on some transcendent blueprint.[22] African Americans, like all humans, are the product of a long process of development, having an unclear origin but with natural and physical antecedents over against the magical workings of a divine figure. This involves a slow crawling through time and space from simple organisms to our current and complex makeup as opposed to any version of the biblically based handiwork of divinity. Rather than divine action or efforts at persuasion, we might consider as primary the biochemical basis for so much of what we call human nature and meaning.[23]

Nature and Meaning of the Human

The human as subject is fragile, never fully captured or defined—but still meaningful. That is to say, the end of modernity left us to wrestle with the uncertainty of identity, the unstable nature of the subject, as we are confronted with the multiple ways in which the subject is arranged and articulated in time and space. Mindful of this shift, nontheistic theological anthropology cannot present an unquestionable understanding or description of the subject, yet this is not the same as saying the subject has disappeared. Only certain assumptions, certain positionings, particular placements of the subject, and a sense of the subject's inevitable progress have vanished.[24] The subject is not unified but instead is better understood as involving "a multiplicity of profiles and perspectives through which the human self moves and is able to come into view."[25] It is a moving target at best, brought into question by a variety of figures with no safe resting place free from deconstruction.

Thinking about this in light of African American culture, such an understanding of the subject as unstable is more in line with the ambiguity found in the blues than the metaphysics of the spirituals. The latter sees this framing of the human as a problem resolved through salvific transcendence, and the former maintains this uncertainty as a basic shape of embodied life.[26]

"Although agreeing with the postmodernists in their assaults on both the classical substance-theory of the self and the modern epistemological or foundationalist construal of self as transparent mind," writes Calvin Schrag, "the principal argument is that a jettisoning of the self understood in these senses does not entail a jettisoning of every sense of self." Rather, what should be highlighted is the subject (as self) speaking, doing, and so on, as they pertain to the making of meaning.[27] In this way, it "knows" something of itself and others, as well as being "known" as the "who" involved in speaking, writing (the production of narratives through the "discursive event"), and doing. The narrative, for instance, begs the question of the "who" positioned between telling the story and being in the story, and while this does not solve all problems suggested by postmodern readings of the disappeared subject-author, it does promote a way of thinking about the subject as multiplicity (perhaps better described as selves) but real.[28] In other words, although far from flawless and full of complications, "to be a self is to be able to render an account of oneself, to be able to tell the story of one's life."[29] Again, the subject here is tender, fragile, with a quality of plasticity due to the often-unreliable nature of memory used in the production and telling of the narratives described by Schrag and others. Yet, the subject or self remains significant.

Related to recognition of the subject through narrative is the formulation of the self through action or activity.[30] Within stories told by and involving the subject is the formulation of action (i.e., experience) as the grounding for the self. As with narrative, action fosters attention to the "who" performing, to the "who" involved in the occupation and shaping of space. The self as aware subject is recognized as that which through doing constitutes itself, and does so in relationship to others.[31] Small actions, as well as larger activities, have meaning in this regard in that they all say something to and about the self as subject. And traces of these actions merit theological attention. Understanding of the self when presented through narrative and action, as Calvin Schrag suggests, offers a way of continuing to think about the subject (self) over against challenges to this thinking offered by postmodern critique.

It is important to realize that speaking, writing, and doing take place within and through the means of particular geographies—both conceptual and physical locations.[32] The self as subject surrounds and is surrounded—is both substance and what is left over when substance is described—and this construction of presence has meaning for the nature of the self as subject on both the level of the individual and in connection to other realities impinging on and responding to that self. Furthermore, the self both utilizes and rejects space in that the self as subject involves the crafting of space, as well as the resisting of space.[33] One gets some sense of this tense relationship to geography as physical space and geography as arrangement of the self in relationship to other selves in these blues lyrics:

> I'm gonna move way out on the outskirts of town
> I'm gonna move way out on the outskirts of town
> I swear I don't want no body, ooo, lord, baby always hanging 'round.[34]

The movement of Richard Wright to Chicago in *Black Boy* (and *American Hunger*), as well as the shifting geography of Helga Crane in *Quicksand*, speaks to a similar geographical disfiguring as both cultural reconstruction and physical transition as the self wrestles for visibility while also resisting the inherent limits of visibility.[35] In fact, shifting geographies—both conceptually and physically—mark much of the literature produced during the Harlem Renaissance, as well as African American literary realism in more general terms.[36] In reflecting on construction of the self, or multiple selves, nontheistic theological anthropology recognizes the manner in which this process has been present within African American relationships to the "new world" for several centuries. A type of connective tissue between particular experiences and moments has emerged and afforded an embodied accounting of agency. Along these lines, African Americans constituted a problem of subjectivity, of the self, in that their enslavement required a matrix of difference whereby their full existence could be troubled and denied when useful, and limited on other occasions.[37] And in response to this situation, African Americans utilized the framework of narrative and action to present self as subject over against various patterns of destruction. The early writings of Jupiter Hammon, for example, or the narratives of figures such as Olaudah Equiano, Frederick Douglass, and Harriet Jacobs establish the African American as subject(s), and the actions of African Americans within the context of North American sociopolitical and cultural life also promote a certain sense of self, as fragile as this might be.[38]

As some are wont to say, self/selves constitute(s) a "hot mess"—philosophically, sociologically, anthropologically, psychologically, and theologically. This is far from a recognized academic articulation of the dilemma, but it is a graphic depiction of the real but complicated nature of the self within articulated and managed time and space. In the moment of history when African American nontheistic humanist theology emerges, it is important to think about the subject as embodied—a body marked by subjectivity and active in the world.[39] The "Black Atlantic World," as Paul Gilroy describes it, for example, houses a particular cultural matrix marked out and constructed by the work of black embodied subjects—those of African descent who signified the assumption they were simply insignificant bodies through their cultural productivity showing the capacity of embodied selves.[40] Such a cultural world speaks to the troubled and troubling nature of subjectivity, the manner in which subjects are constructed and deconstructed (through discourses of race, gender, and so on); yet, central to the story is the perseverance of embodied subjects forging modalities of expression, all meant to give historical weight to a basic proclamation: "I am...." In some ways, this proclamation of self, an embodied self, critiques certain assumptions concerning the nature of subjectivity through cultural creativity. Whereas black and womanist theologies begin with *imago Dei* as the framing for the embodied subject, humanist theological anthropology highlights an impetus for humanity within the evolutionary process.

Scholars involved in the study of African American religion do not dismiss out of hand scientific findings; instead, evolution is simply the theological elephant in the room. This is not to suggest figures in the dominant camps of African American religious studies suggest conflict between religion and science. No, an antiscience posture is not the dilemma; rather, the problem revolves around a dualism that inadvertently privileges spirit over flesh, disembodied theologizing over earthy theological analysis. Furthermore, as a point of clarification, it is important to note that any suggestion that science is objective and free from the taint of sociocultural commitments and concerns is unintended. As Stephen Jay Gould counseled, it is wise to "criticize the myth that science itself is an objective enterprise, done properly only when scientists can shuck the constraints of their culture and view the world as it really is."[41] The slippage between the two—empirical research and culture-preserving intent—is the point of engagement for many within the study of African American religion in that this slippage or tension emphasizes the presentation of bad faith informing certain geographies of medical engagement (e.g., the Tuskegee Experiment) and highlights the need for African American distance and activism. Suspicion regarding intersections between science and culture, in a less explicitly articulated manner, is used also to exemplify the superior moral-ethical arrangement of life offered by African American religion. While the awkward element of theological conversation, the elephant in the room as it were, maintains a strong presence that should not be ignored, talk of humans within black and womanist theologies tends toward liberal religion-influenced interpretations of Genesis using a hermeneutic of liberative allegory.

A turn to issues of science within the theologizing of African American religion is not simply a reaction to an external threat; rather, it involves containment of an internal virus. This makes sense if one accepts the premise offered by Kenneth Manning: "The theoretical basis for racial inferiority came originally out of theology, not science."[42] In this way, human evolution has been a consequence of "gene-culture co-evolution."[43] Accordingly, there is something biological about human nature, just as there is something cultural about it as well. This is not to suggest determinism of any type. We are too well aware of not only the danger but also the oppressive outcomes of determinism. For example, as Gould argued, biological determinism on ethical grounds runs contrary to good science (historically being instead the domain of the pseudosciences, including some versions of anthropology) and is morally indefensible and politically flawed.[44]

African American embodied selves were exposed to damage, and African American religious studies—through liberal religious associations linked to the legacy of mid-century sociopolitical protest—thought itself a good way to expose both the scientific and religion-based underpinning of this damage by means of an alternate ontology. A hermeneutic of suspicion pointed out the bad faith of some scientists and physicians who sought to overdetermine racial minorities through a twisting of scientific language and schemes, thereby supporting irrational cultural markers of negative difference. Figures such as nineteenth-century scientist Louis Agassiz of Harvard University have become for black and womanist theologies iconic representations of pseudosciences as warped challenge to the integrity of humanity. Although these theological discourses could not reject fully a concern with the physicality of the body, the shortcomings of racialized science did affect the scope of their theologizing. They implicitly embraced a dualism whereby the physical body as biochemical reality could be rhetorically affirmed with primary theological power devoted to a disembodied sense of human liberation and "freedom from...." The politics of empirical embodiment became the dressing for theologizing the physical realities of African American life. And the situation is only highlighted in the dominant arrangements of theological discourse where it often seems safeguarding African Americans is done at the expense of their bodily integrity.

The African American embodied self speaks its meaning in that "the expressivity of the body is...the condition for social communication."[45] But this particular body is a stigmatized or marginalized body—one exposed to in/visibility dependent on the needs or wants of the dominant population of bodies.[46] This stigma is not the result of original sin, and it has no connection to any type of ontological damage or flaw. The construction of African American bodies through discursive means in relationship to mechanisms of power results in a fixed "something"—bodies that are rigid, truncated realities that are not to be viewed, understood, and appreciated in diverse ways.[47] This discursive African American body, then, is perceived as having no positive relationship to intelligence, civil liberties, privileged social spaces, and so on. And the African

American material body, likewise, is believed—as a matter of social truth—to have no core relationship to beauty, privileged times and spaces.[48] The African American body is part of the geographies of identity formation and reformulation that are perceived in real ways as a dualism—black and white or abnormal and normal. Put differently, socioeconomic, cultural, and political forces determine the African American body, *but* it also shapes these very forces.[49] It is a moving target of analysis and discussion—an evolving geography (physical and metaphor) for the quest for complex subjectivity.[50] Theological anthropology is premised on "rematerialization" of embodied selves "who experience the material and social world in and through their 'mindful' bodies."[51] Or as Susan Bordo notes, "Our materiality (which includes history, race, gender, and so forth, but also the biology and evolutionary history of our bodies, and our dependence on the natural environment) impinges on us—shapes, constrains, and empowers us—both as thinkers and knowers, and also as 'practical,' fleshy bodies."[52] Or "meaning, in short, resides in the body, and the body resides in the world."[53] Perhaps history, then, is the waste or residue of lived life—and religion a way of "reading" and understanding the experiential nature of this residue.

African American nontheistic humanist theology seeks to adopt a scientifically aware posture as grounding for theological anthropology. Therefore, discussion begins with attention to scientific readings of the nature and meaning of the human animal and from that vantage point applies theological analysis. It does not offer an extensive replay of evolution, but rather it simply highlights some thoughts regarding this understanding of humanity's origin (and the implications) for what it might say regarding an anthropology grounded in biological realities as the detail of human history. Related to this task, nontheistic humanist theology takes comfort in the words of the famed Edward O. Wilson, who, when reflecting on the impact on his religious sensibilities of his growing attention to science as a student, remarks that "we are obliged by the deepest drives of the human spirit to make ourselves more than animated dust." Writing early in *Consilience*, he continues, "and we must have a story to tell about where we came from, and why we are here."[54] African American nontheistic humanist theology is concerned with a version of this realization but one molded to the outlook of nontheistic humanism as religion. Consequently, it argues there is an element of mystery within the structuring of the human story, yet it is not the metaphysical mystery one is confronted with in thinking about a transcendent God. Rather, it is the element of the unknown (but pursued through scientific investigation), such as the workings of the deeply complex and so very vital human brain. The number of genes resulting in the makeup of the brain is far superior to that for any other element of the human's constitution.[55] It has developed its complexities and our capabilities rather quickly over the course of human evolution, enabling and housing a variety of advances in how humans live and how humans think about their living.[56] Our current state, as we know it, shifts over the course of a long period of time (small in comparison to factors such as original for-mulations of "life"). And advancement of the brain is connected to the body because "neurons in the brain gather information from the outside world and from our body," and in this manner the brain "mediates behavior" suggesting how we negotiate time and space. The brain is connected to and dependent on the embodied body.[57]

The neurophysiology all humans share advanced over the course of time as humans, for instance, became upright—freeing our ancestors to use their hands in a variety of tool-like functions, as well as "radical cerebral reorganization that made possible new relations with the world."[58] Greater mental capacity resulted in significant interplay between imagination and construction. This is not a disembodied activity; rather, as neuroscience research has suggested, synergy between body and mind (and how the mind represents the body) provides an "indispensable frame of reference for a sense of self, consciousness, personal identity and awareness of the world."[59] Suggested here is the significance of our developed ability to share information—to tell stories—and the manner by which, through neurophysiologic means, we grow our sense of self (in relation-ship to others). Mindful of this, there are *neurological* ways in which the self is somewhat stable—is not simply the stuff of cultural production—constituting a collection of biochemical activities (e.g., visual engagement, language use) shared across racial and ethnic groups and across time. It also entails something physical in that parts of the body are recognized across cultures as being part of a whole that constitutes the embodied presence of the self as subject used to encounter others, create objects, and traverse time and space.[60]

As Wilson remarks, "The brain is a product of the very highest levels of biological order, which are constrained by epigenetic rules implicit in the organ-ism's anatomy and physiology." There are consequences and advances associated with this. "Working," he remarks, "in a chaotic flood of environmental stimuli, it sees and listens, learns, plans its own future. By that means the brain determines the fate of the genes that prescribed it. Across evolutionary time, the aggregate choices of many brains determine the Darwinian fate of everything human— the genes, the epigenetic rules, the communicating minds, and the culture."[61] Culture, in turn, plays a role in that the environment within which human evo-lution occurs is cultural. Put differently, and with a related framework, "our large brain," writes Gould, "is the biological foundation of intelligence; intelligence is the ground of culture...."[62] It is important for the nontheistic theologian to remember that humans, in this case African Americans, are embodied realities to some degree informed and confined by our biology.[63] Nothing short-circuits this configuration. To theologize the nature and meaning of the human—to think in terms of theological anthropology—requires recognition of this important point in that we grow to know more about the embodied subject through scientific advances, but as noted at the start of the introduction, the humanities, in this case theology, provide a way to link these advances to the cultural worlds in which they take place.[64] And while the hyperoptimism concerning human progress marking the Enlightenment and modernity has been modified for good reason, the body remains the seat of mystery. Science has made possible a knowing of its organs, many but not all of its inner workings and needs. Yet, it remains somewhat elusive and is not easily defined as either a good or an evil. The body, in very real ways, is both. Or as Simon Williams and Gillian Bendelow argue, the body is "Janus-faced: both sacred and profane, purity and danger, order and chaos."[65] This general statement concerning the generic body is intensified with regard to African American bodies based on the legacy and residue of slavery and discrimination.

Human Purpose

W. E. B. DuBois's ontological statement in *The Souls of Black Folk* might be rephrased: What does one do/think when one's body does not house contaminants but is/produces contaminants? When, regardless of the resolution, one's body as flesh prompts the question of how does this "thing" fit? How is the black body to be included in the social workings of human life, when this particular body as metaphor suggests a negative response to this effort—a barrier, a warning? Such questions speak to a basic reality: Humans search for self-awareness and self-understanding. This is our lot. To be human is to continuously seek a better understanding of humanity even as humanity is ever changing, ever evolving. Or as Foucault would suggest, "The responsibility to create meanings and values anew is a perpetual task but nonetheless the foundation of all human endeavor."[66] In this regard, the body is both bound and unbound—a consequence of a thin and shifting movement between internal and external. The question, however, is not so much the destruction of boundaries—as black and womanist theologies' notions of liberation might suggest—but rather recognition of the need to trouble what are the assumed dynamics, purposes, and inevitability of particular boundaries or particular structuring of lived life.[67]

There is a measured realism available to us, one that scholar Sharon Welch has developed to great effect. In *A Feminist Ethic of Risk*, she acknowledges the limits of human reach—the glitches within human nature embedded in the human self and manifested in an array of values. Thinking in terms of the current condition of human society within the context of a troubled world, Welch speaks to a sense of human purpose as discernible through the workings of physical interactions in material spaces. Regarding this, she writes, "When confronted with social evil, many people assert their good intentions, resist feeling guilty, and claim that they are actually decent people. My argument is that such 'good' intentions are beside the point, *for well-intentioned people are responsible for the nuclear arms race.*... The problem is deeper and more complex than a simple manifestation of either ignorance or malevolence."[68] As Welch's book suggests, the implications of the exercise of self are not understandable within teleological shaping of history.[69] The human is a subject desperate to avoid any perception that he or she is anything less but, sadly at times, thinking that she or he is in fact more. As a consequence, human life is marked by a certain mode of ambiguity. Reflecting on human history, it is clear this process strains and pushes humans as individuals and within the context of collectives, and this arrangement is more difficult for those whose identity is a matter of New World "de(re)construction."

Searching for a unified and consistent self continues but without a sustainable outcome. There is something to the questions Howard Thurman believes people all ask themselves: "Who am I? What do I want? How do I propose to get it?"[70] But as Thurman hopes for a set of responses that point to a unified self, the humanist knows better and instead understands that self, as the structuring of subjectivity, cannot be achieved in whole. According to African American nontheistic humanism, to be human is to be aware of and involved in this tangled endeavor—this clumsy desire for embodied life meant as the geography of our subjectivity. It is our nature to want fullness, robust life meaning in line with the quest for complex subjectivity. Yet, and here is the trying element, it is our lot to suspect this cannot be developed in full. (Theism and black and womanist theologies seek to mask this through metaphysical means.) Knowing this, however, does not prevent a sense of purpose because a sense of human will and identity *is process* and not a wearable outcome. And it is important to recognize the manner in which this wrestling with/against subjectivity is chronicled and expressed in/side the visual language of meaning and not simply through the written text.

Renditions of the Theologized Embodied Subject

Having spent the greater part of this chapter arguing for a humanist reading of the embodied self as subject over against postmodern arguments for the disappearance of the self, I am drawn back to the fractured and fragile nature of the subject. In addition to this, I am drawn to the idea of the fragile self as (in)visible and viable, and how it is re-presented to itself and others through the visual arts. As Amelia Jones remarks, the connection between visual representations through art and the embodied and worldly self is keen and allows useful exploration of "our experience of the world as a representational one and of the body/self as itself representational... to point to its limits."[71] This, in certain respects, is a statement concerning the culturally constructed body as porous, with this porosity represented vividly as visual "text" designed and deconstructed by the artist and "viewers." With respect to this marker of porosity, one might think first in terms of conceptual art or performance art by means of which the artist physically alters the body (e.g., cutting, writing on, placing in challenging ways). An example of this type of work is Marina Abramovic's performance pieces, including the piece described by the *New York Times*:

> For "Rhythm 0" a year later she placed 72 objects—including a candle, a rose, a scalpel, some pins and a gun—on a table and invited audience members to apply them to her body in whatever way they wanted as she stood, unresisting, for six hours. Most of the responses were benign, but some were not. Fights broke out between people who wanted either to assault or to protect her. She may have had fears about the direction the ordeal might take, but the important thing for her was that the audience was part of the performance. She fed off its energy, a dynamic she still depends on and solicits.[72]

What the artist offers has something to do with cartographies of subjectivity, the creative depiction of the impact of bodies (culturally constructed and biochemical realities) on themselves and others, as well as the impact of time and space on these bodies and these bodies on time and space. Furthermore, Jean-Michel Basquiat's (1960–1988) short career provides one of the more compelling examples of this connection, as his work often connotes the rawness of life activities spread out on canvas.[73]

Nontheistic theological anthropology is particularly taken by pieces within the early years of Basquiat's productivity, while also admiring and finding compelling the full decade of his work. The full range of his art depicts the nature(s), meaning(s), and purpose(s) of the embodied self in ways deeply informative. In his vibrantly colored and layered presentations of bodies, for instance, there is suggested a way of visualizing and presenting the subject at the point where the traditional language of theologizing reaches its limits. This is not the end or death of language (the written or spoken word) but rather the recognized boundaries, the limited grasp on life meaning it connotes. Pointed out in this respect is the depth of meaning found in the unlikely—the presence in absence and the absence in presence. And for him, the body bridges the two. As Phoebe Hoban put its, "Presence is expressed as absence—whether it's in the spectral bodies and disembodied skulls he paints or the words he crosses out. Basquiat is obsessed with deconstructing the images and language of his fragmented world."[74]

Within an art world marked by the decline of modernism, Basquiat signified many of the tightly held assumptions concerning the nature of art and the process/rate of its production.[75] Drawing inspiration, as he put it, from the drawings of small children, the jazz of Charlie Parker, the innovations of Jimi Hendrix, and a variety of other figures, Basquiat took these influences and wed them to his early work in hip-hop and the sounds and sights of popular culture (cartoons, television, etc.). In his paintings, revising a history of word and image within art, he blurs what viewers might have assumed about communicative media, forcing them to think about his work as it corresponds to the in-between places of embodied meaning. He captured in graphic ways the epistemology and ontological spaces between reading and being. While he positions his work as jazz, there is a quality to his images that speaks to the pathologies—understood here as being the disorienting elements of meaning—of the blues.[76] One can just as easily "feel" Robert Johnson in his work as Charlie Parker, which follows when one considers the presence of both in his painting (e.g., Robert Johnson in "Undiscovered Genius," 1982–1983, and Parker in "Untitled," 1983).[77] In either case, the tragic nature of life is given its form through aesthetics and lodged in the scope, shape, and deconstructive discourse and physicality *qua* bodies. As Rene Ricard writes, "Jean-Michel's identification with tragedy was near total."[78] And the allure of the tragic quality to life others believed to be the framing for his life was not lost on Basquiat. From his perspective, such was a dimension of human nature writ large, and it entailed the full geography of subjectivity. Phoebe Hoban recounts an example of this awareness when chronicling a meeting bet-ween Arden Scott and Basquiat in the latter's studio. Deeply aware of the drug-fueled atmosphere of the studio, Scott, we are told by Hoban, says to Basquiat, he "can either be a great artist or a great tragedy,' Basquiat smiled, and said, 'Why can't I be both?' "[79] (One might expect a sense of human nature marked by the tragic as desirable from one who sought to model his life after Charlie Parker and Jimi Hendrix.) African American nontheistic theological anthropology does not take from this episode the necessity of demise as "sweet" for the fullness of human nature, but instead gathers from Basquiat recognition that the poten-tial for destruction and harm is always present. This is part of the purpose or resolve of the human. Furthermore, great care must be exercised to guard against the assumption that theological anthropology as problem and promise can be read exclusively through the male gaze or masculine construction project. To the contrary, attention must be given to a range of sources—a range of aesthetic consideration—with Basquiat serving simply as an initial attempt to break the grip of the more characteristic attention to theological anthropology vis-à-vis the domain of scriptural stories and other domains of prose.

The geography of expression as Basquiat configured it was not confined to tra-ditional materials—canvases—but instead any hard substance, and cultural arti-fact (e.g., refrigerator) became a modality open to new re-presentations. By this manipulation of sanctioned purpose and intent, he covered human sociocultural construction with new construction—a process of layering meaning. He not only challenges perception of embodied subjectivity, the nature of wholeness, but also our assumptions concerning the ways in which these issues are to be communicated. For instance, there is a clear intentionality at work that suggests there are no mistakes, no missteps or meaningless markings. Even the crossing out of words, what we would commonly understand as the mark of rendering invisible intentionality, became a way to emphasize meaning. "I cross out words," instructs Basquiat, "so you can see them more: the fact that they are obscured makes you want to read them."[80] The construction of embodiment is given thickness, with words taking on a substance as vital and formative as the materiality of the body on canvas. Perhaps there is a bit of postmodernism in Basquiat's work (as is the case with the hip-hop that influenced him early) that understands the body as a troubled terrain—one constructed out of cultural-discursive materials yet also one made of fleshy substance into which markers of identity such as race are embedded.[81] His art in general, through its various phases, involved a blending of found items and creative expression, all meant to speak to and about the yearning that marked human nature and resolve, and the plethora of ways this yearning could be shouted.

In certain of his paintings, the body is pulled (ap)art, exposed—inside out and outside in—and assembled to point out the nature and meaning of the body and to also say something about the embodied quality of subjectivity. The motivation for this approach rests in an early childhood experience:

> At the age of seven, Basquiat became the victim of a traumatic accident. He was hit and run over by a car while playing in the street and rushed to a hospital. An arm was broken and he suffered from a number of internal wounds, one of which required the removal of his spleen. In order to pass the time, his mother made him a present of the classic anatomical work *Gray's Anatomy*. No doubt the oft-repeated themes in Basquiat's works of internal organs and human skeletons owed much to this event, and to the influence of the anatomy book....[82]

While this introduction no doubt had impact, it is reasonable to believe the presence of bodies and the like in his work is also the result of a more thoughtful and philosophical attention to the nature and meaning of embodied life in light of his sociocultural experiences in and outside the art world. There are ways in which this might serve to signify aesthetic presentations of othered bodies as a way of claiming the superiority of those in control of the artistic environment.[83] The *other*-ing of despised bodies through their physical display and cultural reconstruction is countered in his work through a more intense view of these bodies in ways meant to suggest their complexity, their subjectivity. Putting aside misstatements concerning his work as primitivism or the darkening of modernism for good reason—neither captures him, particularly not for these theological purposes—one gathers from Basquiat the vibrant importance of the body's plasticity through approachability and distance. Attached to this is a sense of human nature as multiple, and human meaning as evolving. Subjectivity within this context can be understood as the framing and articulation of disruption, the affirmation of disruption as a necessary dimension of the human self with itself and to others.[84]

> MARC MILLER: *There's a certain, let's use the term, crudity, to your heads....*
> *Do you like it that way or would you like to get them more refined in a realistic*
>   *way?*
> JEAN-MICHEL BASQUIAT: *...I haven't met that many refined people. Most*
>   *people are generally crude.*
> MARC MILLER: *Yeah? And so that's why you keep your images crude....*
> JEAN-MICHEL BASQUIAT: *Believe it or not, I can actually draw.*[85]

Bodies and the arrangement of bodies in space and over against space as marker of cultural contrived meaning, and over against perceptions of ontological depth, is prevalent in Basquiat's work, as reflected in the images of sports figures such as Joe Louis (e.g., "St. Joe Louis Surrounded by Snakes," 1982; "Untitled" [Jackie Robinson], 1982). In addition, body parts and bodies were not the only evidence of a concern with images of the self as either forming, formed, or ended. In some of his paintings, images of bones and skulls dominate. Some critics suggest elements of a *dis*-embodied body in his work speak to a deep concern with the components of the body, while others suggest these images speak to a long-held concern with death and dying.[86] There is something of importance in both explications, particularly as one considers the compromise of his own body through drug use juxtaposed to his dismantling and reconstructing of how bodies are to be presented and experienced—the nature, meaning, and resolve of embodied selves. Perhaps there are ways in which some of his depictions of bodies freeze in time and space the content and inner form of his own materiality. Even so, I would suggest a third alternative to those two explanations: The skulls and bones present an alternate read of the body (beyond gender-based categories of meaning) denied subjectivity—the self reduced to its most rigid and fixed form. This would involve materiality of the body reconsidered in ways meant to promote not necessarily death but static existence with reduced impingement on time and space. The bones are left when the self is pulled apart and the inner exposed.

Issues of heritage, ontological purpose and place, absorption into cultural worlds, socioeconomic ironies, and so on are played out in layered forms—the bodies we look at and through: *body language*. This is certainly one way to interpret "Untitled (Head)," completed in 1981. This piece is part of what some label Basquiat's first phase (1980–1982), including various formulations of the body arranged as if the viewer is looking at and through the body.[87] While it seems to entail a side view of a colorful, layered, and exposed head, it is not simply an empty skull—without vitality and without depth. The eyes are in place and seem to suggest focused thought that drains energy and passion. It is almost as if the viewer is able to dissect the mind, as the various colors and shapes within the area of the brain suggests intense activity. The image implies full concentration on issues that pull at the depth of self-awareness and self-understanding. There is nothing of physical death in this image. "Close inspection," writes Fred Hoffman, "reveals that this head, unlike a skull, is alive and responsive to external stimuli; as such, it seems alert to our world while simultaneously allowing us to penetrate its psycho-spiritual recesses."[88] There is something of symmetry present in this and other images: an evenness produced through a layered effect of meaning, a mirroring of the artist and the image as well as the artist and the viewer (through the self-portraits). Dick Hebdige also recognizes this mirroring but without the theological implications I intend. He writes,

> The crowds of skulls, cartoon characters, masks, and disembodied eyes that stare and peek out from the picture plane are all looking back directly at us, not over us or round us—from a place this is not our place but in which we are nonetheless thoroughly enmeshed and implicated (though we never feel "at home" there). The canvas can suddenly turn into a mirror or (if you're white, as I am) a photographic negative from a book of family snapshots mutated in a dream.[89]

Theologically articulated, one might call Basquiat's presentation the residue of our existential concerns and a visual ontology when the most fundamental and reaching questions of life meaning are done.

Moving beyond "Untitled (Head)," words arranged on the canvas can be said to depict visually the depth and trauma of this quest: "Man Dies" ("Eroica I," 1988); "Heart as Arena" ("Pegasus," 1987); and, "Rest in Peace Who Trust?" ("Untitled [Quality]," 1982). These familiar words composing phrases understandable to viewers suggest a depth of meaning that requires uncomfortable (and certainly uncomforting) attention to detail—to a lingering over Basquiat's testament. Functioning as "brush strokes,"[90] these words expose and explode meaning and purpose. Presented in these vibrant images is more than response to racialization and cultural maneuvering. There is attention to the type of existential and ontological questions and angst that pull at us, pull us apart. What Basquiat offers is not a unified subject, but rather a way of thinking about the fragile and fractured subject as visible and meaningful. He presents this through a combination of signs and symbols, offering us all the while various means of communication (e.g., written words and images) that tie together bodies through a layering of time and space. Basquiat points out both the need to make meaning (as the resolve or purpose of the embodied self) and also the elusive nature of this task. And he ties this to the em/bodied self pulled apart and bound together. Meaning is possible, but it is never complete, and it is always open to further interpretations and dismantling in the same way that the self as subject is already always in process of *de(re)construction*.[91] We, in the end, might simply find our selves fully exposed, with what we once considered our substance stripped away, but through this process also is exposed alternative possibilities and an invitation for new ways to position the self. The cartography of this process might very well constitute the nature of the human emoting an unfulfilled (and perpetual) yearning for life meaning. Suggested by this is the human condition—the nature, meaning, and resolve of the embodied self.

4

On Theologizing Symmetry

African American nontheistic humanist theology does not hold salvation to be a meaningful category, nor does it posit as useful the sense of liberation that has been traditionally presented in black and womanist theologies. However, it does promote a sense of wholeness or fullness in relationship to the signifier of community, consistent with the nature, meaning, and resolve of the embodied self. Readers will recall community does not function in the same way as God does for theists. It is not simply a replacement or renaming of God—a type of semantic shift. Consequently, wholeness or fullness does not constitute the reward or gift given through community as a consequence of moral and ethical standards met. Rather, wholeness or fullness is a push on the part of humans to recognize their possibilities and embodied importance but in light of an awareness of incompleteness—the "*and…*"—generated as a humbling effect of the signifier community. Consequently, wholeness or fullness does not entail absorption into community. Rather, it amounts to a form of awareness that both limits and frees. Mindful of this formulation, the purpose of this chapter is to sketch wholeness or fullness as theological category. And to provide sufficient context, this discussion begins with attention to the nature and meaning of salvation, stemming from the Christ Event, as typically presented in African American theistic discourse.

Howard Thurman provides an intriguing take on the topic by recognizing that racial discrimination meant perpetual threat to his body in that white persons could at any time work out their frustrations—that is, reinforce their assumed superiority—through attack on his embodied self. Segregation meant limited spaces black bodies could occupy with comfort and without threat. (One might assume such a reality would deeply "color" notions of salvation, bringing them in line with a safeguarding of the body.) Thurman addresses this potential impingement on his being by focusing on the quality and health of his inner life, the "place in me untouched by these pressures on my life."[1] Segregation's logic entails a rejection of self, and religion responds to this assault on human dignity and integrity but not in a way that means embrace of the body and all it entails. This is because the assault of injustice is most forcefully felt as an attack on one's *be-ing*. Hence, the explicit rejection of otherworldly notions of salvation does not constitute an understanding of salvation as couched in the human. This approach to salvation framed in terms of Thurman is not the same appeal to loving flesh made by Baby Suggs in *Beloved*: "And O my people they do not love your hands. Those they only use, tie, bind, chop off and leave empty. Love your hands! Love them. Raise them up and kiss them. Touch others with them, pat them together, stroke them on your face 'cause they don't love that either. You got to love it, you!"[2] Thurman's perception of salvation relies on recognition of the radically other in us, and Baby Suggs suggests a modality of salvation arising out of our profound recognition of ourselves in relationship to self and others. For Thurman, salvation involves appeal to the good will, the intentions, of a cosmic *Other*.

Salvation is a meaningless term in Thurman's work if it does not connote a link to the divine other, the great "something more" that pulls us in and allows us to know it and ourselves more intimately. This is one way to frame the following comment by Thurman regarding mysticism: "In the extreme forms of asceticism there is that which is profoundly revolting and sadistic but there is the bold recognition of the fact that nothing not even one's physical well-being and life is quite worthy of obscuring the vision of God. In my opinion this insight represents religion at its best...." He continues, "Flesh does fight against the spirit. In Jesus Christ as symbol, temporary or permanent, the Christian mystic sees the meaning of the triumph of the spirit over the body...."[3] There is, then, a sense in which Thurman as a representative of African American theological discourse during the early and mid-twentieth century understands salvation as a movement toward the human subsumed in connection with God. In other words, according to Thurman, "there is a meaning in life greater than, but informing, all the immediate meanings—and the name given to this meaning is religion, because it embodies, however faintly, a sense of the ultimate and the divine."[4] Salvation here entails liberation from human centeredness to meaning premised on the human being submerged in the substance of a transcendent core to life. This is not a transhistorical encounter, not an otherworldly affair. Rather, it is a new sense of self in relationship to the divine—the "source of life" acted out within the context of history because in the context of our historically situated existence, "God is at stake in man's day."[5] Thurman gives soteriology a twist by focusing primary attention on the manner in which relationship with God involves a transformative impulse expressed through a continual questioning of how religion, in this case Christianity, makes a difference: how it enlivens a sense of meaning, of place and space for those who suffer most. This, for Thurman, is the measure of salvific significance. Yet, the basis for this remains an appeal that highlights the earth-based ministry of Christ, while also suggesting a transhistorical and transpersonal reality orchestrating human existence. And unfortunately, it involves a limited recognition of the body as not only the site of struggle for salvation but also as the source or ground of salvation. Thurman argues for an understanding of Jesus Christ as "subject" as opposed to an "object" of devotion and worship.[6] The implications of such a move are present in black and womanist theologies, even when these discourses make limited, direct appeal to Thurman.

Black and Womanist Theologies on Salvation

Soteriology within black and womanist theologies highlights movement between this-worldly concerns and otherworldly preoccupations.[7] The problems stemming from alleged work toward social transformation posed by salvation vis-à-vis the end of human history (i.e., otherworldly preoccupations) are apparent, particularly when this soteriological perspective is tied to a general suspicion toward the human body. Black and womanist theologies, with few exceptions, seek to modify this more anemic soteriology because of its inability to carry the full weight of African American hopes for transformation in the form of a radically improved existence.[8] As the latter, an otherworldly orientation, has gone out of vogue in many scholarly quarters (even according to fans of prosperity theology), one is likely to find theologians promoting this-worldly approaches, where emphasis is on the merits of high regard for resolution of existential and ontological dilemmas in human history through a teleological drive toward sociopolitical and economic advancement. Accordingly, efforts to overly spiritualize the gospel of Christ and the interpretation of this message involve an oppressive posture that does damage to human dignity and integrity by avoiding struggle against modalities of misconduct *in* this world.

From early missionaries among enslaved Africans who used an otherworldly framework as a way to safeguard chattel slavery, to twentieth-century churches who use this framework to avoid sociopolitical involvements that might compromise their mainstream and middle-class status, a focus beyond this world has served a negative purpose. It is theologically duplicitous, rendering disingenuous Christian piety, and fostering contentment with salvation that has no impact on temporal conditions. Otherworldly orientations misinterpret the meaning of human-divine connection, assuming that it must entail the eventual usurping of the former by the latter. In the words of the spiritual, "You can have all this world, just give me Jesus." To this sentiment, womanist and black theologies say no—hell, no! These theological discourses are mindful of ties to traditionally black Christianity, and they also note the manner in which they deviate from that tradition. Deviation involves a more sustained worldly focus on critique of white supremacy and its impingements on the life options available to African Americans. Regarding this, James Cone notes, "although Martin Luther King, Jr., and other civil rights activists did much to rescue the gospel from the heresy of white churches by demonstrating its life-giving power in the black freedom movement, they did not liberate Christianity from its cultural bondage to white, Euro-American values."[9] In addition, as Katie Cannon insightfully remarks, while useful on some ethical levels, King's vision of renewed life—such as utilization of *imago Dei*, justice-minded love, and expansive community—did not give adequate attention to the nature of sexism and gender discrimination that marked both the oppressive tendencies of the larger society and the manner in which these tendencies are aped by African American civil rights strategies.[10] The academic work initiated by Cone and Cannon and continued by others involves promotion of a hermeneutical shift within and alternate source materials (e.g., popular culture, African American history) for doing theology. Rather than a rehashed hermeneutic of social Christianity, black theology and womanist theology adopt a hermeneutic of suspicion as a way to discern the manner in which the Christian faith in the United States involved an act of bad faith—vis-à-vis movement from an agenda of radical change to complacent service as a tool of the status quo. Both black and womanist theologies argue for existential particularity as opposed to the efforts of dominant theological discourses to universalize the experience of white Americans. With great passion and force, it was suggested God sided with the oppressed to such an extent that God is best understood as ontologically black (as blackness best represented the nature and context of oppression within the late-twentieth-century United States). Through womanist scholarship we learn this God is committed to ending sexism as well as racism. By extension, those who claimed to be Christians had to also become involved in the struggle against oppression in its many forms. The workings of God with regard to liberation of the oppressed are found within the historical struggle for freedom, and it is expressed aesthetically in the black church tradition and in black popular culture—the blues, literature, and so on. In this regard, these theological forms gave traditional categories revised meaning. So, for example, Christology remained central but transformed: Jesus the Christ is presented as a revolutionary (sometimes physically black but always identified with the suffering masses) committed to ending oppressive structures and relationships. So depicted, he represents the ontologically black God who shares pain and "blackness." Womanist theology rightly and convincingly argued for further rethinking of the Christ Event to de-emphasize the historically situated figure and thereby avoid tangled gender issues: Is the Divine best represented in the form of a male, and what does this say about the significance of women? As a corrective, womanist theology focuses on the Christ of community—on the ministry of this figure and the relationships of respect, care, compassion, and transformation that ministry entailed.[11] Pushing against a strictly race-based Christology, womanist theology maintains an awareness of Christ as connected to black communities, but this involves complex relationships cognizant of the manner in which Christ must also be understood as present in the lives and work of black women. That is to say, Christ is concerned with the destruction of racism and a host of other forms of oppression, including classism, sexism, and heterosexism. With this corrective taken into consideration, one might argue that black and womanist theologies maintain an awareness of Christ as a source of God's salvation, as a sign of God's commitment to liberation. Christ is God's revelation, God's yes to human freedom from oppression. Regarding this, "black people," Cone writes, "have come to know Christ precisely through oppression, because he has made himself synonymous with black oppression. Therefore, to deny the reality of black oppression and to affirm some other 'reality' is to deny Christ."[12] Furthermore, as womanist theologian Kelly Brown Douglas remarks, "a vital and effective Black Christ must reflect the complexities of Black reality. A womanist Black Christ is one who can respond to those complexities—that is, the Black struggle to 'make do and do better' in face of racist, sexist, classist, and heterosexist oppression."[13]

Within the context of womanist and black theologies, a reasonable argument can be made for understanding salvation as socioeconomic and political liberation. Clearly, neither theological camp—black male theology or womanist theology—is interested in talking about heaven or the kingdom of God as anything more than a metaphor for a transformed and historically situated reality. All theological categories must say something useful to the struggle for freedom.[14] According to Cone, "Human liberation is God's work of salvation in Jesus Christ...."[15] Salvation is existentially and epistemologically synonymous with liberation within the context of human history. Salvation has nothing to do with conceptions of a nontemporal arrangement as the culmination of God's concern for the oppressed. Such an arrangement is inconsistent with the historical sensitivities of these theologies. Salvation, the argument goes, is not a reward received; rather, it is the outcome of struggle with God for social transformation. In short, "salvation" according to Cone, and most in black theology would agree, "is a historical event of rescue" through which proper relationships are enacted and justice given prominence. It "is the granting of physical wholeness in the concreteness of pain and suffering."[16] The impetus is not a gift from God; one should not "seek salvation," according to Cone, because those who seek it "lose it." Womanist scholars such as Kelly Brown Douglas agree to the extent salvation appears to be the outcome of work, the consequence of sustained and righteous struggle. "It needs to be stressed," she remarks, "that the womanist Black Christ is found where there is at least a struggle for Black life and wholeness."[17] As scripture, a prime source for black and Womanist theologies, says, "He that would save his life will lose it. He who loses his life for my sake will gain it." Hence, rather than seeking salvation, the true task is rebellion "against inhumanity and injustice."[18] In other words, heaven does not connote a future home because "home," Cone asserts, "is where we have been placed now, and to believe in heaven is to refuse to accept hell on earth."[19] Salvation, these theologians want us to believe, is not simply a matter of saving bodiless souls. How can it be, when "any statement that divorces salvation from liberation or makes human freedom independent of divine freedom must be rejected?" asks Cone.[20] Furthermore, Douglas argues for a sense of wholeness as the proper outcome of struggle. In this way, the aim of the Christlike life does not entail a nonhistorical outcome, but rather the perfection of community through the removal of oppressive tendencies and forces.[21] Theologian Delores Williams nuances this perspective by downplaying the role of the cross in salvation history and emphasizing the manner in which Christ, through his ministry, provided survival skills that facilitate salvation. In this way, she seeks to refocus theological discourse away from surrogacy and toward liberative ethics as the best representation of Christ and what it means to be Christlike. In Williams's words:

> So the womanist theologian uses the sociopolitical thought and action of the African-American woman's world to show black women their salvation does not depend upon any form of surrogacy made sacred by traditional and orthodox understandings of Jesus' life and death. Rather their salvation is assured by Jesus' life of resistance and by the survival strategies he used to help people survive the death of identity.[22]

Redemption has to do with a new vision of proper relationship between God and humanity, between humans, and between humans and the larger world of nature. It involves an appreciation for and motivation premised on the deep intersections between all forms of life, all of which hold vitality, significance, and intensity. It is an effort, although African American nontheistic humanist theology argues neither black nor womanist theology abides by it, to create a healthy synergy between body and spirit. This desired but unfulfilled synergy exposes the human to the comforting weight of connection to all that is within the range of the individual's life meaning (body) and within the scope of connection to all that is (spirit).[23] Salvation for these theistic scholars, nonetheless, is not simply a one-dimensional concern with political change. No, relationship with God, with the transcendent, remains the modus operandi. Ultimately, the message is simple and less than a full embrace of humanity's worth: The human has value because the human bears the image of God. In a biblically motivated word, God in the human gives the human ontological importance. Consequently, the fullness of human significance is not realized solely in the realm of human history;

it is also borne out in an undefined future known only by God. This is what theologian James Evans means when saying the Christ Event represents both "our past and future."[24] Kelly Brown Douglas makes a similar theological claim concerning Christ that looks in two directions. "For a womanist Black Christ, here's the thing," she writes, "Christ is inside of my grandmother and other Black women and men as they fight for life and wholeness."[25]

Do the "Saved" Carry Their Bodies with Them?

Black and womanist soteriology acknowledges the body through a vocabulary of embodiment. However, promoted therein is "one-directional" discourse, which begins with transcendental qualities and concern and from there moves toward the mundane as represented by human bodies.[26] While there is benefit to the idea of the divine embodied, this perspective has done little to highlight and center the physical body within African American religion in general and black and womanist theologies in particular. Lurking behind their large claims regarding liberation, with few exceptions, is a troubled relationship to human flesh, to black bodies: Salvation may entail alteration of the space occupied by these bodies, but this arrangement does little to celebrate the texture, the feel and functions, of these bodies.[27] Theological effort to counter the damage done by discriminatory ideologies and sociopolitical structures tends to circumvent these same black bodies. This is because, as Douglas points out, liberation theologies in black communities draw from a Christian tradition that has a troubled relationship with the body, in spite of its theology of the incarnation.[28] Cultural critic and philosopher of religion Michael Dyson puts it this way: "the Christian faith is grounded in the Incarnation, the belief that God took on flesh to redeem human beings. That belief is constantly trumped by Christianity's quarrels with the body. Its needs. Its desires. Its sheer materiality."[29] Traditional readings of scripture only serve to further entrench this disembodied-body perception of human bodies. Much to their detriment, African American Christians with the assistance of their appointed theologians have uncritically embraced versions of this attitude, with deep consequences in that black bodies become at least doubly damned—religiously and socially.

Womanist and black theologies have made clear connections between salvation and liberation but in ways that entail distance from the body. They, in essence, offer salvation as a form of disembodiment to the extent salvation means an appeal to union with an "outside" reality, even when this connection (*imago Dei* in an earth-based struggle) is meant to point in the direction of human history. Put differently, the Christian notion of salvation supported (both explicitly and implicitly) by theistic African American theologians entails a radical push against status as an object without an equal attention to the full merits of subjectivity. While the substance of black and womanist theological formulations of salvation have had some appeal over the course of a rather impressive history, nontheistic humanist theology points out the continuing problems associated with salvation so conceived.

Two Formulations of Beauty

The remainder of this chapter involves a significant departure from theistic formulations of salvation, including their parameters and logic. In fact, the basic framework of salvation as conceived in the discussion so far fails to hold meaning for the nontheistic humanist. Instead of salvation as a perfecting of time and space, and a purging of the body of its more difficult markers of existence, African American humanism and African American nontheistic humanist theology (as the language of the former) offer "beauty" understood in two interdependent and connected ways: (1) the wholeness and fullness of the embodied body over against attempts to dehumanize and "reduce" the meaning of embodied selves as they occupy time and space and (2) symmetry.[30] *Readers might think of (2) as primary beauty and (1) as secondary beauty.*

While both are important in that African American nontheistic humanist theology is concerned with both existential and ontological issues, the more fundamental sense of beauty, the one most firmly connected to community (chapter 2), is the second (i.e., symmetry). And as nontheistic humanists work to resolve issues related to the first mode of beauty (i.e., wholeness/fullness), they do so understanding that the first mode should reflect the second. *Ultimately, there is a tension between these two modalities of beauty that, when maintained, constitutes for humanists what theists might label "salvation." For humanists, it is a realization of life's shape, contours, and scope.*[31] Regarding the second mode of beauty, which readers may initially view as out of place, there are various formulations of symmetry between physics and mathematics. However, I am most interested in a somewhat loose application of bilateral symmetry, translational symmetry, and rotational symmetry, and in the process, I highlight their conceptual significance. The first, bilateral symmetry, involves a left-right sameness often illustrated in terms of the human body, whereby if split down the middle, the two sides would be symmetrical. In addition, if looking in a mirror, the reflected body and the physical body would be symmetrical (i.e., translational symmetry). Furthermore, an object has rotational symmetry if it can be rotated without altering its look. In this case, transformation involves the ability to move and shift a "system" without altering its fundamental properties, without changing it.[32] Sensitivity to the manner in which physics and mathematics work with the world provides a challenging and rewarding posture for the nontheistic theologian who, if honest, must admit working with unavoidable levels of uncertainty because of an interest in describing and "touching" elements of life that cannot be fully seen or understood.[33] Mindful of the speculative nature of theological discourse, even light attention to the grammar of physics on symmetry gives some sense of what might translate into the theological significance and shape of elegance for the humanist's fundamental and contextual awareness of life lived.[34] By extension, posture toward the world sought by nontheistic humanists (and their theological discourse) opens to more creative ways for addressing existential needs and expressing the world in which we "live, move, and have our being."[35]

Finally, this turn to symmetry does not suggest symmetry in the traditional sense of bodily wholeness that presupposes a certain look of the body in ways that condemn those, for example, with physical challenges. I am aware of the ways in which symmetry can be aesthetically loaded as a characterization of a precondition for beauty. However, as I intend it here, it is not a privileging of certain physical body types. Rather, symmetry here functions as a theoretical and conceptual framing of be-ing. In this regard, it raises questions concerning how bodies are perceived in time and space as opposed to suggesting the look of the "perfect" body.[36]

Secondary Beauty and the Embodied Body

Theologies within African American communities neglect beauty to the extent they fail to take seriously the body as more than the target of a negative discourse or an activity of invisibility. What Edward Farley notes in regard to the Western theological tradition is quite apropos: "If giving the body its needed nourishment is 'pampering,'" Farley writes, "how much more would we pamper if we granted the human being its need for beauty? Here is that strand of the Christian movement that is deeply suspicious of the very thing in which beauty finds its initial mediation—the body and the senses, the whole pleasurable interaction with the world that constitutes life itself."[37] Furthermore, Farley remarks, this negative aesthetics is premised not simply on a disregard for the physical form of the human but it is also due to an interpretation of time whereby the present is held suspect and the future, through an apocalyptic preoccupation, is highlighted. With such a scenario, all that is permanent, holy, and worthy of attention (e.g., God) is dissociated from the realm of the body.[38] Regardless of such a predicament and in spite of the limitations of culture and cultural constructions, beauty entails an elusive harmony of meaning by which the African American nontheistic humanist is in accord with the world. And this, of course, requires refiguring the world by opening the humanist to both its content and absence. Furthermore, the idea that religion involves a quest for complex subjectivity pushes beyond sociopolitical and economic arrangements and hints at the centrality of beauty as a marker of wholeness and fullness in that beauty better captures the significance of a deeper being or meaning as fundamental aim: African American "being" as beautiful—a notion fought and denied in an oppressive world. In this respect, African American nontheistic humanists desire a fuller sense of beauty, which connotes recognition of the beautiful as not simply external to the African American (not simply a matter of proportion or transcendence) but rather a matter of internal reality. Thereby, this altered theological perspective celebrates in word and deed connection to the "All" of life that only a full sense of the self "as related to" can achieve.

This wholeness or fullness is not guaranteed. It is uncertain. Hence, beauty has little to do with assured arrangement of ideal relationships between the self and self, self and other, and other and world. Rather, it involves a posture toward those relationships fostered through awareness stimulated by community, as discussed in chapter 2. Beauty is, as Farley notes, a certain type of ethical inclination, not tangible historical outcome—the "way in which the faithful person [mine is a much broader understanding of faithfulness] behaves towards others and in the world."[39] Such a shifting away from historical processes and toward a positioning of the self for deep and meaningful encounters (and absences) entails recognition of fragile possibilities as one approaches self, others, and world in light of what they might become and what they lack. For the African American nontheistic humanist, difficulties and anxiety are never resolved fully but mitigated through an appeal to human potential, expressed in celebration of the human: his or her body, vision, integrity—without appeal to a transhistorical coworker. By extension, wholeness entails a process of self-realization and historical transformation as a human project, a conversion that surfaces (but also fails to sustain) and highlights the beauty of the human *in* the human form.

There is a difference between the Christian and nontheistic humanist perspective related to the best way to locate and focus human dignity. For Christian theologians (black and womanist), dignity is ultimately a matter of the divine making itself available to humanity and redirecting human self-understanding through this "free gift." On the other hand, for the African American humanist theologian, dignity involves an awkward assertion of human agency and creativity without appeal to validation from those who play by the rules of the faith. This assertion, in part, is an issue resolved through a new aesthetic of life.

Embodied Presence—Beauty: Example One

This raises a programmatic question: How is this sense of beauty developed? Drawing loosely on the work of Richard Wright, I propose a way of thinking about wholeness and fullness—the secondary form of beauty—within the context of embodied movement through time and space, in ways that recognize it within the irreverent. Herein beauty is posited within the context of a more fundamental interest in life as marker of ultimate fullness. In turning to Wright, I am concerned with the manner in which African American literature speaks to a revised notion of self-realization in the form of beauty recognized on some level as an embrace of the body. This tends toward wrestling with theological questions and concerns devoid of deep regard for formal doctrine at the expense of creative thinking, which is a problem that plagues much of what qualifies as black and womanist theological discourse. Specifically, I give consideration to a notion of wholeness and fullness as self-realization by turning to Richard Wright's more existentialist writings, particularly "The Man Who Lived Underground" and, to a lesser extent, the activities of Cross Damon from *The Outsider*.[40] In a sense, Wright destroys what Alain Locke labeled "the idols of the tribe." In this case, the "idol" is a soteriology that neglects a deep appreciation for the body, as well as tending to disregard a sense of self-reliance and self-realization as the hallmarks of the best welfare of the human.[41] Notions of self-reliance and self-realization should not be understood as one's will trumping all others, in that the outcome sought does not entail freedom from responsibility to others. Richard Wright's character Cross Damon, who seeks to initially operate through a radical individualism, ultimately realizes the problematic nature of such a stance. Dying on the floor, Damon reflects on the life he lived, the attempt to be completely free from others, and recognizes the search for meaning cannot be done in isolation. Rather, "never alone.... Alone a man is nothing.... Man is a promise that he must never break...."[42] What Wright presents through this character is acceptance of life lived for self within the context of others as the last best option. Cross Damon realizes this before dying. Such is how, as a matter of theological insight, one might interpret Damon's words: "I wish I had some way to give the meaning of my life to others," he says, "to make a bridge from man to man. Tell them not to come down this road.... Men hate themselves and it makes them hate others. We must find some way to being good to ourselves.... Man is all we've got...."[43] The protagonist in "The Man Who Lived Underground," Fred Daniels, expresses a similar commitment to self-realization within the context of others as he reflects on his effort to show the police officers what he had discovered in the cave: "He was eager to show them the cave now. If he could show them what he had seen, then they would feel what he had felt and they in turn would show it to others and those others would feel as they had felt...."[44] Sensitivity to integrity involves an embrace of humanity over against deep feelings of guilt that can only be addressed through surrender to the God/man, Jesus. This certainly seems Daniels's perspective when he viewed a church service from his cave in the sewer. Of the singing about their acceptance of Jesus, he laments, "They're wrong.... He felt that their search for a happiness they could never find made them feel that they had committed some dreadful offense which they could not remember or understand."[45]

For both Cross Damon and Fred Daniels, self-realization at its best entails embrace of who they are through recognition of their embodiment and what that means, and it promotes self-transformation within the context of sensitivity to others. This self-realization is a complex acceptance of the body as important and vital in what philosopher Lewis Gordon refers to as "the constitution of a meaningful world that we may call...life."[46] For the nontheistic humanist, as Richard Wright notes, best welfare means a move to a fuller sense of self in relationship. This interconnectedness involves a confrontation with flesh, the body—and mindful recognition of its ambiguity.[47] Beauty, hence, involves forging identity premised on a realization of the realness of the world and a comfort with the body occupying time and space as it pushes against the perceived twist and turns of this realness. Substituting salvation for "self-invention," one gets a sense of my meaning in a statement made by philosopher Robert Birt: "But to become human and develop a human identity is a process of invention (self-invention), of personal and collective action conditioned by social relations."[48] For the African American nontheistic humanist, beauty (over against theists' salvation) is a process of construction, of identity forged by humans. Turning again to Robert Birt, one finds words that contextualize this meaning of beauty: "struggle for identity, for an authentic human existence which is the core of 'our spiritual strivings,' is a radical effort to transform the world, to transform ourselves, and to give birth to a new humanity."[49] Furthermore, as Katherine Fishburn notes, humans are "metaphysically alone but morally bound to others in a mutual sense of responsibility to life."[50]

Wholeness and fullness is not the end of trouble (no God to guarantee this through the completion of the liberation project). Rather, it is simply the forging of an identity better capable of wrestling with the alienation and other oppressive tendencies (as well as the moments of promise) that mark life in the world. This perspective does not escape metaphysics altogether in that it speaks to a concern with the nature of being and existence. Yet, unlike Christian perspectives, metaphysics here is without grounding in a notion of a divine reality outside time and space. Hence, without this grounding, the picture is rather bleak.[51] Nonetheless, a theological assessment premised on nontheistic humanist sensibilities does not find this portended bleakness so deeply troubling. Rather, this bleakness points to the difficult nature of transformation. And this, I argue, is a much more realistic depiction of human struggle than one finds in the unfilled soteriological promises of black Christianity and its black and womanist theologies. Put another way, black Christian soteriology betrays determinism (based on the workings of God), while African American nontheistic humanist theology seeks to maintain an existential (nondeterministic) orientation.

A distinction between this perspective and that of black and womanist theologies involves the nature of passion and urgency—the (at times) deeply agitated tone of black liberation theologies and the more measured tone of non-theistic humanist theological formulations. This difference does not stem from a lack of concern with oppression and the oppressed within nontheistic humanist theological frameworks. Nontheistic humanism is no less sensitive to the absurdities of social structures and political maneuvering that confine life options, and it is no less concerned with the development of healthy life options within the context of a healthy world. Rather, what many will perceive as an indifference in tone stems from the nontheistic humanist's recognition of life's absurd nature and the notion that we construct this world alone without divine guidance and the (often blind) hopefulness of hope such guidance provides.[52] Black Christian tradition posits something after human history, and even black and womanist theologies that hold talk of heaven suspect do not rule out the plausibility of transhistorical existence in that God exists, and all things are possible through God. However, African American nontheistic humanist wholeness and fullness are limited by death. Furthermore, the nontheistic humanist speaks of wholeness in ways that are preoccupied with the present, while black and womanist theologies focus on the past (the Christ Event) and future (the end of human history as tragedy vis-à-vis social transformation—the "kingdom of God"). Wholeness takes an interesting twist in that it is a push for freedom from unnecessary restrictions that bind people and keep them from an embrace of the embodied self as a sign of humanity's potential *and* limitations. Perhaps this is why Fred Daniels, when hearing the church service from his space below ground, wants so desperately to tell those black Christians to be unrepentant, to embrace themselves.[53] Furthermore, it is the lack of a full sense of their potential, their responsibility for life, that at one point bothers Daniels as he watches people in a movie theater. Those in the theater are "sleeping in their living, awake in their dying," and like the people in church, they were more concerned with "shadows of themselves" than a full embrace of life's realness. They embraced illusions and failed to take responsibility for their living. They were captivated by pretense, illusion, and ignored the potential to transform their existence: They simply "laughed at their lives."[54] Providential proclamations, hence, are inappropriate and without use.

Wright's characters Cross Damon and Fred Daniels seek to re-create themselves, to be "born again," so to speak: Damon after taking the identity of another and Daniels after descending into the sewer. This process, this push for beauty—a new wholeness or altered constitution of life—involves not the grace of a benevolent other, but rather sheer "force of will."[55] For Damon, this entails movement from exercise of will over against all others to exercise of will within the context of communal concerns and obligations. As Michael F. Lynch notes, Wright absorbs in his work a notion of the interconnectedness of human community and "salvation": Individuals are "saved" in community.[56] The outcome is always fragile and temporal but always significant. The importance of this human project, self-realization and creativity, is what Daniels wanted those in church to embrace. Beauty was to be found, as imperfect as it is, in the work of their hands. The singing he hears, "Glad, glad, glad, oh, so glad I got Jesus in my soul," disturbs him. In fact, "he felt," Wright records, "that their search for a happiness they could never find made them feel that they had committed some dreadful offense which they could not remember or understand."[57] Guilt over the alleged offense was unproductive in that it kept people beholden to a bad system of metaphysics, one that did not allow for the full expression of human potentiality and responsibility for self and others.

Fred Daniels enters the sewer or "death" and emerges (or is resurrected) a new man, with an alternate sense of self in relationship to others. Based on this, it becomes somewhat clear that wholeness and fullness (i.e., beauty) involves transformation prompting a different posture toward the world, positioned as realization of what it means to carry (and at other times drag) one's body through the world. Wholeness denotes determination to exercise one's will through the movement and positioning of this body. This is not done through negation, but in ways mindful of its impact on others, thereby discerning of the "secret of [human] existence."[58] The importance of the embodied self is heightened when one notes that Daniels carves out his new existence in the cave and his relationship with others through the physical force of his body pushing against walls and other boundaries. It was the work of his body, the pushing of his arms against tools, against walls that carved out his new space in the sewer—not singing about a place outside this world created by cosmic forces. Wholeness entails humans left to their last best effort, their best devices for self-realization. Old notions of salvation involving Jesus and a life beyond this world sung about by those in the church Daniels observes are done away with, and in their place, Daniels suggests an unapologetic embrace of human existence.

This first form of the nontheistic humanist sense of wholeness and fullness or beauty framed through the body is easily put: The body is given a new value and importance in that beauty involves embodied self-realization and frames wholeness forged within the context of human (im)possibilities. Such is not the consequence of a grand plan; it, instead, requires simple human creativity worked out within the context of vibrant flesh in touch with other pulsating lives *in* the world.

Primary Beauty: Symmetry

This understanding of beauty wrestles with the felt dimensions of life as they correspond to our embodied selves moving through the world, and it seeks to shield (albeit at times in a rather clumsy manner) these bodies from harmful ideological depictions and corresponding confinement in structures of space and time. Again, this is far from an achievable goal in a guaranteed and permanent sense. And while important in and of itself, it is connected to a more elemental and fundamental sense of beauty. Drawing loosely from the sciences for an understanding of this primary beauty, I have in mind what in physics is described this way:

> Much in the same manner that they affect art and music, such symmetries are deeply satisfying; they highlight an order and a coherence in the workings of nature. The elegance of rich, complex, and diverse phenomena emerging from a simple set of universal laws is at least part of what physicists mean when they invoke the term "beautiful."[59]

Beauty discussed in the previous pages involves a statement that can be observed and ordered through cultural shifts and the like and that can be discussed in terms of altered ontological meaning. It involves a certain type of changeability, fluidity of meaning and purpose. However, primary beauty is not concerned with this level of observation. It is more concerned with fundamental structures of life and the deep consistencies that mark these structures. It is, in fact, symmetry. What Brian Greene observes with respect to special and general relativity[60] is key by implication: "This [the consistent nature of physical laws] is symmetry because it means that nature treats all such observers identically—symmetrically."[61] The significance of symmetry (external/space and/or internal/objects) can be further refined: "Symmetry is a sacred word to most physicists."[62] Even if one avoids loaded phrasing such as "sacred," the significance of symmetry is widely regarded. Hermann Weyl noted this decades ago when saying "symmetry, as wide or as narrow as you may define its meaning, is one idea by which man through the ages has tried to comprehend and create order, beauty, and perfection." This, he argues, is evidenced in various modalities of human thought and creation—the arts, architecture, and so on.[63] Whereas the first mode of beauty sheds light on how we occupy time and space, the hope is that this theological attention to primary symmetry will provide a way to think through the very nature and meaning of the time and space we occupy. Combined, these two give the thinking or theologizing (and practicing) of African American nontheistic humanism a defining characteristic.

Suggested here is not a proper or detailed application of physics; instead, it is a theological articulation of a certain element of physics and mathematics in ways meant to help African American nontheistic humanism (and its theological structure) approach those things that theologically matter most. And in this way, symmetry provides a useful way of theologizing African American humanism's aim—the basic structuring of life desired. Symmetry does not entail a particular lifestyle, but rather it involves a certain perception of the "movement" and configuration of life—its layers, complexities, the manner in which it is "built," and so on. This, in turn, as the last two chapters will show, allows for particular modes of action and interaction with self and others.

There is something arbitrary about beauty as described and applied in the first section in that in significant ways it is a signifying (as Charles Long uses the terminology) of restrictive renderings of embodiment. Yet, the primary framing of beauty is not arbitrary in that symmetry (but not simply bilateral symmetry) has to do with the very structure of life exposed as promise and problem on a variety of levels and within a variety of planes.[64] "Symmetries," write mathematicians Ian Stewart and Martin Golubitsky, "abound in the world of living creatures."[65] Through synergy between these two modalities of beauty—primary and secondary symmetry—the nontheistic humanist is able to wrestle with (but perhaps not ultimately answer) two important questions: How does one present life? And on a more elemental level, what is life? This questioning does not produce unchangeable answers but instead enables a certain posture toward life, a way of viewing life more complex and rich than was the case beforehand. In both cases—beauty as the aesthetics of embodiment and the current attention to symmetry—beauty points back at materiality, at physicality.[66] Humanists are not alone in finding symmetries appealing. But nontheistic humanist theology is unique in black religious studies in addressing the fundamental, theological significance of this appeal for the articulation of life arrangements desired through a more robust perception of and openness to time and space as a matter of symmetry. *The real value here is the manner in which attention to symmetry encourages experimentation through openness to life that fosters greater interrogation of our possibilities and clear noting of our current limitations. And all this takes place within the context of the quest for complex subjectivity and while mindful of community as presented in* chapter 2.[67]

A. Zee argues that "many physicists now feel that the big picture may be within our grasp, thanks to the guiding light of symmetry."[68] I am not qualified to either deny or affirm Zee's reaction to this shift. However, the relationship between symmetry and the knowing of the universe can provide a way of thinking about the relationship between symmetry and a guiding sense of community. While not exact, symmetry is to community in African American nontheistic humanist theology what symmetry is to universe for some physicists. Furthermore, the relationship might be thought of this way: To the extent community connotes the encompassing concept framing African American nontheistic humanism— and symmetry involves a means by which to think about the shape and contours of life—one might say primary (theologically understood) symmetry is to community what (physics) symmetry is to a potential "theory of everything" (bringing together general relativity and quantum mechanics) for the scientist.[69]

In either case, and this is not a problem for the nontheistic humanist or the scientist, imperfections can play an important role. In fact, for the nontheistic humanist, such is the nature of community.[70] Symmetry suggests the underlying "sameness" marking life and, as a consequence, develops a more layered understanding of the structure—the shape and contours—of life beyond the more superficial markers of difference. What this involves is greater perspective on life, on the nature of time and space, as we inhabit (and struggle against) both. It, in subtle ways, hints at the *more* noted elsewhere in this book and grounds it in the wonders of multilayered life.

Experience of beauty, then, takes place on two levels: first, the level of surface recognition by which the sociocultural and political markers of negative difference are exposed and exploded. And second, it takes place through base-beauty of life marked correspondences much more fundamental than the accidents of birth we seek to alter. The words of Zee are helpful with the theologizing suggested here. "Nature, at a fundamental level," he writes, "is beautifully designed." By this, he references what appears to be an elegant simplicity that marks the natural world. That is to say, Zee reflects on a beauty associated not so much with content as with design. So arranged, beauty has to do with symmetry. No, to be more precise, "beauty means symmetry."[71] Put another way, "the inner nature of the cosmos is a landscape of exquisite beauty which appropriately underlies the exterior splendor of our experience."[72] Symmetry prepares the nontheistic humanist to view life on a variety of interinformed levels.

Whereas the first form of beauty points out the "how" of life meaning, the second form of beauty—primary beauty—involves more attention to the "why" of life meaning. It, primary beauty, involves a different arrangement of time and space in ways that both encompass and surpass what we know. In saying this, I am concerned with how the sense of wonder and desire generated by this symmetry affects and influences nontheistic relationship to and movement through lived life. This symmetry—related to the structure of life—appeals, motivates, and becomes the basis for engagement with the world. Hence, recognition of this beauty as a marker of community is our ultimate desire. From this basic reformulation in light of the very structure of life, sparked by community, springs forth new opportunities that are about *both* points of opening and limiting. Required is a different perspective on perspective, one by which the nontheist is forced and freed to think deeply about possibilities of action and possible outcomes of action—to look for simplicity. That is to say, theologizing symmetry for the nontheistic humanist procures sensitivity to effects. Herein "the web-like nature of...this and that" takes on a new depth of meaning.[73] *One might say, and it is reasonable to do so, that rather than the salvation of the theist, the African American nontheist gains a more complex view of life lived—one that appreciates the superficial conditions of existence and the symmetry that marks the structures of life on an elemental (but also on all) level[s].* Of additional theological importance is the possibility of symmetry "breaking down" or hidden symmetry, yet maintaining elegance. That is to say, the notion of broken symmetry is intriguing for African American nontheistic humanist theology in that it points to the yes/no of community and fosters a comfort with paradox and tension.

Unlike the theist's salvation—as empty as the theist's claims are demonstrated to be—the humanist's new view of life promises no rewards beyond this view's horizon. It is an increasing clarity that points out both what we "know" and what we don't know—with equal appreciation for both in tension. The combination of these two held together stretch us and pull us, delight us and frighten us. Unlike theistic salvation that seeks to pull apart time and space through destruction of history (e.g., various versions of the "reign" of God), symmetry in the nontheistic context involves thinking about time and space[74] and as a result allowing a different view of, appreciation for, and work within the expansiveness and limitations of our context of being (time and space). It involves an intimate awareness that allows comfortable discomfort in and with the world. Some will undoubtedly claim black and womanist theologies also approach the world, yet they do not allow for the maintenance of tension and uncertainty. If nothing else, the sense of salvation promoted within those theological discourses involves the resolution of this tension, the easing of discomfort—all framed with a strong sense of certainty.

Symmetry—Beauty: Example Two

To recap, secondary beauty points out the manner in which African American humanism challenges the aesthetics of negative difference through critique of theistic formulations of life and critique of accompanying oppressive patterns of living. And this is accomplished, the argument goes, through reenvisioning of relationships to self and others within the sociopolitical, cultural, and economic frameworks marking human history. Emerging out of this beauty is a new aesthetics of life, given clear focus and detail through a fundamental appreciation for embodiment, as embodied bodies leave trails through history in the form of self-realization. Such an arrangement involves attention to both the individual and the "more" than individuality of life—not always a comfortable or comforting proposition. There, despite however desired this may be, is no "bridge from man to man," as Cross Damon observes. While he laments at death that "alone a man is nothing," he dies alone—without substantive connection.[75] Fred Daniels encounters a somewhat similar world, with a similar consequence. Yet, for both, embodied selves are of vital importance because this is the form (while not always achieved) relationships take. Bodies are rendered beautiful in this regard through this realization and because they are carried through the world with a new determination and intentionality. This does not, for example, entail a transformation whereby "movement" leaves either the individual or the "more" than individualness unchanged. It is necessary only to think about the violence committed by Cross Damon, for instance, to see this as so. However, such is not an intrinsic matter. Instead, it is based on a particular reading of beauty, corresponding to the secondary sense of beauty stated earlier. Nonetheless, these Damon and Daniels stories contain more than this in that they offer a way to articulate the primary sense of beauty as symmetry, and it is with this reading of Fred Daniels in light of symmetry that this chapter ends.[76]

In a very real way, the life circumstances of Fred Daniels entail for Richard Wright a fantastic mirroring of the absurdity of "life" within a context of white supremacy. We are to find in them reflections and critiques of the symmetries of racialization. Herein I offer a way to think about "The Man Who Lived Underground" through a theologizing of symmetry, particularly with respect to (1) bilateral symmetry as reciprocity and (2) rotational symmetries as socio-cultural cohesion, (3) the flexible nature of time, and (4) a view of (1) and (2) through an appreciation for the elegance marking symmetry and also through awareness of the nature of symmetry breakdown. While other arrangements are possible and should be explored, I limit this discussion to the forms mentioned in that the goal is simply to give readers a general sense of how a theologizing of symmetry affords an alternate way of thinking about the desired scope of life.

The physical world in which Daniels finds himself is composed of materiality and space—substance and void. For every dimension of the physical world visible, there is so much more beyond his (and our) ability to view and decipher through the senses. This makeup is somewhat mirrored in Daniels's circumstances as they are presented early in Richard Wright's short story. The need to avoid the police forces him underground and exposes him to other dimensions of social reality, unnoticed prior to that moment. While they are not utilized in the same manner and not viewed in the same way, there are some similarities between the upper world and the underworld of the sewer: Both are layered and embedded with the stuff of human activity. There is reciprocity at work in that there is a direct relationship between the interactions expressed in the upper world and the material housed in the underworld. One is dependent and directly reflects the other, and this is without change. The rules of life govern both worlds equally and consistently. In another way, shifting the underworld in terms of how Daniels occupies it does nothing to change its basic makeup. It remains the same, fundamentally unchanged by his attempt to construct a resting place within its confines.

Playing on primary beauty yet again, he enters the sewer to escape, and he finds himself still in the world but below view by others and within a space marked by substance and absence. It is the underworld, the location of the residue of human existence that we would rather hide—waste, discarded items, the signs of the tragic nature of life's end (e.g., the dead baby floating by him), and so on. These things are physically present, open to exploration. They are profoundly knowable. However, the sewer also represents—for those on the surface—an unknown space shrouded in dark emptiness. "Everything," according to Daniels, "seemed strange and unreal under here."[77] There is something akin to moral symmetry—reciprocity—involved here. Like Hades as the underworld in Greek mythology, Daniels's sewer provides balance. Deeds, perceived and real in the case of Daniels, are met with the appropriate outcome.[78] The possibilities at least rhetorically available in the upper world correspond to the dread of the underworld. Shifting them (Daniels's deeds above ground and his construction project below) does not change their fundamentals. The occupation of time and space by embodied selves framing the secondary sense of beauty necessitates the impingement of black bodies on the world through the awakening to their in/visibility, often entailing noise, sounds like the siren, and so on. However, with respect to symmetry (i.e., primary beauty), there is also something to be said about the balance offered to the noise through the intensity of silence at particular moments: "after a few yards he paused," as Wright chronicles, "struck to wonderment by the silence; it seemed that he had traveled a million miles away from the world."[79] Yet, the laws of life remained consistent in that they could not be outrun nor could they be suspended in this new location. There was balance, a type of symmetry between Daniels in the sewer and what he encounters: the upper world mirrored by the under world; the belief and singing of the church service matched by Daniels's disbelief and silence. Furthermore, his position has been rotated through movement to the underworld, but his perception of life (and ours by extension) remains the same, and the physical realities of life remain the same. In correspondence to this point, as Hermann Weyl remarks concerning (mathematical) symmetry and art: "Even in asymmetric designs one feels symmetry as the norm from which one deviates under the influence of forces of non-formal character."[80] Yet, while helpful, this comment does not fully capture the point needing to be made: We are not here talking about art as he intends its meaning. So think of upper world and underworld this way: The latter is a reflection of the former as with a mirror:

> Consider an idealized human figure, whose left side is exactly the same as the right side. Exactly? Well, if your left foot looked exactly the same as your right foot, you'd need two right slippers and it wouldn't matter which foot you put which slipper on. No, the two sides are not exactly the same: you have to flip one over to get the other. This is why the reflection of a human being in a mirror looks like a human being. In real humans there are subtle differences....[81]

The laws remain in force in both locations. The realities of life in both locations entail something of a bilateral symmetry, if for no other reason than that there is at least identity symmetry.

Symmetry can be of differing scopes. It might "break" with respect to a large system but still be present within the context of smaller pieces of that initial system—symmetries within symmetries. Hence, in moving from upper world to underworld, there are ways in which some of the symmetries of life break down or spread around for Daniels. Yet, certain other symmetries remain—a smaller group of the realities of black life (e.g., negative weight of black bodies, the confrontational nature of space encountered by black bodies, the need to critically engage inherited religious assumption). Aboveground or below, the nature of Daniels's life remains unchanged in some basic ways.[82] One can read the theodical implications in his negative reaction to the church service he can hear from his cave in underworld. Also of interest, however, is the symmetry—regulatory laws of black life—he finds so deeply troubling. He is critical of the church members until he remembers that the same laws determine his response to the police:

> After a long time he grew numb and dropped to the dirt. Pain throbbed in his legs and a deeper pain, induced by the sight of those black people groveling and begging for something they could never get, churned in him. A vague conviction made him feel that those people should stand unrepentant and yield no quarter in singing and praying, yet he had run away from the police, had pleaded with them to believe in his innocence. He shook his head, bewildered.[83]

Laws governing black embodied selves have the same effect in the underworld as they have in the upper world. Daniels simply has greater insight into the workings of these laws and the dynamics of the geographies of their influence. Shadow, darkness, the unseen—all these figure into Daniels's relationship to his new world, an inner dimension perhaps of the world he had been compelled to leave. He came to recognize new spaces, new dimensions of existence, embedded within each other as he moved into uncertainty.

Primary symmetry continues within the context of Daniels's life: There was a structure to this new world composed of rooms within rooms, doors across from doors, windows, and so on. What is more, these structures reflected the geography of the upper world. And as had been the case in the upper world, he knew these structures shaped the movement and impact of his activities and offered a cartography of his life. Time, calculations, and creativity were necessary if he was to achieve anything in this new underworld, and at one point, achievement meant getting into the black box, within a room, in a building, above the underworld: "to the right of him, he calculated, should be the basement of the building that held the safe; therefore, if he dug a hole right *here*, he ought to reach his goal."[84] Within the context of these discoveries—the arrangement of his surroundings—the symmetrical nature of the underworld continues. He breaks through one wall of his cave, only to discover it is mirrored by another wall. Daniels stumbles into the basement of a funeral home and discovers a body, like his body, and both bodies have experienced a certain type of death.[85] As he moves along, his exit from the cave is followed by discovery of another location, also an exit for the building he had entered. In so many ways, there is symmetry within symmetry: The pattern of his new life takes him not into a church, but into a movie theater, where reflected on the screen is the sad life of those in the theater. They are seeing the reflection of their meager existence, and they "were shouting and yelling at the animated shadows of themselves ... sleeping in their living, awake in their dying."[86]

Daniels felt all of this and saw all of it through windows and opened doors allowing him to notice others. But at the same time and through the same means, he was also able to see himself reflected as if the doors and the windows were mirrors. No matter what angle he used—whether peering through a window as he held to a rain pipe, or through the glass on a door as he hid in the dark—the basics of the scene(s) did not change. His life was not affected by the movement: He was still bound to the underworld. "Some part of him," Daniels reflects, "was trying to remember the world he had left, and another part of him did not want to remember it.... Emotionally, he hovered between the world aboveground and the world underground."[87] Yet, there were ways in which the upper world marked the "dead world of sunshine and rain he had left, the world that had condemned him, branded him guilty."[88] He believed there was a difference between the two worlds, ways in which symmetry was broken, yet, even in those moments, the two worlds reflected each other.

Drawing on the workings of symmetry as understood in this chapter, at certain points Daniels thinks of the connections between items, a shared relationship to him: "He saw these items hovering before his eyes and felt that some dim meaning linked them together, that some magical relationship made them kin. He stared with vacant eyes, convinced that all of these images [the dead baby in the sewer, the people in church and in the theater, the jewelry and dead body], with their tongueless reality, were striving to tell him something."[89] Daniels could not help being aware of the depth and richness of life's possibilities. For example, when looking at the money he had stolen, Daniels felt as if "he was reading of the doings of people who lived on some far-off planet."[90] But yet, on this faraway planet, they held the same monetary system and the same material wants and needs as those in the upper world. He could think of this other world, but he knew himself to be in the underworld. From both worlds—the upper world and the "far-off planet"—he learned the importance of the spaces, including the seemingly empty spaces upon which our materiality is built. This is certainly one way to read his experiment with the typewriter he stole from the jewelry shop:

> He laughed, then pecked slowly: itwasalonghotday. He was determined to type the sentence without making any mistakes. How did one make capital letters? He experimented and luckily discovered how to lock the machine for capital letters and then shift it back to lower case. Next he discovered how to make spaces, then he wrote neatly and correctly: It was a long hot day.[91]

In the upper world, he saw and felt death, but had he not entered the underworld and experienced it as something along the lines of Hades's realm of death and the dead? He experienced the upper world as definable in part by water, rain, but had not his experience of entering and moving through the underworld involved flowing water in the sewer and more water entering the sewer from the manholes?[92] He was believed to be a murderer in the upper world (having signed a confession, albeit under duress), and in the underworld, he was guilty of crimes and moved through the twists and turns of the underworld with a profound sense of guilt and dread.

He ventured into the upper world long enough to steal the items with which he would decorate his cave, and he felt some guilt for this . . . but not really. There was a balance to these developments. Take, for example, his theft from the safe. Certainly, someone would be punished for his crime; someone innocent would be charged with his guilt. Whatever the case might be for the night watchman accused of taking the money from the safe mattered little to Daniels in that it was all part of a pattern. "Yes, they were trying to make the watchman confess," he observed, "just as they had once made him confess to a crime he had not done. . . . Those were the same policemen who had beaten him, had made him sign that paper when he had been too tired and sick to care. Now, they were doing the same thing to the watchman."[93] Symmetrical patterns of in/justice to be sure were marked by two types of death: The watchman kills himself with a gun, and Daniels dwells in the underworld, dead to those living above him. Death as the final end to human existence is all around, always threatening to present itself. Humans had no soul to save, no divine creator to whom allegiance and obedience are due. On this score and in relationship to these supernatural elements, the church folks Daniels observed living in the upper world were wrong. Assuming otherwise did not address in a meaningful way the traumas of life in either world—upper or under. Instead, Daniels sought to recognize the structures and patterns of human life and thereby to see the connections and intersections as the unchanging dimensions of life. The tragic is already always present, as the laws of embodied life continued to shape and determine him, whether in the upper world or the underworld. Even when he left the under-world for a short time, he felt the circumstance of his life in the upper world forcing him back.

His location changed when he entered into the butcher shop from the underworld. But when approached by a white man and white woman wanting to buy grapes and thinking he worked in the shop, the transformation did not result in a shift to his basic self-perception, and the man and woman did not view him as anything other than a *black* embodied "something." He was still the same, with the same relationship to others. At one point, through an act of defi-ance—pasting money on the walls of his cave—he thinks himself free because he has signified the materialist inclinations of the upper world. But he is still in the underworld, bound in real ways by the rules and signifiers of time and space he thinks he has suspended. He could not outpace the measures of time (e.g., watches) of the upper world. Daniels—as he hangs watches from the walls of his cave—is still bound to the dynamics of time that hold fast those who dwell in upper world. This obedience to time was matched by an adherence to sym-metry within symmetries: He hung rings (with crystal symmetries) on the walls and piled diamonds (more examples of elegant structure) along the floor, even-tually spreading them along the dirt floor as if placing them as stars in space. The diamonds in/on the floor, envisioned as stars in the sky, also reflected an image of the lights of a vast city. He used these diamonds to image both symmetries of human construction and of natural development. Time and space were brought together, and the patterns told him something about himself and those in the upper world:

> He lit a cigarette with shaking fingers; the match flame revealed the green-papered walls with militant distinctness; the purple on the gun barrel glinted like a threat; the meat cleaver brooded with its eloquent splotches of blood; the mound of silver and copper smoldered angrily; the diamonds winked at him from the floor; and the gold watches ticked and trembled, crowning time the king of consciousness, defining the limits of living....[94]

He would feel the two worlds pulling at him, and he would eventually reenter the upper world. He looked different—dirty, caked with mud, inarticulate hav-ing had no one with whom to talk—and his meaning to those in the upper world remained marginal, although for a different reason. Marginal. Tangled in a web of life forces. This had not changed simply because he changed loca-tion: the same laws of sociocultural importance and visibility remained intact. Daniels wanted to bring these two worlds together—"he saw the cave next to the church…"[95]—to draw together and recognize the sameness of the patterns of life and life meaning found within the two worlds. That is to say, he sought deep understanding of the symmetrical nature of the worlds between which he lived and died, and he wanted to share that appreciation:

> If he could show them [the police officers] what he had seen, then they would feel what he had felt and they in turn would show it to others and those others would feel as they had felt, and soon everybody would be governed by the same impulse of pity.[96]

As Daniels demonstrated in a terribly fantastic manner, recognizing the patterns of life through the structuring of the space and time occupied is the goal, and this goal changes us but only in certain, subscribed ways: "when I looked through all of those holes and saw how people were living, I loved 'em."[97] His final encounter with the church and the police—two manifestations of authority: natural law and state regulations—simply enforced the unwillingness of those inside and outside the fictional story to embrace symmetry as the manifestation of beauty. Both, the church and the police, refused to "see what he had seen" and "feel what he had felt."[98]

Finally…

As the various examples of secondary and primary beauty drawn from the work of Richard Wright detail, focus on symmetry demands an interest in, if not embrace of, the physical world, whereas theistic soteriological formulations run the risk of leaving the world behind.[99]

For the theist, salvation must entail something of a complete process, or at least—as is the case with liberation—a process that holds a teleological promise. But this is not so with symmetry in that it pricks us to view life without offering anything complete and fully understood. Although not necessarily the way in which physicists understand this phrase, African American nontheistic humanist theology finds something of this perspective in the remark "symmetry dictates design."[100] *Time and space, based on symmetry as understood by the African American nontheistic humanist, has more depth, more layers, more possibilities than formulations of salvation can allow. We interact with it, move through and in it, and it interacts with us. Lived life as embodied selves, in light of this and within the framework offered by nontheistic humanist theology, becomes recognized for its dynamic nature. And there is something elegant about this arrangement.*

Through Daniels, Wright promotes the transformative significance of symmetry in ways that support the theologizing project of nontheistic humanism and the manner in which it undergirds physical existence. And when acknowledged, symmetry alters attitudes and postures toward the world. (Wright is a kindred spirit on this score.) Yet for Wright, as with African American nontheistic humanism (and its theological form), recognizing the fantastic structuring of physical existence, and moving through the various dimensions of life meaning, is more substantive than traditional notions of salvation. It requires both mental and embodied work—no easy task—but the rewards might be substantive, if (and it is unlikely) they are every secured.

5

African American Humanist Ethics

Outside Boston, a short drive from the city's major markers of cultural structures, communal engagement, and conflict—monuments to war and a demand for political independence—is serene Concord, Massachusetts.[1] This wooded space, kissed by Walden Pond, is a place of legend. Henry David Thoreau, philosopher of nature and writer, moved to Walden Pond to write and to, as he put it, "live deliberately." He built a cabin and stayed in Walden beginning in 1845 for a little more than two years before becoming "a sojourner in civilized life again."[2] In words that continue to inspire, Thoreau shares the intent behind this departure from "civilized life":

> I went to the woods because I wished to live deliberately, to front only the essential facts of life, and see if I could not learn what it had to teach, and not, when I came to die, discover that I had not lived.[3]

He recounted the substance of this experience of intentional and intense living in *Walden, or Life in the Woods* (1854). This book sparked the imagination of many and guided them into a sense of life experience marked by simplicity and recognition of connection to others that requires justice. Visitors come to this spot, go to Thoreau's small cabin—complete with a bed, three chairs, a green writing desk, and wood-burning stove for warmth—and then cross the road to see the pond. The water spreads out in front, and it is easy to imagine this view from Thoreau's perspective. "It is a soothing employment, on one of those fine days in the fall when all the warmth of the sun is fully appreciated," he writes, "to sit on a stump on such a height as this, overlooking the pond, and study the dimpling circles which are incessantly inscribed on its otherwise invisible surface amid the reflected skies and trees."[4] Thoreau found this beauty enchanting, the scope of life within natural surroundings appealing. However, I am not convinced he would have appreciated the addition to this surrounding, the marker of industry: Across from Thoreau's home for those two years (and two months) is the gift shop. As one might imagine, there are ample copies of *Walden* and additional works related to Thoreau. Moving around the store, one also encounters food items (e.g., huckleberry lollipops), stuffed animals, cards, gold-covered leaves, and so on. Perhaps these are all the typical items admirers of Thoreau would expect (and want) to find in the gift shop.

On my last visit, a series of bracelets for children caught my eye. They listed, as mantras of sorts, key ideas from Thoreau: "simplicity, simplicity" and, of course, "live deliberately." The idea was somewhat obvious: Thoreau provides insights that can be used to shape the good life by providing reminders of proper posture toward the world and right living in the world. What made this implicit ethical stance obvious was a set of T-shirts selling for $19.95 on the other side of the story: "What Would Thoreau Do?" Obviously, the question turns the recent "What Would Jesus Do?" campaign on its head by finding in Thoreau's writings such as *Walden* and "On Civil Disobedience" the earthy ethical platform that parallels the code of conduct associated with the teachings of Jesus Christ. Perhaps this was an effort to be linguistically clever and nothing more; perhaps it has a much richer and more challenging motivation. Nontheistic humanist theology finds intriguing the latter possibility. The shift from a Christologically arranged ethics to an anthro-ethical platform could not have been lost on the Thoreau Society of Concord, Massachusetts, responsible for the T-shirts. But perhaps their intent was not to produce a system of ethics with such a strong sense of humanity that it might give a nontheistic humanist pause, not out of disgust but rather as a moment of familiarity—a shared sense of ethical challenge and possibility. Somewhere between a small cabin and a jail cell, through his reflections on the simple life and his demand for justice for all humanity Thoreau might offer principles of conduct proving useful in the development of humanist ethics appropriate for an African American nontheistic humanist theology.[5]

Here the intent is to highlight the ethical advantages of Thoreau's thought, accompanied by that of figures such as Frederick Douglass and Harriet Tubman. And this is done while mindful of the physical presence of Africans within Thoreau's *Walden*, as well as the significance of the African presence to the overall context of Concord. In fact, the literary and historical significance of Concord is shadowed by the presence of a small number of enslaved Africans. "From its founding in 1635 until after the Revolution," writes Elise Lemire, "enslaved men and women helped to build what would become New England's most storied town."[6] African Americans once freed from enslavement in the Concord area had restricted mobility and little visibility because of limited economic and social opportunities.[7] Some of the few places they could reside without overt resistance were wooded areas with poor soil quality, places like the Walden woods.[8] They were pushed to these woods before Thoreau because of socially coded patterns of interaction and also as Concord's way of enforcing various mechanisms of difference worthy of discrimination. Thoreau's was a temporary and quasi-hermitic existence that amplified the feel and experiences of his body, and theirs was a forced isolation meant to render their bodies invisible to the residents of Concord. Acknowledging the plight of these *other(ed)* occupants, Thoreau nonetheless experienced Walden in a different manner: His embodied existence in those woods was shaped through the aesthetics of social capital and the privileges of voice. It is worth noting Thoreau's critique of the failures of democratic living and liberative thinking and action in "Civil Disobedience" and "Slavery in Massachusetts" comes after his time at Walden. Hence, I highlight *Walden* over against subsequent lectures and writings because I am interested in the manner in which his ethical posture is formed, which has implications for humanist ethics, and less concerned with the particular targets—slavery, for instance—of this ethical posture once developed.

Engaging the World and the Good Life

As George Shulman argues, one need not understand Thoreau as advocating a nonpolitical individualism grounded in a simplicity that ignores sociopolitical need. Instead, it is possible to view Thoreau's turn to the deliberate life premised on romanticization of connection to nature and his prophetic stance with respect to slavery as involving a creative tension. That is to say, "By inhabiting the office of (moral) witness and by creating a poetry of wilderness regeneration," Shulman writes, Thoreau "engages a political world he always distrusted and maligned, always wished he could escape, and always dreamed of transforming."[9] Thoreau proposes the individual's obligations and commitments must be premised not on blind conformity but on independence of thought. His critique of social existence outside Walden, for instance, involves rejection of life that does not promote integrity of relationships and that is not premised on the development of complex and reflexive persons. To further clarify the point, life deeply lived *is* the good life.[10] Or as my grandmother instructed, "Move through the world knowing your footsteps matter." Involved here is a freeing of persons to engage life and in the process understand the "weight" of their existence. To rework a scriptural reference, one cannot carry new wine (i.e., transformative relationships) in old skins (i.e., individuals with improper sense of self). In a dynamic relationship, African American nontheistic humanist theology, as does Thoreau, makes use of the familiar vocabulary of the Christian faith but not as a way to exalt it but rather to bring it under the authority of embodied life in connection to embodied selves.

I imagine the deepening of the self poses little trouble. However, more challenging is the assumption that Thoreau's stance promotes healthier social existence as opposed to simply breeding greater egotism and an ethics of selfishness as virtue. It is important to note his "training" in self and thoughtful connection to others is short-lived, only a little longer than two years, after which he returns to the social connections he finds problematic. His movement between Walden Pond and Concord suggests the need for a productive paradox: The inevitability of existence within the structures of life less than ideal matched the possibility for effecting change regarding the self and the self in connection to other relationships of life and meaning. Furthermore, while a transformative experience for him, Thoreau's time in the wilderness does not involve a strong rejection of the trappings of social life—money, career, and so on—but rather entails a temporary push against a rather unimpressive career path and limited conformity to the dominant markers of success. The experiment at Walden means connection to the impulse of life freed from the unreasonable trappings of unity as a means for disinterested living; freed in this manner, connection to life promotes concern for others.[11]

Thoreau's experience, so conceived, pushes against the manner in which individuals entrap themselves, rendering themselves subject to self-understandings and perceptions that limit reach because "what a man thinks of himself," he writes, "that is which determines, or rather indicates, his fate."[12] Such a life is one of "quiet desperation."[13] Ethics in this context is a matter of measured progress determined but incomplete movement toward wholeness of life.

Thoreau reconfigures the geography of meaningful engagement and promotes cartography of the same premised on an ethics of inward clarity generating outward activism sensitive to individuals and communities—multileveled forms of obligation to think for oneself and with concern for others. The key to this system of ethics is to live life with earnestness and in pursuit of fullness.

Thoreau and the Ethical Implications of "Being Good"

Ethics as culled from Thoreau—and African American humanist ethics draws from this perspective but extends it beyond a strict concern with the male as central ethical agent—on a fundamental level does not involve construction of new social mechanisms and structures of existence.[14] Not fundamentally concerned with communal existence, ethics has as a core concern the creation of space and time wherein individuals and groups are able to refine the embodied self—to better develop their humanity—and from that internal improvement generate patterns of and postures toward our external commitments and relationships. Such a stance toward what we ought to do demands questioning of those things enabling comfort with the world as it is and a struggle to fix attention on the elemental structures of our existence. To achieve this outcome, one must first, as a matter of ethical necessity, strip away illusions and empty appeals and instead push inward as a way of extending oneself outward. Reflecting on Thoreau's sense of life, Philip Cafaro remarks that "deliberation is the key to living well, affirming human freedom, and meeting life's challenges. Life is glorious, Thoreau insists, and so the stakes are high." Awake and experience life, and as one learns more of life, one is better positioned to extend goodness (but also, I would add, oppressive tendencies) beyond oneself and address the pressing needs (and again I would add extending or redressing these needs) of others.[15]

Thoreau appreciates the potential impact of simplicity and all it entails in spite of its limited connection to majority opinion. As humanists should understand, he often makes use of the grammar of Christian faith but does so in a way that centers it on humanity over against appeal to ethical reasoning on the whims and desire of a divine figure. Ethical commitments and frameworks are earthy for Thoreau. He develops his ethical insights through writing, manual labor, keen observation, and limited social interactions that heighten his sensitivity to the significance of the ordinary and mundane.[16] "No way of thinking or doing, however ancient," Thoreau advises, "can be trusted without proof."[17] Experience is to be valued, and a variety of life paths acknowledged. Metaphysical assumptions and claims to a fixed model of proper life pale in comparison with the ethical lessons learned through reflection on embodied connection to the physical environment. The promise of life in the United States is not symbolized by the refinement of a city on a hill; rather, the potential for (not promise of) substantive and meaningful life is in the sights and sounds, the feel and challenges, of the simple and deliberate life. This is the type of life that demands the most and best from one and, in turn, prepares one to offer oneself to transformative opportunities for responsible living. For Thoreau, this is in part accomplished because life in the wilderness exposed the damage done by structures of social engagement as they render bodies docile and promote conformity to unreasonable rules of collective life.

To live deliberately in the wilderness is to strip away layers of stultifying social expectation and conformity. This, like all commitments, requires what Thoreau references as "a genius," a fundamental inclination and capacity. For him, this motivation and inclination flies in the face of socially orchestrated humanitarianism that in the long run is usually void of solid thought and internal persuasion. Based on the usual assumption that the social good is rightly one's primary concern and motivation, what Thoreau proposes seems an ego-centered and nonprogressive approach to collective need. Yet, it is not a rejection of concern for others that motivates Thoreau; rather, it is a different place of origin for such concern that distinguishes him. In his words, "a man is not a good man to me because he will feed me if I should be starving, or warm me if I should be freezing, or pull me out of a ditch if I should ever fall into one. I can find you a Newfoundland Dog that will do as much. Philanthropy is not love for one's fellowman in the broadest sense."[18] Such a stance toward philanthropy, the one rejected by Thoreau, does not recognize appeal to and push for the best of ourselves, but rather assumes a somewhat low opinion of (and minimal requirements for) humans. What some outline as ethics gives little attention to root causes and instead is content to labor around the more superficial dimensions of human need in ways that require little personal moral commitment. This posture is not the proper starting point for Thoreau's ethics. In the colorful language of Thoreau: "There are a thousand hacking at the branches of evil to one who is striking at the root, and it may be that he who bestows the largest amount of time and money on the needy is doing the most by his mode of life to produce that misery which he strives in vain to relieve."[19] It is not the "good which society demands of me" that marks proper ethical posture; rather, action premised on conscience and substance is preferable, regardless of how such activity is categorized within the dominant social order. Notions of the good typically require little of the person, demand limited correction of the self. Instead of doing "the" good based on such a model, Thoreau privileges proper action—"doing good"— stemming from a deep commitment to "being good."[20]

Religions, like Christianity, involve an effort to live life through the experiences of *another* (e.g., Jesus Christ), to see as the focus and end of life a mirroring of another's will.[21] So arranged, the important moment is always a past or future moment, with the present only a problem to solve. Instead of this approach, nontheistic humanist ethics tutored by Thoreau urges an effort to "live deep" in the present, to appreciate and fully commit to life, and to remove all distractions from this engagement with ourselves, with others, and in the world.[22] "My practice," reflects Thoreau, "is 'nowhere,' my opinion is here."[23] There is in this statement a conviction, a determination not based on conventions and traditions. Instead, he speaks a position that would later be mirrored in Martin Luther King Jr.'s theologizing of social protest: "If a man does not keep pace with his companions, perhaps it is because he hears a different drummer. Let him step to the music which he hears, however measured or far away."[24] Nontheistic humanist ethics, while purging King's theistic (and theodical) intent, shares with him an appreciation for the vitality of Thoreau's approach to ethical vision and involvement. Referencing King serves several purposes, including an implied juxtaposition of Thoreau's experience with that of other figures noted for ethical insight who mark out these insights within the context of mundane space made meaningful.

Thoreau is not the first to have a wilderness experience and not the only one to create a time of separation meant to foster something new by means of an altered consciousness and a new perspective on ethical and moral obligation. Earlier encounters with the wilderness, through Jesus or the Buddha, for instance, maintain a certain metaphysical necessity, and time does not remain intact (as it does for Thoreau). Yet, Thoreau's wilderness experience shares with that of Jesus and the Buddha, for example, a sense of crisis confronted within the context of embodied self. In this sense, as Delores Williams frames the wilderness experience for Hagar, it involves a moment of relief from absurd social obligations and structures.[25] But whether Jesus, the Buddha, or Hagar, this wilderness experience involves the human in connection to metaphysical issues and concerns that point to the individual's role within a larger and cosmic devel-opment—a significance that can dwarf the body/embodied self. These three (Jesus, Buddha, and Hagar) seem to pick spiritualized obligation over the body, but not so for Thoreau.[26] To think about Thoreau's notion of authority and right-ness as connected to even an earthier notion of "god" is not a move one makes of necessity. He seems more humanistic (certainly some would oppose this claim) than that, arguing instead for an eco-anthropology that serves to ground thought and activity in a simple regard for "the gift of life."[27] In this way, we are able to keep the great charge to "make [one's] life, even in its details, worthy of the contemplation of [one's] most elevated and critical hour."[28] Meaning is not external to the individual, but rather it entails the larger framework of life when observed, embraced, and experienced. This is what constitutes and con-firms, in the moment, an internal substance. Proper ethical conduct reflects a trace of this inner impulse—goodness based on the depth of the ordinary— and allows for work toward "justice" as opposed to self-aggrandizement in the guise of concern for others. One's "goodness," writes Thoreau, "must not be a partial and transitory act, but a constant superfluity, which costs [one] nothing and of which [one] is unconscious."[29] Acts of goodness, in counterdistinction to Thoreau's proposition, more often than not reflect a concern with self, based on attention to one's situation and concerns. There is a tendency to seek the lofty— to target and attack on grand narratives and superstructures. And while there is something to this approach, it fails to the extent that it is not grounded in rec-ognition and correction of the self. Proper action based on sound ethics should involve sharing "our courage, and not our despair, our health and ease, and not our disease, and take care that this does not spread by contagion."[30] One can find in *Walden* a rationale for embodied self as the antisocial figure or as the reflexive person also concerned with the context of the collective.

Does Thoreau's attention to the individual go too far, and does his concern with life stripped down to its most fundamental forms promote a romantic sense of human qua nature (with an embedded sense of stewardship over the earth)? Does he promote an epistemology of the wilderness (or deification of nature) that allows for "pure" isolation as right living?[31] No. Grounding of the self in a desire to "be good" over against simply "doing good" does not result in isolation. Thoreau, in spite of what critics have said, must be acknowledged for the con-nection to others he maintained even when at Walden Pond: "Even in *Walden* there are many references to visitors to the cabin, trips into town to gossip, social rambles, shared fishing idylls, and other pleasant social interactions.... During the fifteen years left to him after he returned from the pond, he remained a beloved member of his family and an increasingly valued and respected member of his community, performing useful duties as town surveyor and keeping his neighbors alert and a degree or two more self-aware and honest with his sharp tongue."[32] What one gathers from *Walden*, then, is sensitivity to the weight and seriousness of both individual awareness and social engagement. Each is more than superficial encounter without effect. Both involve uneasy confrontations and delicate balance between different impressions of the world. Again, for African American nontheistic humanist ethics the world is deliberate... deliberate experiencing of life in ways meant to expand understanding and enrich encounters with self and others, often articulated in the action-based language of an identifiably naturalistic quest for complex subjectivity. There is here a pushing of the individual in the direction of others (thereby grounding a desire to be more than sympathetic toward those who suffer injustice), an immersion of the individual in the mundane.[33] Given the strategies of discrimination encountered by African Americans (the ways in which the integrity of the African American self was challenged and denied as a mechanism for maintaining the inferiority of African Americans), the framework offered by Thoreau can be used to reconstruct the African American as a moral and ethical agent who matters in a world that matters. Yet, it is also important to recognize that care of the embodied self is not a contained task. Ethics as implied in *Walden* has to involve the good individual's lived experience as self with others and nature.

"Simplicity, simplicity, simplicity," as Thoreau announces, is not only an appeal to less stuff—his three chairs, desk, and bed, for instance, and fewer pieces of clothing—but also an alternate hermeneutic by which individuals determine those things fundamental to meaningful life. As a consequence of making this discovery, individuals are better able to focus energy in ways that enhance their humanity and mark significant points of life potentiality through intense contact with the ordinary. Ethics, then, gains a great deal by diving deep into the common and unspectacular. After all, it is within these spaces of the familiar that embodied humans "move and have their being." For Thoreau and African American nontheistic humanist ethics, traces of the self litter the world as we experience it because "we are in the world" *and of it*. There is inherent tension in this statement and in its felt and spoken consequences.[34] But this tension does not prevent moral activity; instead, it informs the rather modest claims ethical vision and behavior should entail.[35] Thoreau appreciates the integrity of the individual as one who thinks and lives, but he does not forget the connections of this thinking and doing individual to larger social arrangements. He simply laments the shortcomings of these connections.

Development of the individual as one who is good opens that person to relationships that draw from that ethical foundation. Hence, this fundamental effort on the part of the individual provides a moral compass usable for critiquing oppression's structures and public policies. Not "tradition and conformity" but rather what is important is a deep effort to be good and have that goodness guide all one's dealings.[36]

The written word for Thoreau is bound to proper action, and it serves as flexible encasing for the rhythms of our embodied intentionality. Or as Robert Richardson notes, "Writing cannot be separated from life for Thoreau. It is linked to it, built upon it, and dependent upon it."[37] Because of this concern for capturing the vocabulary and grammar of his life, the ethical insights garnered during those twenty-six months at Walden push beyond their initial moment. Insights gained from his time apart in Walden belong to Thoreau, of course, but they have a life beyond his effort to be deliberate in his personal thinking and conduct. He did not want them to rest only with himself. "The very language of Walden," notes one writer, "creates the impression that while the experience at the pond is Thoreau's own, the conclusions and lessons to be drawn from it are common property...."[38] He seeks to leave society for a finite period of time with the intention of reestablishing the self so as to affect society upon his return in ways that do not leave it as it was found. A measured realism dominates here in that Thoreau understands the limits of human capacity and the manner in which human interactions have their confinements and proscriptions. African American nontheistic humanists fully understand that embodied selves seek to do the best they can to make the living of life an act of justice, while recognizing the shortcomings of this strategy from start to finish.[39]

Thoreau's comfort with paradox (privilege versus simplicity) and tension (individual and the collective) also allows for an ethical posture by which to encounter the absurdity of sociopolitical and cultural arrangements defining our occupation of time and space. We are left with the certainty of uncertainty, and, while this might trouble more teleological discourses such as black and womanist theologies, it is enough for nontheistic humanist ethical thinking and living.[40] In fact, scholars such as Mary Elkins Moller depict Thoreau as a humanist because of a perceived (although questioned by some others) "determination to 'serve the public good'...despite, or even because of, those instances and scathing criticism."[41] Thoreau argues too many are so concerned with the outer trappings of social existence they fail to note the true substance of life. And he laments this when saying, "I am sure that there is greater anxiety, commonly, to have fashionable, or at least clean and unpatched clothes, than to have a sound conscience."[42] Such an approach, this shallow digging of sorts, involves a faulty aesthetics of existence. It does not support life lived with integrity and meaning, marked by movement through the world based on determination, thoughtfulness, and awareness of all that surrounds us.[43] The style of *be*-ing rejected by Thoreau is cheap. Yet, as he notes, things have an expense that extends beyond material exchange; rather, the "cost of a thing is the amount of what I call life which is required to be exchanged for it, immediately or in the long run."[44]

Wilderness living is not long-term but rather offers a moment of revelation, an opportunity for fostering perspective and greater clarity concerning obligations to self and to the collective.[45]

Making a difference in the world is an embodied activity that must be undergirded first by reconstitution of the individual, and it does not require any particular devotion to religious institutions or doctrinal formulations. The process is more natural than that. One might suggest the Walden experience makes possible for Thoreau an ethics of sensitivity and mindfulness that prompts the individual to contribute to the collective good, not by thoughtless conformity but through embodied resistance. This resistance seeks to make real the type of awareness and integrity of existence generated through an individual's poetic discovery of self. And this is achieved in part through embrace of the everyday as the arena of transformation and the individual as the starting place for social renewal. Sensitivity to how the individual as embodied self occupies time and space is the launching point for rethinking the dynamics and commitments of the social body in ways that counter tendencies toward the subduing of life as lived. This subduing, to Thoreau's lament, denies recognition of what can be life's fullness, and as a consequence, they are "cultivated, just as nature was increasingly becoming the material for consumption and industry." And what is more, with this limiting context "lives took on predictable shapes and activity conformed to expected patterns."[46] Such is the stuff of life as a superficial and dronelike existence, whereas Thoreau petitions readers to recognize that "it is life near the bone where it is sweetest."[47] Ethics in this context begins with the development of "capacities for judgment, dialogue, and action."[48]

African American nontheistic humanist ethics appreciates Thoreau's framing of response to the social body as posture toward the world that values the margins as the location for more clarity and maturity of insight concerning the stranglehold conformity has on individuals and therefore communities. There is vulnerability associated with this ethical stance, entailing a level of uncertainty and risk: The posture toward the world and the action it seeks to promote may be insufficient to the task, and conformity to social regulations and political confinement will continue to rule the day.

Thoreau's time in *Walden* meant departure *and* a moment of arrival. And while there are benefits or elements of growth and freedom in this time apart, it is not a framing for life that can be sustained indefinitely: Thoreau leaves Walden (just as intentionally as he went) and reenters the social machine, somewhat transformed, but still connected to a rather troubled system. Involvement in this system or work against it ends with death, and this progression should serve to point out the importance of digging deep into life. In this way, to die means one has actually lived.[49] This is a compelling response in that for African American nontheistic humanists there is nothing after this embodied self stops wrestling in time and space. Any continued existence is only socioemotional (and perhaps physical space, such as graves and shrines) as we are remembered by those still living. Proper ritual and proper belief do nothing to prevent this end; as Thoreau knew, Walden was replete with the in/visible markings of embodied selves no longer wrestling with life—both white and black.

Frederick Douglass and the Ethical Implications of Claiming "Space"

The African presence shadows Thoreau's Walden. While the African American population in Walden struggled to survive, the challenges and limitations were too great, and their numbers dwindled. Nonetheless, Thoreau was aware of and influenced by the legacy of enslaved Africans in the Concord area; they haunt his narrative.[50] He is sensitive to their impact on the land, and his obligation to be good through rejection of social structures and political mechanisms is built on their pain; yet, this is not enough for the African American humanist seeking a theologically influenced structure of ethical conduct. Thoreau remembers the complexity of life in the woods—the various communities represented there, including free Africans—and this reflecting on the deliberate life in light of this complexity is vital. But although Thoreau critiques and engages the problem of slavery and racial discrimination as a destruction of humanity and a contamination of the environment, African American nontheistic humanist ethics must partner his framing of life with additional ethics-driven commentary from other vantage points.[51] Along this line, important for nontheistic humanist ethics is more direct contact with the world as experienced by this diverse system of wilderness dwellers—and in this way pushing them out of the shadows and putting them front and center. Understand, I am not suggesting a crude and gross assumption that African Americans have epistemological privilege in these matters.[52] Rather, attention to an African American presence allows one to incorporate a measured sense of challenge and progress made necessary by the troubled history of the United States.

It is to another one-time resident of Massachusetts—this time, New Bedford— that we turn for insights gleaned from the experiences of enslaved (and free) African Americans. In 1845, the year Thoreau packed his few material items and moved into the woods, Frederick Douglass published his first autobiography and thereby exposed the mechanics of enslavement and the ethics of personhood as a way of claiming embodied space.[53] Thoreau was familiar with Douglass, and as his thoughts on civil disobedience would suggest, he shared Douglass's commitment to development of the full reach of human integrity and consciousness. African American humanist ethics recognizes this link—Thoreau and Douglass—and understands it as a useful bridge. Douglass and Thoreau held differing relationships to land and the working of land, with Douglass unable to afford things associated with a romanticized embrace of nature known to Thoreau. Yet, there is a shared sense between the two by which truth is experiential, and the individual must develop the capacity for being good as a precursor to acting good. And furthermore, for both Thoreau and Douglass, this work entails the mind and a strong relationship to fleshy bodies.

Prior to securing his freedom, Douglass used the pretext of religious devotion (in the form of religious instruction) as a means by which to teach enslaved Africans to read. A troubled relationship with institutional religion marks Douglass's thought, but open to less questioning is his sense of ethical conduct guided by and responsible for the shaping of human experience. Douglass, one could argue, remains committed to the idea that the Christ Event provides a model of morality of some benefit, and, to the extent Christianity has something to do with the presentation of the model, Douglass maintains some of its vocabulary and grammar.

It is a mistake—a matter of desired connection between the contemporary moment and Douglass—to suggest, however, that Douglass's rhetoric "anticipates" liberation theology (meaning black theology).[54] Not every call for justice when couched in the grammar of public moral precepts constitutes such a theistic theological formulation. Perhaps Douglass provides a certain type of religious (filtered through a strong anthropology and, at times, something resembling religious naturalism) argument for the advancement of African Americans, but this does not necessarily constitute a liberation theology. To the contrary, effort to render Douglass the prototype of a liberation theologian is a lament of the declining significance of so many post–civil rights theological discourses. Furthermore, the lament is couched in a determination to give these discourses historical weight and continuity beyond the merit of their argument. Such a move involves effort to revive these discourses through appeal to the heroic personalities of the past as if this lends significance to contemporary theological proclamations that have failed to bear fruit consistent with their claims. It is a backward look that fails to acknowledge the danger in the uncritical transference of paradigms and heroic personalities into the current moment.[55]

Douglass would not be the first or the last to attempt a disentangling of moral possibilities found in Christ from the problematic trappings and theological nonsense of Christian religion. This, however, is not the same as suggesting he embraces Christianity as a pattern of ethical conduct. He seems much too grounded in a type of naturalism. Douglass strays from many of the central markers of the social gospel of his period, let alone the discursive moves that would come to mark liberation theologies. For example, the redemptive suffering matrix dominant in African American Christian thought during the nineteenth century (and later in the twentieth century as well) gives way to a more anthropodical perspective on the part of Douglass. Unlike much nineteenth-century thought (extending through the twentieth century), Douglass does not posit a robust Christology as the center of theological and ethical commitments. To the contrary, Douglass privileges anthropology, whereby he offers a grounded framework for thought and action, informed by historically positioned determination to ethically situate oneself to oneself and others.[56] Hence, one must let Douglass be Douglass, and liberation theologians be liberation theologians.

In like manner, the argument here is not that Douglass offers an earlier version of African American nontheistic humanist theology. My claims are more modest and revolve around the ways in which Douglass's ethical sensibilities might inform nontheistic humanist ethics.[57] Perhaps Douglass embodies tension between belief and disbelief, and the movement between these two poles is based on the dynamics of and shifts within mundane human experience. Black and womanist theologies tend to give primary attention to the development of institutional forms and doctrine as the birth of religious sentiment within African American communities. But why would embrace of borrowed creedal forms and institutional structures best mark the quest for complex subjectivity? Does not the physical movement highlighted by Douglass exemplify the manner in which this quest is enacted as both material demand and symbolic gesture—affecting a more complex arrangement of the body? African Americans as presented by Douglass are subjects, with growing complexity—yet without complete independence of thought and movement. And this raises anew certain questions of ethics: How should increasingly complex subjects act in the world?

Douglass speaks to the development of a certain type of consciousness resulting from a sense of education as a dangerous thing—the tool by which slavery is destroyed. "Learning," remarks Mr. Auld, who controlled Douglass's body while he was in Baltimore, "would spoil the best nigger in the world." And to this, Douglass responds, "I now understood what had been to me a most perplexing difficulty—to wit, the white man's power to enslave the black man."[58] This realization prompted greater awareness of the mechanisms or genius of enslavement. Yet, all is not language and discourse, as Douglass discovered. Reading, for example, resulted in greater awareness of the measurements of both mental and physical control exercised against him. In other words, "it opened my eyes to the horrible pit," he writes, "but to no ladder upon which to get out."[59] The power of slavery had an expressed embodiment that meant the need for knowledge and the claiming of place. But in demanding time and space, and holding his place,

Douglass was able to damage the cultural construction of his body as despised and was able also to point out the strength and merit of his materiality as strike against white supremacy and the ways in which class, race, and gender attach to and inform bodies. The ramifications of this are significant for a nontheistic humanist understanding of ethics and religion.

Douglass recognized confinement as the manner in which he was created and monitored, while privileging truth gained through the integrity of the self over against blind compliance with popular opinion (or tradition?). "I prefer," he writes, "to be true to myself, even at the hazard of incurring the ridicule of others, rather than to be false, and incur my own abhorrence."[60] Out of what does this mental and physical integrity arise? Douglass's fight with Edward Covey, the overseer, represents an example of the connections between the lived body as nexus of culture (body as discursive) and nature (the body as related to other human and "nonhuman" bodies, vulnerable to age, disease, confinement, etc.). According to Douglass, he is put under the control of Covey in 1833 to break him, to render him docile and therefore useful.[61] Covey targeted the body—organizing its confinement and deconstruction—as a way of capturing the mind, along the way seeking to make both pliable. On one occasion, after some difficulty controlling an oxcart that eventually damaged a gate, Covey took Douglass to the woods. Douglass recounts the experience: Covey, he writes, "rushed at me with the fierceness of a tiger and tore off my clothes, and lashed me till he had worn out his switches, cutting me so savagely as to leave the marks visible for along time after. This whipping was the first of a number just like it, and for similar offences."[62] The regular beatings had an effect on Douglass, a consequence that Douglass labels the breaking of his total being—"body, soul, and spirit."[63] To borrow Thoreau's structuring of conduct and consciousness, Douglass knew himself as slave—moving him from doing the work of a slave to *being* a slave. Although traumatic, this process of construction and control through power flow, as Michel Foucault makes clear, is incomplete. There are deficiencies, or ways in which the practices of docility do not achieve their ends and can, in fact, be recognized for their shortcomings. Or as both Foucault and Thoreau note in different ways and for different purposes, social structures and stories of meaning are nonessential. And both the partial and fragile nature of these structures provide an opening for ethical (re)action based on a simple maxim phrase: "No man has a Right to make any concessions to Tyranny, which he would refuse to make if *he* were the victim."[64]

The rule of conduct is simple but not simplistic and involves something of a negation. Do nothing that prevents fullness of life lived. This does not prevent or hamper justice-driven action ("benevolence without justice is a mockery")[65] but rather frames ethical thinking and conduct in terms of full humanity over against efforts to reify particular depictions of the proper self in relationship to other selves.[66]

In the case of Douglass, the sparking of consciousness and moral outrage happens as he reflects on his suffering and determines to seek aid from Thomas Auld. He sees this as a way of easing the abuse encountered at the hands of Covey. Douglass asserts a limited sense of self by which pain is recognized as contrary to one's proper state. However, it is not a fundamental strike against the ontological damage of enslavement, but rather a call for a gentler type of oppression. It seeks from those in control only a posture of leniency and an ethics of measured compliance. Even this move, staged through an appeal to the one who claimed ownership of his body, and whose land had been the location for his work and existence, gained Douglass little in that Auld maintained the social economy, as well as the rules of property. Could Douglass, after his various experiences, really have believed Auld would take the side of a slave (a "something") over the cultural contract understood to exist between two white males (even if they are of different social classes)? More likely this effort on Douglass's part served as a marker of his desperation and evidence of oppressive webs of contacts and relationships—mechanisms of control and domination. Further evidence of Douglass's desperation involved reluctant embrace of the spiritualized aid of one Sandy Jenkins, who offered him a "root" capable of protecting him from harm. This device, if anything, offered an alternate focal point—an object of direction that charged the material body in a new way and gave it a heightened sense of time and place.[67] Perhaps the root served to reframe the connection of the self to the body.

It is worth noting Douglass's hesitant use of the root (a dimension of root work or hoodoo) connects to a critique of Southern ("status quo") Christianity as a discourse of compliance running contrary to what one would assume to be the ethical commitments of Christians based on their theological rhetoric.[68] Slavery, according to Douglass, exposes the mechanics of control and warped anthropology, and Southern ("status quo") Christianity seeks to distinguish types of existential and ontological bodies through adherence to a social discourse of black inferiority. As a process of epistemological and ontological dissonance, root work challenges the integrity of these mechanics of control not by hiding bodies but rather by a new type of visibility qua the harnessing of *natural powers* (over against artificial modalities of dominance—social regulation and so on). Southern ("status quo") Christianity disconnects white discursive and physical bodies from the world of nature, and root work's value lies in its ability to connect Douglass's discursive and material body to the power and balance of nature over against tying him to depictions of nature as savage, dangerous, and in need of strong restraint. Whatever the case or rationale, Douglass had the root with him at the time of his life-transformative encounter with Covey.

"This battle with Mr. Covey," Douglass recounts, "was the turning-point in my career as a slave. It rekindled the few expiring embers of freedom, and revived within me a sense of my own manhood. It recalled the departed self-confidence, and inspired me again with a determination to be free."[69] This claiming of self was not full freedom; rather, it was promotion of a new being (the "embers of freedom") made possible through an alternate ethical relationship to self and others, one premised on exercising humanity through the demand of embodied time and space. Or in the words of Douglass, this moment of struggle released an ontological shift from *slavery in being to slavery in form only.*[70] This restructuring of the discursive self encouraged in Douglass a push for a more robust physical self, and all this was in counterdistinction to the construction of slaves: "to make a contented slave, it is necessary to make a thoughtless one. It is necessary to darken his moral and mental vision, and, as far as possible, to annihilate the power of reason."[71] Douglass fought against the structures of racial difference through a limited controlling of his body over against the interests and desires of other bodies. Douglass gave focus to a new blend of action and words, with the latter premised on a proper grammar of social transformation. That is to say, "Douglass's view of grammar is pegged to a broad humanism. To be human is to be free, and to be free is to have the full cognitive powers characteristic of human inner life. Grammar is the skeleton over which those powers drape, hence it is essential for full, modern humanity."[72]

Thoreau, on the other hand, sought to control the white body through a short-term rejection of the more explicit trappings of privilege: to live simply and with determination and to reflect on life lived. Ultimately, this was to involve taking active responsibility for the space and time occupied by the privileged body. What Gail Weiss says in critique of Foucault and Merleau-Ponty speaks to this point: "Bodies are marked by assumptions made about their gender, their race, their ethnicity, their class, and their 'natural' abilities." And, she continues, "these assumptions, moreover, often tend to go unnoticed until they are violated by a body that refuses to behave as it should."[73] Douglass's position on morality holds a similar sense of restriction based on social status. He argues, for instance, enslaved Africans are free to behave in ways generally considered unethical or immoral because of their current sociocultural state of being. However, this rethinking of proper behavior is based on confrontation with a false status—an inauthentic restriction and a corruption of humanity. When one's embodied humanity is recognized, via physical struggle, for instance, new possibilities and responsibilities take form. One then acts from and in light of a demand for fullness or wholeness, and through this focus, one also undertakes a certain awareness of the necessary welfare of others.

It was not just a fight for Douglass and Covey; instead, it was the blurring of cultural boundaries, the challenging of what were considered essential arrangements of place whereby certain bodies were at the service of others. The discourse of inferiority framing the cultural bodies of Douglass and Covey was fractured through the violent contact of their material selves. Both reconstruction of the cultural body and the claiming of the physical body have something of an ethical component at work in that both have something to do with the processes and patterns of living life.[74] Both involve shifting circuits of power, with Douglass's body no longer constructed as docile. His was a different relationship with the world and a different posture toward himself in the world. As a result of this struggle with Covey, Douglass's body is not a body violated and ripped apart through word and gaze or a passive body handed back to its "owner."[75] Douglass's domination of space/place over against an instrument and symbol of dominance and control (i.e., Covey) suggests an active and resistant body—but one not completely free from the workings and shape(s) of oppressive/freeing power. This is not to argue Douglass understood slavery as the proper lot for those who do not strike back.[76] (He is not as pedagogically demanding as David Walker appears to be.[77]) Slavery is an evil that seeks to diminish the possibility of resistance through the process intended by Covey—the fostering of flexible bodies and compliant minds. Race-driven slavery is an arrangement of power through mechanisms of control and discourses of epistemologically justified discrimination. *And one works to expose and challenge these mechanisms and discourses; doing so, as Douglass teaches and African American nontheistic humanist theology affirms, is an ethical act.* Covey is forced to confront Douglass as an embodied being with significance and meaning. Douglass reconfigures space as freedom-infused geography of self-recognition and embodied visibility.[78] The particulars of Douglass's response do not translate, but the manner in which ethics and epistemology run through the occupation of bodies in time and space is of value in the construction of African American nontheistic humanist ethics.

Douglass's interior body was at least momentarily free from the constraints of particular modalities of power, and his external body moved in physical space in opposition to the rules of occupation and the geography of docile objects. This involved ex/changing bodies.[79] Hence, he provides an important dimension to African American humanist ethics by offering a platform highlighting the physical geography of life—the embodied occupation of time and space—as the proper venue for ethical thinking and acting. In addition, Douglass highlights the importance of a system of ethics that centers on the necessary integrity of consciousness and deep regard for the welfare of the physical body as a primary concern. In this way, talk of justice and equality, for example, is given felt and physical manifestation. Maintenance of the embodied self's welfare is fundamental, and effort in solidarity with others flows from this. In a sense, this is a gritty presentation of Thoreau's desired development of the "good" person as primary ethical act, and good actions as a secondary move stemming from the first.[80] Appeal to metaphysical assumptions yields little in that "all the prayers of Christendom," writes Douglass, "cannot stop the force of a single bullet, divest arsenic of poison, or suspend any law of nature."[81] The ethical insight from this for African American humanist ethics is clear: "What [humans] can make, [they] can unmake."[82]

While the type of narrative provided by figures such as Frederick Douglass may offer the first written expressions of African American self-understanding as means by which to rethink sociopolitical life as a collective American reality,[83] his narrative is not the most fundamental mechanism for getting across this message and critique. Before the written response to oppression, the embodied body provided the text of African American life within death-promoting environments. The aesthetics of the African American body—the scars and the like— told in part the story of the nature and meaning of the African American presence in North America. And so without contributing an autobiographical narrative to the corpus as did Douglass on several occasions, Harriet Tubman's attention to and presentation of her body and the bodies of other African Americans speaks to the nature and meaning of African American life, as well as the sober facts out of which and in response to which bodies are formed. Movement of these bodies—South to North—connotes the shifts in this story of embodied selves, as well as serving as the substance of this story. And there are important lessons of ethics valuable to nontheistic humanists and their theological discourse in this movement.

Tubman: Geography of Ethics, or the Ethics of Embodied Geography

In presenting Tubman in this regard, while not overlooking it, I am not concerned primarily with the underground railroad as a general mode of anti-slavery effort stemming back well beyond the period of Tubman's activity.[84] There are no records or accounts that give precise indications of how Tubman conducted her work with such success in that all aspects of her activities seem bound by her general caution to safeguard information. We merely tie together bits of information by using speculation and ongoing investigation.[85] Hence, my concern here is not to develop African American humanist ethics through a detailed accounting of the mechanics of the underground railroad as ethical symbol set. Rather, my interest here is the ethical lessons one might gather from a particular figure's—Tubman's—praxis honed over the course of better than a dozen trips South.[86] That is to say, further framing of African American nontheistic humanist ethics takes place through attention to Tubman's signification of "right" territory.

This discussion of Tubman is important for a variety of reasons, beginning with the manner in which her rearrangement of enslaved bodies to make them free (while acknowledging this is not the full range of her abolitionist work) sheds light on an approach to ethics that takes seriously the nature and meaning of embodiment as mapped through the trope of physical space configured and negotiated. In addition, although less has been written on Tubman than on Thoreau and Douglass, she provides an important marker of historical and cultural memory with respect to the deconstruction of geography as confinement—one that has benefits for ethics.[87] Related to the last two points, she seems to ground freedom or fuller humanity not in discursive shifts but rather in new occupation of space, and a determined claiming of time.[88] As Tubman states in terms of her own escape north: "When I found I had crossed that line, I looked at my hands to see if I was the same person."[89] Finally, attention to Tubman and her mission has significance in that it is vital to avoid the implicit assumption that the ethics of African American humanism can (or should) be outlined strictly in terms of the male body and a masculine posturing toward movement in and against the world. Through Tubman, one is able to challenge dominant reified gendering of struggle in that she "defied every antebellum notion about what women were supposed to be."[90] The stories by and about Tubman's exploits of the slave system's geography of meaning and placement "help disrupt or at least complicate the classic linkage in antebellum fugitive slave narratives of masculinity and the quest for freedom." Furthermore, "both in Tubman's actions as a 'character' in her life history stories and in her narrator's voice, genteel Victorian gender norms are implicitly (and even sometimes explicitly) questioned."[91] In this way, we gain a more balanced perspective on the shape and meaning of freedom beyond the establishment of a "manly" claiming of time and space articulated through a grammar of masculinity.

There is a tendency toward the mystical in Tubman.[92] Yet, if anything, it is a mundane mysticism that, like Thoreau's experience of nature (or certain aspects of Thurman's centering of the human in the world through mystical sensibilities), redirects the individual to embodiment and finds its ultimate expression in the experience of life lived.[93] It is not a spiritualization that pulls her out of the world and renders human experience suspect as a guide to the real. Instead, it is an experience that better focuses her commitment to changing the lived circumstance of African Americans and demands activity in the world.[94] Even prayer, as Tubman notes, does not do away with the human factor—although it can, from her perspective, influence the arrangement of human history in ways that maintain the need for human accountability and responsibility for conduct and its consequences.[95] And as some religious humanists might argue, prayer may provide a centering moment—an opportunity for focused attention on pressing issues in ways that isolate their importance and their mutability. So conceptualized and arranged, prayer becomes the activity of humans bringing about the twists and turns of encounter and life commitment. That is to say, Tubman prayed and worked, thereby training her thoughts through the embodied context of lived experience. As Frederick Douglass was wont to remark—to the lasting pleasure of nontheistic humanists—he "prayed for emancipation for twenty years but received no answer till I prayed with my legs."[96]

Tubman's concern for the fleshy nature of humanity is highlighted in particularly intriguing ways in that humanity is not achieved through reasonable argument (i.e., speeches) or compelling narratives (e.g., autobiographies) but through forced confrontation with the geography of oppression whereby new cartographies of life are sketched.[97] Tubman seems to share with Thoreau an understanding of the wilderness or the natural environment as a place of mystery wherein one never fully grasps existential and ontological shifts. (Surely Thoreau would also appreciate the assistance Tubman offered John Brown in securing "soldiers" for his mission.)[98] For him, this mystery allows a centering of the careful observer whereby simplicity of life allows for a greater sense of life. For Tubman, the mystery of the environment has to do with the manner in which it can provide cover for the movement of despised bodies, both visible and invisible. Her activities and relationships provide anthropological and ethical insights guided by a measured sense of the risks embedded in actions, in that human nature entails the possibility of betrayal or failed will. One could argue Tubman knew and embraced risk more fully than others involved in similar work because of not only her trips to the South but also, more specifically, her trips to locations putting her in close contact with her former residence.[99] Such a posture connotes an ethical stance based on comfort with paradox and uncertainty.

There is intrigue surrounding what has been known as the underground railroad.[100] Secrecy necessary for its success promotes some of this ethos, but it is also due to the vast network of unlikely partnerships and relationships and the signification involved—the physical being both present and invisible.

> She resorted to various devices, she had confidential friends all along the road. She would hire a man to follow the one who put up the notices, and take them down as soon as his back was turned. She crossed creeks on railroad bridges by night, she hid her company in the woods while she herself not being advertised went into the towns in search of information.[101]

Cartographies of domination and the status quo are altered to produce unintended pathways opening to the possibilities of full humanity (as full as possible within the context of racialized and gender-biased North America). The danger of the journeys undertaken by Tubman required attention to the individual within the context of the collective, which is a framework of activity of great importance to humanist ethics:

> The expedition was governed by the strictest rules. If any man gave out, he must be shot. "Would you really do that?" she was asked. "Yes," she replied, "if he was weak enough to give out, he'd be weak enough to betray us all, and all who had helped us; and do you think I'd let so many die just for one coward man."[102]

It was always clear to Tubman that great thoughtfulness and deep commitment were required because her work was more than rhetorical maneuvers meant to disprove the integrity and correctness of the slave system (although she would become a much sought-after speaker).[103] Certain situations could not be written but instead required the nontextual (yet textured) response of action. Life, within the scope of this struggle for places of more freedom, is tragic in nature. And like Douglass, Tubman understood this movement to take place within the context of a world troubled through the workings of race-based discrimination, gender bias, and class. Lives were at stake, which makes sense considering Tubman's depiction of the condition of being escaped as being "the next thing to hell."[104]

There is something of Tubman in Toni Morrison's preacher, Baby Suggs Holy, who calls her listeners to love themselves—their bodies—in opposition to the demonizing of these same bodies in the larger world.[105] As Anita Durkin remarks, "Baby Suggs's sermon attempts to redefine African American identity through the flesh, to transform the inscriptions inflicted by whites into a radical self-love of the African American body."[106] One could argue that Tubman demands the same deep appreciation for embodied black bodies through a determination to move them to places of greater appreciation. In both instances, through safeguarding black bodies vis-à-vis movement and through preserving the worth of black bodies through celebration, an embrace of embodied selves as fundamental is achieved. Such a connection between Baby Suggs and Tubman is not so very odd. Both were called and anointed for service to safeguard the abused and vulnerable, and both found the proper location for this work in the rough geography of a troubled country. *With respect to African American humanist ethics, the key to this similarity and to the larger significance of this embrace of flesh is not found in metaphysical assumptions but rather in the logic of encounter: Proper conduct requires recognition and embrace of flesh-full bodies as a first act of life.*

Tubman, like Douglass and Thoreau, understood ethical activity to involve steady effort to *be* good, and from that inner determination would flow proper care for and interactions with others—both those with whom we are most familiar (e.g., Tubman's work to free her family) and a more general commitment to response to pressing need within the context of a more elaborate matrix of belonging. Yet all this was done with recognition that each ethical action is likely to be met with countereffort to maintain stultifying situations. Hence, according to Douglass and Tubman, the North, the location inhabited by Thoreau, while called the Promised Land, was not the end product of ethical conduct. Without doubt, it was a place allowing a greater range of life options, affording a more robust framing of life meaning. But it did not entail, through discourse or practice, the complete restitution of full humanity. It offered more humanity for embodied selves but not full humanity.

Framing African American Nontheistic Humanist Ethics

Taking all three—Thoreau, Douglass, and Tubman—together, one gets a sense that ethics entails struggle with and in bodies that is short-term but determined. As such, it is premised on consciousness of "being good" (Thoreau) shaped within the context of embodied p(l)ace (Douglass) and framed by new geographies—p(l)aces of life and meaning (Tubman).

Drawing on this understanding, nontheistic humanist ethics promotes a sense of proper conduct or action as the fragile consequence first of grounding the individual in an appreciation for life lived as fundamental (instead of a privileging of systemic mechanisms and metaframeworks), with a sense that life so understood is embodied and has to do with the real occupation of time and space in new ways. It is a simplified cartography of life meaning that sees p(l)ace as flexible and vibrant. Furthermore, in all three cases, there is a perspective on anthropology beneficial in the establishment of African American humanist ethics: Recognize both the limits and potential of humanity—the ability toward both great good and great harm. All three figures expose soft spots in the structures of existence, the points where embodied life can be rethought and reformulated: simplicity as mark of contact with the world for Thoreau, movement of bodies as freedom for Tubman, and the challenge of docility as normative for Douglass. These three bodies—black and male, black and female, white and male—also serve as an example of Bryan Turner's theory: "to be born and to be embodied do not in themselves guarantee social membership. The transfer of bodies out of culture back to nature is equally ritualized...."[107]

Nontheistic humanist ethics learns from Thoreau, Douglass, and Tubman that struggle involves fostering short-lived spaces of greater body control over against (but from within) structures and arrangements of domination. As Gail Weiss says with such great insight, "We need to make our bodies just as central to our moral theorizing as they are in our moral practices."[108] This makes sense because bodies are central, always central, in that "everyday life is therefore fundamentally about the production and reproduction of bodies."[109] Through physical struggle, Douglass makes a claim to both—physical life and social existence—as does Tubman through the self-determined movement of bodies across unfriendly terrain. In one sense, they struggle against the body constructed as other, but they also embroil themselves in a very modern and imperialistic move: dominance over and normalization of territory, even if it is only one's double body. And as for Thoreau, he attempts to bring into question the value of the social body as traditionally conceived and arranged but in the process (as must be the case) also reinforces the privileges of the privileged body. Simplicity can be both a necessity and an exotic privilege, with the latter also framing a romanticized posture toward the world that would inform and influence movements such as Transcendentalism. In short, the living of life is already and always managed, *but* the means of management are also always and already open to critique and some (albeit short-term) alteration.

Structuring African American Nontheistic Humanist Ethics

Nontheistic humanist ethics involves trans/formation—meaningful, but hardly permanent reconstitution of the cartography of life, mindful of the contours and altered *limits* of embodied selves. Forged within this arena is a sober (or skeptical) and measured response to how embodied selves should maximize short-lived but vibrant opportunities for more complexity, and this involves much more than struggle against the persistent challenges of racism, sexism, gender discrimination, and classism. Humanist ethics here involves an effort always incomplete to, borrowing language from Cresddia Heyes, "think ourselves differently" and to "practice ourselves into something new." However, there is nothing certain about this process, and even the presentation of this approach as ethical conduct is open to a variety of interpretations, based on one's position in relationship to the mechanics of power and privilege, as well as one's particular connection to the "normal."[110] Nontheistic humanist ethics, then, is as much concerned with noting the limitations of action/thought—what has not worked and the limited long-term benefits of struggle—as it is with mapping out a tentative plan of action/thought.

Religion as mundane engagement with/in the world does not afford teleological notions of historical development and does not allow for the types of grand ethical schemes found in many modalities of womanist and black theologies. There is no sense that we can step outside structures of meaning and obtain a "true self" or a perfect social geography of life. Instead, African American nontheistic humanist ethics, borrowing from Thoreau, Douglass, and Tubman, works from the premise that we are porous—both representing the issues we seek to confront and also entailing the means of struggle against these issues. As a result, we are (and are not) the problems we seek to end. The situations we confront are thick and complex, evolving, mutating, but not ending in a manner that qualifies as "liberation from...."

There is no ethical platform—no way of doing things—that circumvents the arrangements and challenges noted. Those "things" against which African American humanists and others struggle can be somewhat fragile, vulnerable— but capable of mutation and transformation. What is of value here with respect to ethics is the manner in which every expression of power, every modality of the presentation(s) of power, is effectual.[111] Yet, Foucault's caution should be observed. "I have always been somewhat suspicious of the notion of liberation," he notes, "because if it is not treated with precautions and within certain limits, one runs the risk of falling back on the idea that there exists a human nature or base that, as a consequence of certain historical, economic, and social processes, has been concealed, alienated, or imprisoned in and by mechanisms of repression."[112] Foucault is aware of the struggles of oppressed peoples to gain more life, and he remarks that the effort of the oppressed to free themselves "is indeed a practice of liberation in the strict sense."[113] However, he provides a cautionary remark in noting that this "practice of liberation is not in itself sufficient to define the practices of freedom that will still be needed if this people, this society, and these individuals are to be able to define admissible and acceptable forms of existence or political society."[114] Mechanisms of liberation have some meaning, some vitality; but they alone are insufficient. I would add that they promote notions of human capability that are reliant on mythology and metaphysical assumptions for their sustainability. And even if no one person or group owns or "has" power, as Foucault suggests, I think it reasonable to assume some persons and groups have more access to knowledge concerning the structures and mechanisms of power and, therefore, have greater opportunity to utilize or manipulate such discourses.

The privileged (taking a variety of forms) have what is necessary to give these discourses of power felt consequence and, in this way, suggest themselves as the owners of this power: It appears power is associated with and embedded in particular bodies. As a result, what has been typically termed liberation by black and womanist theologies (and in much of my earlier work as well) must be held suspect and challenged as the model of desired outcome within a non-theistic humanist system of ethics. Foucault advocates "practices of freedom" over against liberation, and this reformulation of struggle is helpful in the development of nontheistic humanist ethics as a structure for enhancing life in line with the quest for complex subjectivity.[115] While the body in question, the body participating in this quest, is molded in certain respects through culture, it is also physical. This recognition is important in that attention to the physical or material is necessary for any efforts toward political maneuvering or ethical practices meant to make a difference in this quest.[116] Bodies are real in that they live and die, and African American nontheistic humanist ethics is concerned with the consequences and connotations of this realness.

What Ethics Yields...

Again, within this system of nontheistic humanist ethics is a continuing concern with improved life arrangements from dehumanization, but it is understood that struggle may not provide the desired results.[117] However, *in place of this outcome-driven system, a humanist ethical outlook locates success in the process.* That is to say, we continue to work. We maintain this effort because we have the potential to effect change, and we measure the value of our work not in terms of outcomes achieved but in the process of struggle itself. More robust occupation of time and space is the norm; perpetual rebellion is the process. Struggle is our last, best option.

I am in agreement with ethicist Sharon Welch. There is no foundation for moral action that guarantees individuals and groups will act in productive and liberating ways or that they will ultimately achieve their objectives. Therefore, ethical activity is risky or dangerous because it requires operating without the certainty and security of a clearly articulated "product."[118] This is a more sober—somewhat less passionate—approach to ethics. It lacks the unfocused urgency of some modalities of womanist and black theologies, but it has a clearer sense of how life works within the context of sociocultural geographies of experience and a more measured (historically borne out) sense of what can be achieved, based on the nature and meaning of embodied selves. It understands that human relationships (with self, others, and the world) are messy, inconsistent, and thick with desires, contradictions, motives, and a hopeful hopelessness.[119]

African American nontheistic humanist ethics involves proper action and behavior in the context of concrete and historically arranged life. As such, it concerns a wrestling over both language and materiality. In wrestling over language, African American humanist ethics exposes the fragility of discursive constructions that oppress—exposing them as nonessential structures of meaning that can be challenged. With respect to materiality, this ethical platform concerns itself with promotion of more fulfilling and free modalities of our occupation of time and space. This ethical system recognizes that the battle takes place from within systems that we resist but also support as embodied selves. As Edward Casey remarks, "Embodiment acts as the covert basis of human experience and of coherent connection among human beings: a basis and connection that occur not only in time but in space (and more particularly in p[l]ace)."[120] Susan Bordo's framing of the history of the body as materiality gives some sense of the scope or cartography of ethical insight. She writes, "We need to get down and dirty with the body on the level of its practices—to look at what we are eating (or not eating), the lengths we will go to keep ourselves perpetually young, the practices that we engage in, emulating TV and pop icons, and so forth. Our assessments of gender and race inequalities must consider not only the most avant-garde images...but what people are doing to their bodies in the more mundane service of the 'normal.'..."[121] These are the dimensions of the "practical life of our bodies," as Bordo phrases it, and they bear both religio-theological and ethical import.[122]

Modalities of meaning sought cannot be dissected to make them addressable in isolation. Rather, frames of meaning draw on and from each other. Hence, positive movement regarding racism or homophobia could be reinforcing other oppressive patterns. Unlike black and womanist theologies, African American nontheistic humanist theology promotes a sense of ethics guided by the assumption that there is no preoppression existence, no underlying free existence that we must move back toward. Power mechanisms are always present—in our oppression, our struggle, and within anything we experience resembling freedom. Structures of power are present in auctioning off enslaved Africans, lynching African Americans, and presenting discourses of white superiority and black inferiority undergirding these activities, and they are in the accompanying institutions that highlight and seek to stigmatize difference (read black and/or female, gay, lesbian, and so on). This machinery is also present in slave rebellions, the civil rights movement, and other modalities of praxis meant as attempts to transform the construction of bodies through moments of reconstruction on the level of language and praxis. But such efforts do not destroy power; rather, new modalities emerge, and the battle resumes through disobedience. Consequently, the sources for African American nontheistic humanist ethical engagement of thick problems must mirror the complexity and layered nature of the issues at hand.[123]

Finally, nontheistic humanist ethics suggests a reciprocal relationship between creative impulses expressed in culture and the activities we consider appropriate and right. We are moved to behave in certain ways, value certain interactions, and disregard others through the power of our creative impulse (artistic expression in its various forms). Hence, understanding cultural production and the celebratory nature of this productivity teaches lessons concerning values, choices, and power that can move us ethically. It is with this thought in mind—the cultural encasing of celebration or ritualization of the ordinary— that this chapter ends and the last begins.

6

Humanistic Celebration
as the Ritualizing of Life

Several years ago, I received a phone call from Greg Epstein, the energetic humanist chaplain at Harvard University. He called to gauge my interest in delivering the thirteenth annual Alexander Lincoln Lecture. I was intrigued, and after a few minutes of conversation, I agreed. But the invitation was a bit more complicated than I initially anticipated in that we concluded the conversation with Greg asking me to move beyond my current work and address a more practical question.[1] These, of course, are not his exact words, but what he said was along these lines: "I know your work on humanism, and I'm hoping you might be willing in this lecture to extend it into the area of practice, to think about African American humanism as practice, not in terms of political activism but as something more celebratory—its shape on the ground as a matter of ritual." It is true, much of what I had done with respect to African American humanism involved theories of development, conceptual frameworks, and historical-theological analysis, but Greg was asking me to address African American humanism from the angle of engagement: How is it practiced as celebration or ritual?

This second orientation—ritual or celebration—made perfect sense, and perhaps it is what colleagues in the study of religion have had in mind when probing and interrogating the nature and meaning, the value and contributions, of African American humanism to African American life. (Or for some the suggestion might seem oxymoronic.) In other words, what do humanists actually *do*? One might even sharpen this question: "What do African American humanists, those who don't go to churches, do," not in terms of ethics per se but rather along the lines of what might be called "religious" communion? In other words, how and where do African American humanists present and celebrate their deep regard for the wonder of the embodied living of life?

Harold Bloom, in *The American Religion*, positions African American religion in a way that gives it significant impact on the nature and meaning of religion in the United States. In fact, he suggests African American religion, by which he really means African American Christianity, was a "crucial element" in the inception of American religion born, as he puts it, about 1800. In making this case, he comes to a question that has some importance for this chapter. "When is one made free," he queries, "in solitude, or in community?"[2] That is to say, is freedom—a major impetus for religion within the context of African America— a matter of individual development, or does it require a communal positioning? His is a telling concern, although my line of investigation is not the concern motivating his writing, and although my purpose in this chapter does not reso- nate with the intent of the chapter out of which his question comes. In response, individualism (or group identity) is not the problem with respect to celebration within African American nontheistic humanism. Attention to self in a focused manner also points outward and engages at least the shadow presence of others. The nature and impact of divinity (in the form of the Christ, for example) has no real significance for the workings of African American nontheistic humanism. The latter is much too earthbound, too centered on the ordinary and everyday- ness of human existence to be distracted by the metaphysical claims of theism and the resulting structure of self-understanding. The dualism so very present in African American theism(s) does not function in African American nonthe- istic humanism, and disregard for personal bodies and other external markers of embodiment does not taint African American humanism.

Differentiating Celebration from Ethics

It is important to distinguish ethics from the challenge to articulate the celebra- tory or ritualized dimension of African American nontheistic humanism. The former, as discussed in the last chapter, concerns what nontheistic humanists understand as proper behavior regarding pressing issues on both the individual and collective levels. Celebration or ritualization involves not this wrestling with the reconstruction of life worlds, but instead it demands organizing moments of reflection meant to revitalize and renew the humanist (individually or within the context of community) to provide the wherewithal necessary for ethical prac- tices. In this sense, celebration or ritualization provides moments of intention- ality for the nontheistic humanist either as individual or as individual within the context of relationship. Celebration or ritualization involves humanists (as indi- viduals and/or as groups) arranging time and space (p[l]ace) to feel and reflect on the quest for complex subjectivity and center the self/selves in light of the reality of this quest and sense of community (presented earlier) related to it.

African American nontheistic humanist ethics is concerned with a two- pronged development regarding the "substance" of the quest for complex sub- jectivity: (1) fostering greater opportunities for high-quality embodied life lived and (2) stretching out over time and space the reality and consequences of complex subjectivity. And both say something about the concern for developing good people as a precursor to doing good actions. In distinction to this, celebration is the arrangement of opportunity for humanists to acknowledge (and linger over) the feeling this quest for complex subjectivity entails and also to address episodes of doubt and personal challenge. Celebration and ritualization concern the practiced recognition of possibilities of embodied life meaning as they emerge, and where they emerge. More to the point, a primary concern is consideration of the somewhat everydayness of celebration—the manner in which African American nontheistic humanism recognizes and ritualizes the sacrament of life.

Within Dedicated P(l)aces

Algernon Black framed the challenge of ritualization and celebration in the 1970s for a general humanist audience in a way that continues to have impact. "Ceremonies had always seemed to me," he writes, "to be a survival of traditional rituals based on the myths and creeds of the old religions of supernaturalism. I regarded them as external to the real struggles of life, decorative, empty forms, signs of human weakness." Here is the rub: "How could ceremonies," he continues, "be part of Humanism?"[3] He would conclude that ceremonies could be a vital element of humanism's self-understanding and expression. Consequently, Black, during the course of his work with the New York Society for Ethical Culture, would come to recognize the centering possibilities of thought practices. "I began to see that there was a wisdom in some of the traditional practices of religion," he reflected, "even though I differed with their dogmatic theological doctrines, their mythology and fixed, repetitious, symbolic, and mystical basis."[4] The happenings of life—human need and desires both to particular life changes and the encounter with one's existence in less traumatic terms—have to be acknowledged and reflected on in ways that advance the embodied existence of individuals within the context of larger groupings of life. To some extent, we are following the contours of his thought by giving attention to the "where and how" of humanist celebration and ritualization.

While African American nontheistic humanists maintain a shadow presence within traditional Christian denominations, the two religious organizations reflecting the basic elements of humanist theological sensibilities, including a similar anthropology and system of ethics, are the Unitarian Universalist Association (UUA) churches and the Ethical Culture societies (the American Ethical Union), the latter being the location out of which Black spoke.[5] These two, like their theistic counterparts, maintain a ritual and celebratory structure revolving around Sunday and taking place within buildings—physical spaces—set apart for this purpose. Conceptually marked by the chalice with flame, the Unitarian Universalist Association, with some variations on the local level, maintains a sense of celebration or ritual revolving around heightened awareness of human connection to other humans and to other realms of life. Drawing in an overt manner from a variety of traditions, such as Judaism, Christianity, Buddhism, and Paganism, it would be extremely difficult for the UUA to develop a system of ritualized activities too dependent on any one religious system. Instead, to the chagrin of some, its celebration patterns tend to be mosaic in nature. Still referred to as worship, although any referent beyond physically shared life is uncertain, UUA churches have scheduled services described in this manner:

> Our worship services usually begin with the lighting of the Flaming Chalice (our symbol of faith) and include both instrumental and vocal music, a prayer or mediation, readings, and a sermon. Many worship services include either an intergenerational segment, such as a "moment for All Ages" in the service. The sermon…may be about theology, social issues, holidays, or issues of importance to the life of the congregation.… Services may also include announcements and a time for worshippers to share their joys and concerns. Many congregations collect money in offering plates or baskets during the service. Visitors are welcome to donate during the offering, which is usually accompanied by music, but do not need to do so. What members and visitors wear for Sunday services varies from congregation to congregation. Respectful dress is appreciated, but few congregations expect formal business attire.… Following the service, there is often a "social hour" or other casual gathering where visitors can get to know one another and members of the congregation.[6]

The UUA provides this as a flexible template, recognizing all the time that there can be no one "worship theory" in place to cover the needs and wants of all Unitarian Universalists. But this does not rule out, as far as the association is concerned, the need to develop frameworks of celebration that have purpose for individuals within the context of current social and historical situations of need and meaning. In this sense, UUA worship tends toward an educational and celebratory model, reflecting a need to be mindful of and engaged with the current historical moment in all its depth and complexity.[7] Put another way, for most members of the UUA, "the validity of worship forms and the order in which we use them depend on how well they help us shape and celebrate worthwhile experiences and values and how well they help us make use of the healing and transforming forces present in the world."[8]

Mindful of this intent, some UUA congregations—either implicitly or explicitly—follow Von Ogden Vogt (former leader of First Unitarian Society in Chicago), who called for worship as "celebration of life" guided by an overwhelming "ideal" to which we respond. This process is beholden to five thoughtful acts:

Act 1. Attention/Vision
We state and affirm our ideals and aspirations.
Act 2. Humility
We are humbled by the realization that we fall short of our ideals.
Act 3. Exaltation
We regain our strength, feel empowered, give thanks.
Act 4. Illumination
We consider wisdom from the past and present.
Act 5. Dedication
We reaffirm our ideals, resolve to act responsibly.[9]

The structure offered by Vogt was not without its limitations, and over time it has been modified to reflect shifts in history and in the UUA, with some congregations using something resembling:

Act 1. Centering
Entrance Song, Call to Celebration, Invocation, Opening Words, Processional Hymn, Doxology, etc.
Act 2. Embracing the Limitations
General Confession, Acknowledgment of Struggle to be Whole, Poetry or music touching the depths, Reading illustrating human folly, Silent Meditation, etc., followed by Doxology, Gloria, Words of Assurance, Hymn, Psalm of Praise, Litany of Thanksgiving, Hand clapping, etc.
Act 3. Declaring the Possibilities
Readings, Sermon, Dramatic presentation, Dance, Dialogue, Panel, etc., perhaps followed by congregational discussion.
Act 4. Community Building
Peace Greeting, Sharing of Concerns, Offering, Affirmation, Covenant, Communion, Signing a Petition or other Social Action Commitment, Hymn, Closing Words, Benediction, etc.[10]

The plasticity of worship within the UUA is always present in that the leadership of the association does not insist that any particular model (including use or disavowal of particular symbols and signs within the worship context) be used within the context of its congregations. Rather of more importance than format is the quality of experience whereby those gathered gain something that meets their needs and connects them to the world in which they live. African American humanists who participate in these services and call humanism-centered UUA congregations home embrace a mode of celebration or ritualization that is to some degree theologically distinctive from what they would encounter in historically black churches, but the structuring of ritual is somewhat reminiscent of black church worship practices: songs, centering moments, collections, a "sermon," and so on.

The American Ethical Union holds to a similar perspective when arguing: "Ethical Culture is a humanistic religious and educational movement inspired by the ideal that the supreme aim of human life is working to create a more humane society."[11] There is no formal theological platform embraced by all members of this union when undertaking this ethical task, nor is there a standard pattern of worship embraced by all members. Each is free to develop its own patterns of ritualized interaction and celebration in keeping with the larger aim of a "more humane society" and the particular needs of the members and visitors to the twenty-six individual ethical culture societies, the oldest of which is the New York Society for Ethical Culture, founded in 1876.

The New York Society offers a host of meetings and gatherings, including a Sunday meeting with an arrangement of activity similar to what one would find in many nontheistic UUA congregations. The intent of these weekly community gatherings is to educate, stimulate personal growth, inspire reflection and action, and build a sense of community. Sunday meetings usually begin with a musical prelude that is followed by greetings, songs, and a talk given by a society leader, member, or guest speaker.

> Talks cover a variety of topics that reflect current events, social issues and Ethical Culture philosophy. A collection basket is passed and money is shared between the Society and a charity selected for that day. While contributions are always appreciated, Sunday meetings are free and open to the public. Each Sunday a Society member is available afterwards to welcome newcomers, answer their questions and accompany them to brunch in our Social Hall.[12]

Like all such activities, there are a variety of possible outcomes. For some, these gatherings hold only insignificant importance and meaning, serving instead to satisfy a sense of obligation and mark out an act in line with a family tradition. Others might engage the time/space of such a traditional setting in a much fuller way and may even be fortunate enough to wrestle from this situation a p(l)ace for *more*.

For some African American humanists, these organizations provide an institutional base from which to undertake deep investigation of the self within the context of a group concerned with larger issues of life meaning and ethical behavior. But I would argue there is also the possibility that these are the exceptional outcomes of architecture and building and of sacred space imagined and constructed in a modified theistic framework. All of this, and I say this as a member of the Unitarian Universalist Association, is complicated when one considers the low number of African Americans involved on a regular basis in the Unitarian Universalist Association and the American Ethical Union.[13]

It is possible one issue affecting levels of participation by African American humanists stems from the manner in which the somewhat traditional structuring of time and space for celebration in these organizations might not appeal to those seeking to move beyond the structures marking the traditions they find problematic. In this scenario, the theological stance of the UUA and American Ethical Union is appealing but not adequately presented outside the social activism available (but also available through a variety of organizations) during the non-Sunday-related workings of both organizations. Sundays in these organizations, then, may present to African American humanists a somewhat derivative pattern of interaction that does little—in a sustainable way—to engage the embodied self through a heightening of the body deeply consistent with nontheistic sensibilities. Derivations on a traditional model might even serve to hide a troubled relationship with the body, one that maintains a priority of the mind over the body: Celebration is primarily thought in this context, and this does not require full investment of the self. That is to say, the format of celebration within the UUA and the American Ethical Union are beneficial and productive on some level but may still strike some African American nontheistic humanists as entailing the need to surrender their embodied selves—the very thing they have attempted to rescue from black churches.

The problem is this: Humanists have often attempted to express themselves in substantial ways using theistic frameworks—the liturgical style, the ritual space, and so on—of those who view their activities as expressing, enticing, or mimicking the transcendent. How does an African American humanist ritualize or celebrate a push for an increasingly robust sense of meaning and being? To sharpen the question a bit: How might one describe the celebratory or ritualized activities of African American nontheistic humanists who do not find a home in formally and traditionally arranged church structures but think of architecture for the religious in very different terms?

Without doubt, some African American humanists ritualize life in ways suggestive of the modes of celebration, practice, and worship found within theistic organizations. And in this respect, the most significant differences between these humanists and theists revolve around a lack of "*god*-talk" associated with the typical framing of practice around contact with divine forces. Yet, with this structuring of ritual comes a somewhat traditional sense of meaning-affirming space (or sacred space for the theist). Theists privilege physical spaces for celebration that presents these locations as subject to divine presence(s) that modify the content and intent of the space. Over against this, humanists within the context of built space hope to foster a sense of p(l)ace through the centering and impact of embodiment, not divinity. By its very nature, p(l)ace, drawing again on Thoreau, entails the arrangement of surroundings in ways meant to highlight and take in the value and meaning of life lived—its details, its depth. It, then, is the (unfixed) "location" for the humanist ritualization of life.

African American humanist modes of celebration should reflect the tone, the texture, the content, and language of the naturalism that undergirds them. Nonetheless, maintaining this stance is difficult and not accomplished without slippage. Yet even with this slippage, it is hoped that the manner in which nontheistic humanism focuses on embodiment and the prioritization of the historical/mundane entails a strong point of differentiation between African American humanism and African American theistic traditions.

Ritualizing Everyday Happenings

African American nontheistic humanism does not recognize a fixed distinction between types of space. There is no sacred and secular split within the humanist worldview; instead, differentiations are more a matter of intentionality and conscious arrangement. Other traditions, many African-based religious systems, for example, would agree.[14] However, there is dissimilarity in place with implications for ritual in that African American nontheistic humanism is also opposed to the differentiation of time and space through notions of transcendence. Ritual or celebration does not, in either implicit or explicit ways, suggest a connection to supernatural realities. Instead, it is a deepening awareness of connection to all life, expressed and known only within the context of history. Celebration for African American nontheistic humanists involves the deep appreciation of, or ritualizing of, the ordinary—the everyday—in that the quest for complex subjectivity and the fragile outcomes of the quest are lodged in the historicity of daily developments and occurrences. While this can take place with the individual, it can also take place within the company of others. In either case, however, the constitution of p(l)ace is vital.

Besides humanists involved in church-modeled communities, the significance given to humanity, the value given to life within the existential contexts of human history, without appeal to transcendence, invests what theists might consider mundane and nonconsequential (in an ultimate sense) activities such as eating a meal with loved ones or taking a walk with deep meaning. In this respect, acts of living within the context of others can involve sacraments of sorts, rituals of the ordinary that mark time and space. Christian rituals of Sunday worship distinguish a particular time within the context of a certain space as having significance because of its affirmation of the deep and interconnected nature of human existence, and the daily life activities of the humanist also mark time and space as important and have the potential to transform them into p(l)aces. This, for the humanist, is not distinction of time and space based on separation of the mundane from the transcendent in keeping with the manner in which Christians might make the distinction; rather, for the humanist, time and space are ritualized through the remembering of connection, of relationship to self, others, "world." This remembering can take place anywhere, under numerous circumstances, alone or in the company of others.

The framing of ritual or celebration for African American nontheistic humanists owes something to (but isn't synonymous with) the tradition of liberal religion in the United States, and I have in mind here Howard Thurman and Thoreau and the radical (humanistic) spirituality of figures such as Alice Walker.[15] While the rationale for attention to Thoreau should be apparent at this stage, a word of caution is important regarding the next figure. Use of Thurman here is rather liberal, and appeal is made to him because he offers elements of language, a vocabulary and grammar for constructing notions of celebration and life that short-circuit some of the problems for the nontheistic humanist in traditional modalities of Christianity. Nonetheless, this borrowing from Thurman can be taken only so far in that he might ultimately understand the humanist appeals to sacraments of living as a push toward togetherness as idol. "We have made an idol of togetherness," he laments. "It is the watchword of our times, it is more and more the substitute for God."[16] While humanists find nothing troubling in his cautionary statement, for Thurman, the properly centered self, a profound and robust sense of self as the grounding for all interaction, must ultimately take its cue from the reality and presence of God. African American nontheistic humanist theology, however, suggests a different articulation of the point: The properly centered self, a profound and robust sense of self as the grounding for interaction and relationship as the substance of sacrament, must ultimately take its cue from community and symmetry as they harness the quest for complex subjectivity.

While some might argue the African American humanist sense of community accomplishes the same dwarfing of self, this assumption is inaccurate. The organizing effect of community does not negate the value of the self as a subject (to the extent this subject can be known) embedded in history; rather, it serves to enliven the self as robust and within the context of other robust selves—but it does so in a way that recognizes the importance of "absence" as a part of this robustness.[17]

In Alice Walker, African American nontheistic humanist ritualization of life finds a useful sense of praxis as celebration, or act of devotion. Yet, this does involve a holding in tension or bracketing some of the terminology (i.e., God) held over from the Christian faith that framed her childhood. While attempting to control for Thurman's theistic tendencies and Walker's panentheism, the non-theistic humanist still gathers from them an appreciation for the depth of the mundane, an effort to reflect on the human in ways that both exalt and humble. In particular, Walker helps African American nontheistic humanists refine this posture toward the world through recognition of relationship between life forms as profound. For example, in reflecting on her youth within a small church, Walker seeks to shift the reader's gaze from a transcendent heaven to the goodness of the earth. She writes:

> Life was so hard for my parents' generation that the subject of heaven was never distant from their thoughts. The preacher would gleefully, or so it seemed to me, run down all the trials and tribulations of an existence that ground us into dust, only to pull heaven out of the biblical hat at the last minute. I was intrigued. Where is heaven?...I was told what they sincerely believed: that heaven was in the sky, in space, as we would later describe it; that only the best people would go there when they died.... The truth was, we already lived in paradise but were worked too hard by the land-grabbers to enjoy it. This is what my mother, and perhaps the other women, knew, and this was one reason why they were not permitted to speak. They might have demanded that the men of the church notice Earth. Which always leads to revolution.[18]

If Walker's emphasis on the "saving" energy of human engagement with life is somehow missed in her reflection on heaven for the folks in her childhood church, the title of the essay from which her words are drawn certainly makes the point: "The Only Reason You Want to Go to Heaven Is That You Have Been Driven Out of Your Mind (Off Your Land and Out of Your Lover's Arms)." In other words, those who want to transcend the earth have been denied the joys of earthbound and complex relationships. These earthy relationships, according to Walker, are worthy of celebration in that they are sacramental. But there is a qualification here (a sort of normative stance) in that such relationships are sacramental to the extent they represent progressive and life-affirming arrangements.

Nonetheless, recognition of Walker's meaning and finding ways to enact it are two different things—both damaged by traditional Christian theism.

What Walker says in terms of paganism's struggle for ritual recognition could just as easily be said concerning African American nontheistic humanism. Using words dripping with critique, she writes, " 'pagan' means 'of the land, country dweller, peasant,' all of which my family was. It also means a person whose primary spiritual relationship is with Nature and the Earth. And this, I could see, day to day, was true not only of me but of my parents; but there was no way to ritually express the magical intimacy we felt with Creation without being accused of, and ridiculed for, indulging in 'heathenism,' that other word for paganism. And Christianity, we were informed, had fought long and hard to deliver us from that...."[19] Such is the conceptual framework: African American nontheistic humanism and its theological discourse as entanglement with all that is. And when recognized and embraced, this heightened awareness amounts to a celebratory posture toward the world. "Worship," then, is not something we must learn; rather, it involves recognition of the sacramental nature of the interactions we take for granted. Or as Walker notes, "We are born knowing how to worship, just as we are born knowing how to laugh."[20]

The African American humanist finds in these moments of connection or relationship renewed appreciation for the shared nature of existence, the intersections between modalities and forms of life—but without appeal to engagement beyond human history, beyond the world we know. This entails a stance of mindfulness and recognition of the weight of our existence—noting our promise and our problems, our abilities and our shortcomings. African American nontheistic humanism notes the fragility and tender nature of life, celebrates it, and seeks to work toward its integrity. This process, of course, is not without a sense of life's tragic nature. There is a mild wish connected to an abiding realism concerning humanity that rings true for the African American humanist.

While remaining a theist, Thurman's turn away from a preoccupation with proselytizing for a declining institutionalized Christianity opens religious engagement beyond strict doctrinal sensibilities. And this allows for the shadow presence of some of his approach in African American nontheistic humanist notions of celebration. Thurman also sheds additional light on the solitude, the status of the individual in both African American humanist ethics and celebration, whereby life meaning is framed and acknowledged. In addition, Thoreau points in the direction of this perception and expresses it in a variety of ways, but the style of expression found in *Walden* can often make this simple message difficult to capture. In Thurman, however, the sentiment is clear and straightforward. Value solitude because "in solitariness, a person is often most profoundly aware of the underlying unity of life for it carries with it, often, a dimension of sensitiveness to life, and awareness of others well nigh unique."[21] Thurman's waning interest in theological uniformity and correctness, combined with a life-affirming orientation above all doctrinal commitments, when viewed pedagogically by the humanist, promotes something very useful. "We seek to bring together all of the fragmentation of our lives," he writes, "the wide diversities of our interests, with the quiet hope that they may all be seen as one event, one experience, one life. We seek meaning for the commonplace, for the ordinary, for the nondescript; we seek strength to walk the ordinary path, to do the ordinary task; we seek wisdom to live fully, that our minds and our spirits may be filled with a quiet tranquility, that we may walk with dignity and meaning in our way, on our street, in our home, in our tasks, by the light in our hearts and by the light in the sky."[22] While the tensions and paradoxes of life are ultimately resolved through centering moments in which we reconnect with the ultimate source of life, God, there is still something valuable in Thurman's articulation of the quest for connection that rings true even for those who seek no solace in the supernatural.

There is a vocabulary and grammar framing Thurman's sentiment that projects a simple beauty, an unpretentious and penetrating gaze into the thoughtful "aha!" moments. And it is these instances of shared recognition that cut to the quick. He writes, and I quote at length:

> So much of our common life is spent in seeking ways by which we may break the isolation and solitariness and loneliness of the individual life. There is within us the hunger for companionship and understanding, for the experience of free and easy access to the life of another, so that in the things which we must face, the enemies with which we must do battle, we shall not be alone. Sometimes this isolation is brought about because life has eliminated from our world, one by one, those who have won the right to companion us on our journey. Sometimes the isolation is due to evil things which we have done deliberately or against our conscious wills, rendering those around us afraid and injured, and we are alone. Sometimes the isolation is due to a demand which our hearts make upon ourselves—the right to be free from involvements, the right to experience detachment, the right to take the long, hard look in solitariness and in isolation. But whatever may be the cause, it is so very good to sense the common character of our quest and the mutual support by which we are sustained.[23]

Thurman frames his sense of worship through a focus on something singular— the integrated presence of God. And there is something about the mindfulness, the sensitivity to life as posture of celebration, that African American nontheistic humanist theology finds useful.[24] Thurman's words regarding a reverence for life as general context for worship holds meaning in that it provides a mechanism for deep sensitivity to the awe inspired by life itself. "We celebrate the sacrament of life," writes Thurman, "the simple delights of being alive with varying measures of health, strength, and vitality. We are blessed," he concludes, "with so many things that we did not create ourselves, but are ours because of the labor, the work, the sacrifice, and the dreaming of many people whose names we shall never know—all of the little things by which our days are surrounded to make us secure, to make us happy, and to give to us a quiet sense of joy in being alive."[25] And "to be alive," notes Thurman, "is to participate responsibly in the experiences of life."[26] Thurman shares Thoreau's attention to the depth of the everyday, the manner in which clear attention to the dynamics and workings of the mundane have importance beyond what one might anticipate through their typical use or their usual spaces in the course of our lives. Thoreau's hands-on encounters with his surroundings—whether through his daily walks, picking berries, or other embodied activities—says something for him that extends beyond the immediate utility of the berries or the health benefits of walking. These activities take him away from Concord, but they also bring him into a better sense of self, a deeper connection with the self within the context of a greater matrix of life.[27] Through hungry engagement with the natural environment, Thoreau nurtures himself. And by extension, he gains a greater connection to the world through which he moves. The implication here is not the need for African American humanists to also become environmentalists or naturalists in this sense (although such a move does have its merits).[28] Nor is abandonment of the urban context in pursuit of rural splendor necessary or in most cases even plausible. Rather, the suggestion simply points out the diversity of encounters qualifying as celebratory and that fit the scope of a theologizing and living of the quest for complex subjectivity. While this nontheistic humanist theology shies away from using the term *spirituality* to describe the geography of the quest for complex subjectivity, what Robert Solomon says has some merit here: "The place to look for spirituality, in other words, is right here, in our lives and in our world, not elsewhere.... There is also spirituality in our sense of humanity and camaraderie, in our sense of family... and it can be found in the best of friendships." [29] Every activity, every location has the potential to be consciously arranged as a p(l)ace for encountering and celebrating the depth of our being, and our being in connection to other realities. [30]

In this sense, even alone in a location turned into p(l)ace is an environment marked by the hint of ritualization of life. So understood, what Thoreau promotes is not a full isolation, and African American nontheistic humanist theology finds it worthwhile to remain mindful of this.[31] It is not total abandonment of the other, in that in the woods at Walden Pond, Thoreau's activities, while not usually in the physical presence of others, were always shadowed by his awareness of other humans. And for sure Thoreau's time in the woods was always within the context of other embodied human beings (including the shadow of the Native Americans and African Americans who once lived in the woods near Walden Pond) and embodied beings not always human, but always impinging on his sense of self. Walker's writings and practice encourage for nontheistic humanist theology a similar recognition: The earth in a basic way provides a context for humanist ritualization of life, and deep attention to and appreciation of the qualities of life—large episodes and minor details—qualifies for the humanist as celebration or ritualization. There are links between the sense of everyday encounters as the stuff of celebration in Thoreau and in Walker.

Expansive and elaborate epistemological, existential, and somewhat ontological connections are also privileged in the work of Alice Walker. Think, for example, of Walker's words that begin *Living by the Word*, where the desire for solitude as the launching point for self in relationship is apparently even more compelling than one finds in Thoreau: "For years I'd long to be alone in the middle of fields and forests, silent, without need of words," writes Walker. "Knowing how ecstatic I can be simply lying on a hillside in the sun," she continues, "I realized I will probably be happiest—anticipating all of my possible incarnations—as a blade of grass." This desire for radical alteration foregrounds a depiction of society as troubled, something along the lines of Thoreau's troubling of social regulations and structures: "Besides, the daily news of death and despair coming in newspapers and over the airwaves began to seem the very breath of the planet itself: ominous and foul."[32] But like Thoreau, Walker's rather bleak depiction of society does not constitute a clean and complete break with relationships and social mechanisms. Instead, her sensitivity, as his, to the nature of life lived with intensity and with a sense of fullness actually draws her back to others with a clearer understanding of herself and a greater, but still measured, sense of possibility. And this movement is the stuff of life ritualized and celebrated. "Every small, positive change we can make in ourselves," Walker reflects, "repays us in confidence in the future."[33] Comfort with the world we encounter becomes vital, according to Walker. Perhaps the effort to live deliberately, as Thoreau instructs, helps to promote this comfort and celebratory posture toward the marks of our living?

Walker and Thoreau posit a connection to physical earth that has been difficult for African American nontheistic humanism and even more challenging for African American Christians. Yet, these writers are not the only ones to recognize the value of this type of deep connection. For instance, the 1990s group Arrested Development promoted a similar earthiness as fundamental when urging, "Children Play with Earth":

> Gain knowledge of the big but small earth around you
> Dig your hands into the dirt, the dirt that made you
> Get acquainted with the earth, the earth that eventually will take you
> And the world that hopefully will appear to wake you.[34]

These lyrics speak to a relationship with earth that is not always present in African American religious imaginaries. The relationship is complex in that as often as African American Christians have touted the wonders of connection to the matrix of life, they have also announced at least in song "the world is not my home" or the mantra "in the world but not of it." Both have connotations extending beyond moral abstractions to a general discomfort with embodiment and the feel of earthbound existence.[35] Particularly in traditions such as Christianity over against the more earth-friendly African-based traditions (e.g., Vodou and Santería), there develops a troubled connection to the earth based on a lingering attention to stewardship and subduing as the proper structuring of involvement. Nontheistic humanist theology does not argue celebration must involve engagement with the woods or other elements of the "natural" environment. Rather, the suggestion here is that such attention to the quality of our surroundings, and recognition of ourselves as part of the natural environment, does entail one of the more underappreciated dimensions of the ritualization of life.

P(l)aces, discussed earlier in this book, are also the location of celebration and ritualization of life in that we are confronted with the opportunity to recognize ourselves (and ourselves in connection to others) within the context of community, as defined earlier, and for the purpose of expanded and embodied life meaning. This, in significant ways, entails a rethinking, a reformulation of connection to our geography. Some attention to this process was given when discussing Starbucks and barbershops as p(l)ace. But in what follows, a turn is more forcefully made to less likely contexts not simply of p(l)ace formation but the context of celebration within those p(l)aces.

Celebrating in the Rough

My turn to the nontheistic humanistic dimensions of wilderness geography is out of the norm in that the wilderness is often seen as a space in which the body's importance is reduced or mitigated by divinity. It is a place of renewal but one that highlights the metaphysical over the physical. As Melvin Dixon remarks, "The slave's religion pointed out territories, both physical and spiritual, beyond the reach of the moral, if not the political authority of the plantation." Furthermore, "slaves songs," he continues, "pointed out the geography that had to be reached, encountered, sometimes conquered, in order for the new name or the new identity to have effect."[36] This sense of wilderness geography present in the period of slavery, according to figures such as Delores Williams, is combined with a less than positive response after reconstruction:

> The wilderness was a place where the slave underwent intense struggle before gaining a spiritual/religious identity, for example, as a Christian. But the struggle itself was regarded as positive, leading to a greater good than the slave ordinarily realized....Immediately after slavery, then,

African Americans apparently had two attitudes toward wilderness. One, deriving from antebellum days, emphasized religious experience and projected positive feelings about the wilderness as sacred space. The other sense of the wilderness seemed shaped by new experiences of economic insecurity, social displacement and the new forms of oppression ex-slaves encountered in a "free" world.[37]

As Williams suggests, one has reason to think of African American encounters with wilderness as transformative but also good reason to view this experience as detrimental, as a negative. The record provides examples of both, and in either case, Williams centers this geography of encounter in uncertain space as focused on the transhistorical—either meeting with God or the despair of not finding God.[38] The everyday quality of p(l)ace and ritualization of the everyday as celebration is difficult in an environment where one is on constant lookout for the impingement of the divine. Whereas the physical space for this process became secondary, according to Williams,[39] what remained primary was the manner in which wilderness served as a mechanism by means of which the individual was distanced from his or her bodily life. The spiritual takes priority over the physical.[40] On the level of the embodied self, wilderness within theistic frameworks entails a recognizable frailty of the physical individual, based on which only divine intervention makes possible life worth living. Williams notes the outcome of this time apart is not always the growth sought. And within the context of theistic theological formulations, this raises a question regarding moral evil that she conceptualizes through the existentially and ontologically framed notion of surrogacy.[41] This posture toward the world, whether fought or not, hampers the significance of physicality and embodied existence. In other words, there are ways in which the unsubstantiated nature of transformation found within wilderness cannot escape, for the theist, a troubling theodicy not in place for nontheistic humanists. Such an understanding of celebration or the ritualization of everyday happenings runs contrary to the theological anthropology and organizing principle of community, as well as the fundamental meaning of religion defining African American nontheistic humanism.[42]

Theistic traditions, by and large, do not connote an opportunity to better engage self through encounter with life. For instance, the wilderness as Delores Williams demonstrates through a post–Civil War analysis can be a place of transition or discovery, but seldom does this result in a celebratory posture toward this contact with nature, and—again—it does not maintain its everydayness.[43] The wilderness does little to secure Hagar's sense of self. Instead, it allows a dynamic of surrogacy to gel.[44] Characters do not often linger over these encounters with earth but rather experience them as having limited direct benefit. The geographies of movement not controlled by slaveholders or "Jim and Jane Crow," as Harriet Tubman shows, were not places one could linger for long, and they provided a limited but still terror-filled break from the immediate dread of dehumanization. They combat the total destruction of the person—bringing together bits and pieces of identity—although they do not constitute, as Thoreau would describe it, the person as "good being." Rather, they provide enough rest from terror to allow the person to contemplate the doing of good. That is to say, they do not necessarily invest life with a quality of deliberateness. There is trauma involved, even for the likes of Walker and Thoreau, but the end of trauma does not involve for those two release from the wilderness, as it does for Williams and enslaved Africans who exist in the shadows of the spirituals and folktales. All wilderness entails, for Walker and Thoreau, celebration or ritualized reflection. Hence, unlike in theistic thinking, p(l)ace is not a spot of celebration because of guaranteed outcomes. As this example of wilderness is meant to demonstrate, the celebration of ritualized everyday happenings is based simply on a measured realism whereby the quest for complex subjectivity and its fragile realizations are enough.

With Williams and Dixon, the wilderness is required to lose its mundane status, its regularity, to have deep significance, and after the period of slavery, encounter with geographies such as wilderness surrenders their embodied quality even more fully. In the context of the wilderness, embodied selves are surrendered to the will of an other transcendent figure. In this way, it does not constitute p(l)ace in that the experience serves to surrender self—not enlarge self. The embodied nature of the celebratory dimension as presented by Thoreau is vital in that, as Shannon Mariotti summarizes, "for Thoreau we change what the head does by changing what the hands and feet do; the recuperation of our critical capacities, for Thoreau, is strongly connected to his body's movement in space."[45] The takeaway from Thoreau involves the manner in which p(l)ace allows a stripping of the unnecessary elements of space and a reformulation of time that allow more concentrated attention on the self and the self in relationship to others in ways owing to the quest for complex subjectivity. The concern and outcome of this quest detailed in p(l)aces is nature, not in the sense of unspoiled physical locations but instead meaning there is no extrahistorical and noncontingent source, no divine authority orchestrating the whole drama of human life from some exalted location beyond our physical and mental grasp.

The woods do not open to something but rather close in on the visitor. Or as Walker recognizes, "all fear of natural things leads us: to fear of ourselves, fear of each other."[46] Furthermore, as Thoreau reminds, celebration or the ritualization of life through the arrangement of p(l)ace is not restricted to any particularity. It is fluidlike, marked by a type of placidity, and highlights the significance of the ordinary. Thoreau and Walker, of course, do not provide identical takes on the nature of ritual or celebration. Yet, beyond their differences—and there are many—is a similar posture toward the value of deep contemplation, the importance of experiencing life in its simplest terms, and experiencing it as a precondition for changing the nature of collective, social existence. A similar stance is at times reflected in the words of bell hooks, whose autobiographical depiction of experience with earth explores the connection between African Americans and land that is not only of existential significance but "also spiritu-ally life-sustaining relationship with the land they were cultivating." For hooks, there is an ironic twist in that the search for greater liberty and opportunity—a greater and more robust sense of self and life meaning—framed by the many decades of the Great Migration, served to damage this relationship to earth with the consequence of distance from the meaning of the embodied bodies once connected to the earth. Correcting this holds something of the deliberate life marked out by Thoreau. "Even in my small New York City apartment," writes hooks, "I can pause to listen to birds sing, find a tree and watch it. We can grow plants—herbs, flowers, vegetables."[47] One could easily understand such moments, particularly in light of hooks's connection of land contact and spiritu-ality, as providing opportunities for recognizing in p(l)ace celebration as vital.

Thoreau, Walker, and hooks speak of open land, of green space, that draws them back to themselves and then out toward others. But surroundings forged through steel and cement, without much green, can provide the same framing for the ritualization of life. While Starbucks and barbershops, as discussed ear-lier in this book, can play this role, I want to provide additional examples beyond those two, examples just as graphically situated in the ordinariness of human existence. Take, for instance, the "living room," the location within many houses and apartments where much activity takes place. I have in mind a particular depiction of the living room—as location for life dynamics associated with the yearning for meaning—provided by Lorraine Hansberry in *A Raisin in the Sun*.[48] Located in Chicago, this living room is the central location of "home" for the Younger family. It is where the young boy, Travis, sleeps; where his father, Walter Lee, talks with his friends; and so on. Because so many activities take place in this room, the movement between each must be intentional and orchestrated. For example, before sleeping, Travis must gather the materials to transform the living room into a bedroom, and in the morning, he must deconstruct the bedroom by removing his bedding to his mother and father's room. For Walter Lee, the living room invites communion with his friends, talk of better economic times, and by extension, a new relationship to himself, others, and the world. It also entails some conflict with his wife, Ruth, over the mechanisms envisioned as the means to this newness:

> That's it. There you are. Many say to his woman: I got me a dream. His
> woman say: Eat your eggs. Man say: I got to take hold of this here world,

baby! And woman will say: Eat your eggs and go to work. Man say: I got to change my life, I'm choking to death, baby! And his woman say— Your eggs is getting cold![49]

This conversation scopes out the arrangement of embodied life and says something about the geography of existential desire and ontological yearning. It is not so much a matter of how Hansberry through the characters articulates the nature of the time/space called living room. Rather, it is the conscious and intentional arrangement of time and space that constitutes it as p(l)ace where, for example, Walter Lee can wrestle with the meaning and quality of embodied life as a mundane ritualization of the ordinary.

Ruth, Beneatha (Ruth's sister-in-law), Walter Lee, and Beneatha's mother discuss and play out the gendered nature of life meaning in the context of this p(l)ace. And for most of these figures, what happens has little to do with notions of the divine.

> MAMA (KINDLY): 'Course you going to be a doctor, honey, God willing.
> BENEATHA (DRILY): God hasn't got a thing to do with it.
> MAMA: Beneatha—that just wasn't necessary.
> BENEATHA: Well—neither is God. I get sick of hearing about God.[50]

Beneatha does not conclude with this statement but instead promotes a synergy between ethics and disbelief:

> Mama, you don't understand. It's all a matter of ideas, and God is just one idea I don't accept. It's not important. I am not going out and be immoral or commit crimes because I don't believe in God. I don't even think about it. It's just that I get tired of Him getting credit for all the things the human race achieves through its own stubborn effort. There simply is no blasted God—there is only man and it is he who makes miracles![51]

The living room often serves as a site of introspection and exchange for the individual members of the Younger family—Walter on economic life as subjectivity, Beneatha on cultural return as subjectivity, and their mother on the shifting sense of life meaning from generation to generation. However, the insurance money due ($10,000) after the death of the mother's husband serves as a centering element for all members of the family. For once, their individual wrestling with social expectations and life meaning are focused together within the context of the home. As Walter Lee's mother remarks,

> MAMA: It's dangerous, son.
> WALTER: What's dangerous?
> MAMA: When a man goes outside his home to look for peace.[52]

Conversation revolves around money because, as Walter Lee proclaims, money is life.[53] And as Walter Lee's mother insists, home—this living room—is the p(l)ace for wrestling with issues of such deep importance.

For the Younger family, immersion in nature is not possible—mother is mindful of the one sickly plant in the window that marks nonhuman construction—they must arrange p(l)ace in the context of cement and steel. Yet, as is the case for Walker and was the case for Thoreau, this quest and the fragile outcomes (whatever they maybe) are already and always embodied. *It involves ritualization of the mundane, of the typical occurrences of life. The outcome of this process is not necessarily fantastic or extraordinary—perhaps a simple changing of a mind on issues, a greater sensitivity to the nature of one's relationship to self, others, and the world.* In other words, it involves the nature and meaning of "home." As mother says to Walter Lee, "It makes a difference in a man when he can walk on floors that belong to him...."[54] Within the context of those determined conversations about home, Walter Lee and his mother forge new modalities of identity, and this involves pushing for a greater sense of life meaning in the shape of complex subjectivity. While one does not always achieve the desired outcomes, in that subjectivity does not always have the tone and texture imagined, it is important to entertain the quest, to provide a p(l)ace for this engagement. As Asagai, Beneatha's friend, reminds her, "Never be afraid to sit awhile and think."[55] It, p(l)ace qua living room, is where Walter will come to some final thoughts on life: "Talking 'bout life, Mama. You all always telling me to see life like it is. Well—I laid in there [the bed in the bedroom] on my back today... and I figured it out. Life just like it is."[56] Yet a new reckoning follows this realization, as tragic as it may appear, and it promotes a fuller sense of his, and his family's, place in the world.

The darker corners of social life are capable of spawning p(l)aces for the ritualization of the mundane. This, African American nontheistic humanist theology argues, is one way to read Lorraine Hansberry's presentation of the Younger family. There is also a way in which the more graphically tragic dimensions of collective life can open to similar possibilities. Take, for instance, the predicament of Richard Wright's character Bigger Thomas in *Native Son*.[57] Bigger has struggled through the course of the novel with notions of personhood and being within the context of a society bent on his irrelevance. Ultimately, his response is to establish himself through destruction, to establish meaning through negation. In this case, negation involves the murder of Mary—whose naivety with respect to racialization of black bodies entails attempts to enter his world, not realizing how such a move serves to further his marginalization—as well as the murder of Bessie. Near the end of the novel, readers encounter Bigger in a new environment of punishment but one Bigger transforms into a p(l)ace of contemplation and self-discovery, with all the dread and terror involved. This unlikely context is not simply Foucault's physical space of discipline, a location housing mechanisms of domination meant to create docile bodies and weak minds. It also serves as a potential arrangement in time and space to foster a p(l)ace where Bigger explores life meaning in alternate ways.[58]

Time is reconfigured for Bigger after his arrest. "There was no day for him now," Wright remarks, "and there was no night; there was but a long stretch of time, a long stretch of time that was very short; and then—the end."[59] And space is redefined intentionally as a location of vague difference. Note the words of Wright as he reflects on the aftermath of Bigger's conversation with his attorney, Max, back in his prison cell:

> He was balanced on a hair-line now, but there was no one to push
> him forward or backward, no one to make him feel that he had any
> value or worth—no one but himself. He brushed his hands
> across his eyes, hoping to untangle the sensations fluttering in
> his body. He lived in a thin, hard core of consciousness; he felt
> time slipping by; the darkness round him lived, breathed. And
> he was in the midst of it, wanting again to let his body taste of that
> short respite of rest he had felt after talking with Max. He sat
> down on the cot; he had to grasp this thing.[60]

Once a location of punishment, of humanity reduced, for Bigger it becomes a p(l)ace where meaning presses upon him. Bigger confronts himself, the limitations of his identity, and connects subjectivity to agency. Somehow this agency, with all its terrifying implications and possibilities, had something to do with what Bigger claimed to desire but could not be achieved within the time/space of Christian architecture: "I wanted to be happy in this world, not out of it."[61] This is because "life is all life had."[62] Within the context of this p(l)ace, Bigger Thomas attempts to envision himself anew. "He stood up in the middle of the cell floor and tried to see himself in relation to other men, a thing he had always feared to try to do, so deeply stained was his own mind with the hate of others for him," Wright recounts. And he continues by contextualizing what was occurring and outlining its fragile composition: "with this new sense of the value of himself gained from Max's talk, a sense fleeting and obscure." Bigger now approaches himself and his existential condition. "For the first time in his life," says Wright, Bigger "felt ground beneath his feet, and he wanted it to stay there."[63]

What happens in p(l)ace need not amount to "progressive" or "positive" transformation. The ethos of the religious and the ritualization of its markers are not defined in this way. Hence, even where and how Bigger is presented—even the tragic nature of life—says something about the ritualization of the mundane. Think of the questions and reflexive thought surrounding the time of his trial. He is presented with an option for (albeit weak, stereotypical, and laughable) Christianity as the end product of the quest for complex subjectivity. No. Instead, the trail and jail cell become the p(l)ace of fuller humanity vis-à-vis agency (i.e., the ability to act on the world over against the world's rules of interaction). As Joyce Ann Joyce notes, "The trail that demands his physical death brings with it his spiritual awakening."[64] This is celebration within p(l)ace in that celebration should not be associated with the stylistics of theistic modes of expression, nor necessarily with the activities in built spaces discussed earlier in this chapter. Instead, celebration simply involves an intentional sensitivity toward and recognition of the quest for complex subjectivity and its implications as found within the common occurrences of life. It, then, is a matter of impactful awareness. For Bigger Thomas, this amounted to "a will to believe in a new picture of the world." Yet, even this involves a measured realization, a dim acknowledgment that in Bigger's case, "a knowledge of how to live was a knowledge of how to die."[65] But even in this moment of dreadful recognition, Bigger gains something—the sense that he occupies the world in a manner no longer invisible. This visibility will kill him, but it also constitutes something of life in a very material, felt, and concrete manner.

As we learn from Bigger, there is no guarantee these intentional p(l)aces will not collapse before those present are able to make any gains, there is no guarantee that those present will maintain a commitment to the quest for complex subjectivity in productive ways, and there is no guarantee the quest for complex subjectivity will promote what we have in the past referenced as "good." Consequently, celebration and the ritualization of embodied quest involve a certain degree of humility and an ethos of measured expectation within the realm of the ordinary. The African American humanist who is more certain than this, who assumes a teleological take on history, betrays the residue of theistic inclinations still needing removal.

And So...

Celebration, as I told the audience at Harvard that evening, is simple and requires little in the way of preparation or tools. It can take place in grand locations or in the most despair-filled environments. Celebration—the ritualization of the ordinary—takes p(l)ace and entails intentional and thoughtful recognition of, openness to, and embrace of the intimacies of the quest for complex subjectivity as found in mundane activities and places.

Readers may find my response to the question of celebration or ritual far too easy and not without its limitations, in that it does not give shape to time and space in ways that render them easily recognizable as distinct or, as Christians might say, "holy." Rendering acts of celebration out of the details of human interaction and relationship makes the idea of *religious* activity (marking a certain arrangement of experience) unintelligible to some. Even if one were not thinking along these lines, attention has been drawn to the nebulous nature of nontheistic humanist theology's ritualization of life. But this is done without apology and without correction because intentional movements through the world within various arrangements of meaning are profound and the substance of our embodied existence. In this case, such stuff is worthy of celebration with every breath and every movement we can manage, and with every opportunity we can muster.

Conclusion

Theologizing at the End of God-Talk

With African American nontheistic humanist theology constructed, one might wonder how it fits the existing theological landscape. How is it positioned?

African American nontheistic humanist theology shares with many forms of liberal theology a concern for the human and an understanding of theology as grounded in (and responsive to) existential realities. In this regard, it takes theology in African American communities in the direction of a constructive theology that recognizes as central the role and consequences of the human in theological discourse. However, it is distinguishable from liberal theology (including "Death-of-God" theology) in that it is not premised on God as anything more than a matter of language, a human construct, and it gives little attention to the importance (symbolic or real) of the Christ Event as a cipher for human self-understanding. Finally, while certain figures in modern theology would also maintain theology is anthropology, African American nontheistic humanist theology makes such assertions from within the context of (and in response to) African American life. In a word, it draws from the best of the liberal theology tradition and the existential edge (and social critique) of black religious thought, and it distills them through a rejection, among other things, of transcendence and the divine. This move is not as far-fetched as one might initially think. In fact, humanism is a long-standing modality of orientation within African American communities, and it is present in two primary forms: weak humanism and strong humanism.

Weak Humanism

As philosopher William Jones argued almost forty years ago, progressive black church practices and doctrine present a modality of humanism, a Christian or theistic humanism that preserves the best of the Christian faith and combines it with something resembling appreciation for the existential reality and historical needs of African Americans.[1] Or to borrow from Karl Rahner, one might consider certain modalities of African American Christianity a type of humanism to the extent "one can...designate any affirmation of man's worth and value, of responsibility, of freedom, intellect, the social dimension of man as already being 'humanism.' In this sense," he continues, "one may designate Christianity as humanism...."[2] This is a form of what Jones has labeled "humanocentric theism" or the makings of what I have elsewhere (to the chagrin of some) labeled "weak" humanism. *By this terminology, weak humanism, I mean to conceptualize the assumed workings of God through human muscle and mission found within the arena of human life, whereby flesh becomes a particular encasing for God.* In this way, anthropology is made significant but not so significant as to trump all formulations of the divine.[3]

Even prior to the creation of its institutional structures, African American Christianity presented this understanding of the intersections between the transcendent and the immanent in song and image. The spirituals, the theological language of the proto-African American church, outlined such a connection by framing a robust anthropology through which, and in connection to which, divinity is presented. In this way, humanity is recognized as a weighty reality, one through whose mark on the world God is seen and experienced. This is the significance of the *imago Dei* as found in the religious songs of the enslaved, as well as in the nascent theological proclamations of the early African American sermonic tradition and the testimonial oratory of the laity. Most important, this framing of the world, this cartography of human development, is considered the best way to map the movement of God in the world, and the cipher for this is Jesus Christ. This is certainly one way, for example, to understand the large number of songs exploring the triumphant presence of God in human flesh:

Ride on, King Jesus; no man can a-hinder me.[4]

The biblical world and contemporary movement are brought into harmony. Time and space as related to religious meaning are collapsed. In a significant way, the presence of Christ—God and humanity in perfect harmony—marks the spirituals as a significant articulation of weak humanism: human struggle and existential movement as irrepressible statement of who and where God is found.

Deliver Daniel, deliver Daniel;
Didn't my Lord deliver Daniel;
An' why not-a every man.[5]

Framed by the spirituals and the development of a nascent religious language, a shadow or weak humanism *lurks in* the secret meetings of enslaved Africans—the hush arbor activities during which African Americans worked through, among other things, their theological positions over against the dominant presentation of the gospel message. This is not to say these meetings are a formation of weak humanism; instead, I am arguing that elements of weak humanism develop within the context of the intellectual and cultural space of these meetings.

The African presence in North America was more than a century old before this hidden religious worldview took sustained and somewhat independent institutional form with the development of churches. Yet, it is within these African American churches that this weak humanism took its most explicit and celebrated form through combining commitment to the reality of the divine and a sense of human progress and reason. According to Alice Dunbar, "the mode of the time clearly favors applied Christianity in its most humanitarian forms." Yet, many fail to recognize this proper business of Christian churches: "It is not a religious club for the education and help of the congregation, nor is it primarily for divine worship; its real purpose is to give real help to the world."[6] This is certainly a viable way to interpret the words of Robert Pope, who says, "Our religious creeds conform more nearly to the life and teaching of the Christ. The old idea that theology is stationary, while every other science is progressive is absurd and must go. As more light is turned on, this science becomes more comprehensive in its scope, more responsive to human need, and expresses more full the thought of God."[7] Furthermore, according to Pope, "Modern theology is not a theology for the few, nor a theology for the strong; but it is a theology for the rich and the poor, the lord and the peasant, the noble and the ignoble, the classes and the masses; it is a theology for humanity."[8] Even more telling than Pope's words is the perspective of Norman Brown regarding doctrine of God. In an article in the *AME Church Review*, Brown notes, "A people's God is no bigger than their needs, no higher than their aspirations."[9] Doctrine of God is measured against anthropology. That is why Brown could write, "The only God that will satisfy and that is practical is the God in you; and if you cannot find God in you, it is useless to search for him amid the stars."[10]

Prior to these statements by Pope and Brown, pronouncements in support of a version of liberal theological formulation of weak humanism were made by figures such as Bishop Henry McNeal Turner of the African Methodist Episcopal Church, who proclaimed the blending of transcendence and immanence with the bold statement "God is a Negro."[11] By this, Turner meant to counter white supremacist manipulations of doctrine of God by signifying it as he linked African Americans to some of the more significant metaphysical and ontological notions available. This intertwining of God and humanity also points to the continuing importance of humanity for a proper understanding of reality: God is real and present in the world, and humans are accountable for acting consistently with this belief and required to bring this belief to bear on practices of struggle for existential improvement. Human growth and development is vital—that is, a religious truth—that works in conjunction with a deep and abiding confirmation of the reality of God. The Christ Event is the primary example of how this blending of transcendence and immanence works. Accordingly, theistic (weak) humanism within African American churches amounts to a weighty and persistent Christology as the centerpiece of thought and the model of historical action.

The Great Migration brought this concern with a humanized gospel into greater relief in that it highlighted debate regarding the proper orientation of churches—this-worldly versus otherworldly. The latter, for the most part, has been downplayed within progressive theological discourses and within social gospel–minded churches in that it tends to represent an embrace of transcendent concerns vis-à-vis salvation as nonhistorical development. The former, however, understands the significance of God's movement in the world in terms of historically situated transformation—the increase in life options and greater possibilities for human existence. The this-worldly orientation was also given both explicit and implicit attention during the civil rights movement, as churches were called through the social Christianity posture of certain leaders to give an account of their commitment to human progress as the hallmark of God's concern and character. In a word, churches were challenged to live out a posture of theistic humanism that made consistent, if not synonymous, salvation and liberation. This theistic or weak humanism involved a sense of communal concern with transformation over against the radical individualism of the counterpoint other-worldly orientation. Thereby it, weak humanism, entails a social gospel type of synthesizing of God and history in ways that point out the humanity of God—the Christ Event as model for proper conduct in the world. The efforts of figures such as Martin Luther King Jr., a student of the Boston University School of Theology, known for its personalism called for social transformation as the proper business of those devoted to the Christian faith and the task of churches. In less academic guise, activist Ella Baker expressed this perspective in plain terms and laments what she perceives as a shifting theological and ethical terrain: "My grandfather had gone into the Baptist ministry, and that was part of the quote, unquote, Christian concept of sharing with others. I went to a school that went in for Christian training. Then, there were people who 'stood for something,' as I call it. Your relationship to human beings was more important than your relationship to the amount of money that you made."[12]

This humanization of God's presence in the world takes an odd turn in the late twentieth and early twenty-first centuries through the megachurch phenomenon and the prosperity gospel movement. Whereas the early this-worldly (social gospel) orientation involved a commitment to the Christ Event as a call for a theistic (weak) humanism devoted to both a devotion to God and a deep regard for the needs and responsibility of humanity, prosperity gospel at its worst entails disregard for the needs and responsibilities of humanity as the centerpiece of the Christ Event and replaces them with a superficial appeal to the economic and social conjuring of scripture for the benefit of individuals measured in terms of material acquisition and sacralizing of the American dream. At its best, however, segments of the prosperity gospel movement might entail an opportunity for increased theo-ethical conversation concerning the look and content of the liberative processes of African American Christian faith. In either case, for good or ill, embodied humans are given attention as the litmus test of religious vitality. Perhaps much of the recent (and energetic) critique of the prosperity gospel movement stems from the manner in which it seems to push against dominant trends in theistic humanism to modify anthropology (e.g., human need, want, and reach) through a corrective doctrine of God (e.g., one that places material acquisition within the larger framework of the Beloved Community).

Black Theological Thought as Reflection on Weak Humanism

While not as heralded as some in African American theological circles, Howard Thurman provides one of the more interesting articulations of weak humanism—*complete with its anthropological limitations*—within African American religious thought and life. For Thurman, the human soul has tremendous importance and can achieve profound connection to the divine, and through such connection, the human becomes responsible for transforming this soul energy into healthier spaces for physical bodies. Yet, this does not translate necessarily into a profound appreciation for the body in and of itself. There is no doubt, as Thurman scholars note, that his mysticism did not preclude recognition of social settings and the need for sociopolitical and economic justice. But this commitment to praxis was motivated by a higher regard for the health of the soul, the intangible "thing" housed in the body, as opposed to the significance of the body. Hence, according to Thurman, "The time and place of a man's life on earth is the time and the place of his body, but the meaning or significance of his life is as far reaching and redemptive as his gifts, his dedication, his response to the demands of his times, the total commitment of his powers can make it."[13] Thurman, like many others, recognized the manner in which the body was a target, the battlefield on which racial discrimination played out.[14] Yet, lamenting this did not result in an epistemological rescue of the body. Salvation remains something that neutralizes the significance of the physical body, while also recognizing the spaces the body occupies. It is a type of uneasy truce with the body that allows him to talk about salvation in this manner. In Thurman, there is a struggle: the mystic aware of and connected to the world. This is quite a dilemma in that it involves disciplining the body while simultaneously trying to create more socio-economic and political areas of historical comfort for that body.

In talking about Jesus' message in light of his historical context, living in a land dominated by a foreign entity, Thurman says, "I do not ignore the theological and metaphysical interpretation of the Christian doctrine of salvation. But the under-privileged everywhere have long since abandoned any hope that this type of sal-vation deals with the crucial issues by which their days are turned into despair without consolation.... The basic fact is that Christianity as it was born in the mind of this Jewish teacher and thinker appears as a technique of survival for the oppressed."[15] Jesus is humanized, but this seems to do little to alter Thurman's theological anthropology and a general slighting of the human body. This is because the embodiment of Jesus continues to point beyond rather than to the body. In other words, Jesus represents in flesh a transpersonal reality in that he is "the product of the constant working of the creative mind of God upon the life, thought, and character of a race of men. Here is one who was so conditioned and organized within himself that he became a perfect instrument for the embodi-ment of a set of ideals...."[16] Perhaps this limiting anthropology results from (1) the influence of Augustinian thought, the theological anthropology that marked the work of Thurman's contemporaries, and (2) his appreciation for mysticism that developed early—during the summer of 1929 spent at Haverford College under the tutelage of Quaker mystic Rufus Jones. In spite of his more inward-turning posture, Thurman's theological perspective and ethical sensibil-ities, such as the ministry of Jesus over against the formal structures of church politics as both theological posture and model of ethical obligation, have had implicit influence on later theological developments as expressed by figures such as James H. Cone and J. Deotis Roberts.

Cone and Roberts, perhaps two of the most recognizable names in black the-ology's first three decades, called for human activity and ingenuity as require-ments for living out the Christian faith. Both suggested in strong terms that black theology is an extended Christology in that through the Christ Event one gathers a sense of God's commitment to human progress, as well as the manner in which this commitment is expressed in human history, in conjunction with human activity and struggle. Deeply critical of theological discourse that over-inflates human potential, theologians such as Roberts have noted the manner in which such theological formulations are "for the suburbs, for the 'haves.'" Yet, while rejecting the sociocultural position of such theologies, black theology has maintained a not dissimilar concern with human accountability and respon-sibility for the world—a mode of weak humanism but within the context of a continuing commitment to the transcendent. The deep disagreement with a turn to the human, if Roberts is representative, is not situated in a fundamental rejection of anthropology. Rather, it is a matter of certain forms of liberal religion's anthropology that fail to recognize the existential condition of African Americans. Regarding this, Robert writes: "Affirmation of human manhood [*sic*], the movement from anxiety to responsibility, the awareness of human strength, and the like belong to the radical shifts in theological focus. But while these insights survey the general theological terrain, crucial aspects of the black experience are untouched."[17]

In a certain way, Roberts points out and critiques efforts to render synonymous the angst of white Americans and the core of theological inquiry and concern. This evaluation is based on a conclusion similar to that reached by Charles Long in casting Death of God theology as reference to disillusionment and as recognition of the faulty nature of Western constructs and arrangements: "When, for example, Thomas J. J. Altizer speaks of the 'death of God,' is he not in fact trying to refer to the decline of the West, or the death and end of the American Dream? Why assign the category of death of God when you really mean something else?"[18] Roberts agrees with Long and extends theo-anthropologically his commentary, noting in his critique of the Death of God theology, the continuing centrality of the divine tied to some recognition of humanity, over against a radical anthropology with a limited Christian grammar: "A Christian humanism rather than a 'Christian Atheism' would appear to be more to the point." The type of humanism Roberts highlights entails synergy between divine presence in human history and human accountability for and activity toward liberation.[19] It, again, is the type of humanism with which African American theologians (and African American religionists in more general terms) can be comfortable. This is because black theology's approach requires a God present in the world, working through and with humanity to bring about liberation. Such a posture does not reduce the significance of humanity; rather, it is heightened, Roberts would argue, through God's immanence. In this way, African American weak humanism involves a partnership between God and humanity, a working together for the transformation of oppressive circumstances. Roberts and his colleagues are concerned with the "moral attributes of God," not the existence of God.[20] To the extent this understanding involves the death of God, it is the God of oppression and white supremacy because "the white God is an idol created by racists, and we blacks must perform the iconoclastic task of smashing false images."[21] The question for Roberts is not "does God exist?" but rather "does God care?"[22]

Although one might make such theological moves based on the general posture of black theology—particularly in response to liberal approaches like Death of God theology—James Cone does not want to suggest religion is reducible to ethics.[23] Instead, ethics involves a response to contact with the depth of the religious quest. The activity of God within the context of human life is the source of theological energy, and it is this preoccupation with the presence of the divine within the context of human existence that shapes black theology and black religion (as expressed in churches) in the mode of weak humanism acted out: "How do we dare speak of God in a suffering world, a world in which blacks are humiliated because they are black? This question, which occupies the central place in our theological perspective, forces us to say nothing about God that does not participate in the emancipation of black humanity."[24] Black theology, particularly in the writings of Cone, affixes doctrine of God and theological anthropology in a rigid manner, through a process of correlation by means of which to speak of one means to speak of the other: "We can know God only in relationship to the human race, or more particularly in God's liberating activity in behalf of oppressed humanity."[25] Even with this said, it remains understood that God is not captured or fully known through human experience. Historical reality only provides a glimpse of God, and one that affirms the importance and integrity of human life. Black theology argues for an understanding of immanence and transcendence in ways that reinforce each other in that "transcendence refers to human purpose as defined by the infinite in the struggle for liberation."[26] In this case, within this theistic humanist perspective, social transformation becomes the litmus test for the relevance of God in that the existential experience of African Americans is the hermeneutic through which truth claims are assessed— accepted or rejected as the ideological trappings of white supremacy. "We do not want to know," Cone argues, "how we can get along without God, but how we can survive in a world permeated with white racism."[27] Black theologians, as exemplified in early incarnations by Cone and Roberts, maintained a somewhat awkward and self-conscious connection between what they perceived as the best aspects of their training—the best aspects of liberal theology and its counterpoints in neo-orthodox theology—and the demands of the black experience.

By the 1980s, black theologians would come to realize that tension with the Western (male) theological tradition was not their only challenge. Their failure to take seriously the experience of black women as a major element of black experience would face significant critique in the form of womanist theology. Maintaining the weak humanism of black male theologians, but carved out of the experiences of women, womanist scholars suggest human accountability and responsibility for liberation are not outweighed by God's presence and workings in human history. Rather, there is a connection between these two that makes it difficult to distinguish the work of God from the work of humanity. The obligation for moving in ways promoting health and well-being are God's orientation and humanity's responsibility. What womanist theologians suggest is in keeping with the old saying: "God has no hands but your hands, no feet but your feet."

Black and womanist theologies are a messy blend of liberal theology—centrality of experience and the importance of culture, for instance—and critiques of liberalism, such as suspicion concerning notions of human progress and reified modes of identity.[28] Black and womanist theologies as a dimension of U.S. religious liberalism have, nonetheless, a different perspective on the secular world, one that is much darker, marred as it is by the continuing legacy of the slave system through which black bodies were reified and denied the freedom that marked the modern quest for life. On this score, I would agree with Peter Hodgson, who places these theological developments within the framework of liberal theology while recognizing some of the alterations they suggest. He says, "Feminist and liberation theologies share many of the central concerns of the liberal tradition, recontextualized in a much more diverse cultural and intellectual situation."[29] To the extent black and womanist theologies have attempted to distance themselves from liberal theology, it has not been because of fundamental disagreements on the stated relationship between humans and the divine or the moral and ethical insights and obligations present in history through this relationship. Rather, attempted (but failed) rejection comes from the overall failure of liberal thinkers to extend (in their work) to all peoples in all places inclusion in divinely inspired freedom and liberty within the historical intersections of human and divine contact. That is to say, the freedom and liberty that mark the liberal tradition in the United States and the radical presence of God through the promise of Christ did not reach the African American section of James Cone's Arkansas or Katie Cannon's North Carolina.

Black and womanist theologians deny the existence of certain god formations—those inconsistent with the demand of the oppressed for liberation. In making this statement, I am suggesting a connection most will find objectionable—the idea that black and womanist theologies have anything to do with humanism. And what is more, I propose links between Death of God and black and womanist theologies that will come across to many as unjustified and unthinkable, particularly in light of statements made by Roberts, for example, to the contrary. Death of God theology and its brand of humanism involve language games through the questioning and reevaluation of Christian vocabulary (e.g., "God") and grammar. To some extent, black and womanist theologians have participated in a similar process. That is to say, there is something of the "death of God" in their work. The words of William Hamilton have some meaning in this context, although they must be understood within a particular socio-political context: "The death of God in 1965 served as psychological preparation for the black theology of the late 1960s. It made black theology possible as ideology, if not convincing as theology, for—as James Baldwin had earlier observed in *The Fire Next Time*—the God that died in 1965 was white."[30] In essence, one might argue, black and womanist theologies advocate for weak humanism in that they give so much weight to doctrine of God understood through the humanization of God in the Christ Event, with a sense of real optimism premised on the presence of God in the struggle for liberation. God is infused in human history through Christ, and humans participate in this divinity to the degree they take on—in an ontological sense—God's character.

The Limits of Weak Humanism's Theologizing

While weak humanism and its theological platform have been helpful, fueling and animating various dimensions of the theologically guided struggle, it has failed to sufficiently challenge all religious signs and symbols, safeguarding some (e.g., God) from critical attention. Consequently, black and womanist theologies contain both potential tools of transformation and the seeds of their own demise. They house the signs of contradiction and inconsistency that prophesy their current status as espousing great rhetoric without evidence of great involvement in the struggle and without clear signs of the change prophesied. And rather than addressing content and constructive problems, black and womanist theologies as modalities of liberal and postliberal theology remain silent on the flaws within their systems. These weak humanism-driven theologies throw empty challenges at rather watered-down projections of oppression. The theological advocates of this posture appear more concerned with rhetorical appeals regarding their connections to the folk than with attempts to work through the shape and meaning of their theological pronouncements in light of the embodied struggles of the community of concern.

The problem, as I see it, is not that black and womanist theologies embraced European theology (Karl Barth and Paul Tillich, for instance), American liberal theology in the form of figures such as Walter Rauschenbusch, or the neo-orthodoxy of Reinhold Niebuhr. *No, the dilemma involves a failure to see the ways in which the weak humanism they represent raises internal questions concerning theological anthropology and the viability of the divine.* Regardless of focus on race or gender, black and womanist theologies fail to see the dilemma associated with their metaphysics. As evidence, readers might think in terms of Cone's call for the death of gods unsupportive of the black liberation agenda. Yet, does the ability to demand such a profound metaphysical shift—in light of human want and need—really speak to the human construction and constitution of the God idea? (Where's the Barthian infinite and qualitative distinction between God and humanity, the distinction that forges such a profound divide between the divine will and human will that Cone seems so fond of in his early work?) Is God, as Ludwig Feuerbach remarked, simply the (African American) human projected onto a cosmic screen? Is the persistence of the Christian faith (e.g., weak humanism) in African American communities a matter of fear and complacency over against anything of real cosmic substance? By extension, is it not possible that the positioning of black and womanist theologies (e.g., limited attention to them within church circles) speaks to the manner in which church communities sense a break with their metaphysical sensibilities, a soft (and inadequate but nonetheless present) confrontation with metaphysical fear and complacency on the part of theologians who by pretense claim these Christianity communities? Such questions are not typically asked, but nonetheless they point to an internal tension in black and womanist theologies—a tension that, I believe, begs the question of a more robust depiction of humanity in the form of "strong" or nontheistic humanism. If nothing else, this tension calls for this book—an exploration of the nontheistic humanism alternative and its accompanying theological discourse.

In spite of the presence demonstrated through cultural production and institutionalized mechanisms, African American humanism had gone relatively ignored by scholars and the general public through the mid-twentieth century. However, within the past four decades, scholars of African American religion have begun to recognize the existence of African American humanism as one of the ways in which African Americans express themselves religiously. While most of these scholars are Christian, their work is increasingly sensitive to the nontheistic strands of African American practice and thought as representing a "marginal orientation" evident but without, these scholars argue, great impact on the life agenda of African Americans as a collective.

As I have argued for a good number of years, not all African Americans embrace theism or weak humanism as their orientation toward life, and the signs of this alternate religious framework—nontheistic humanism—run as deep as those of theism and weak humanism.

Nontheistic Humanism as Religious Orientation

To sum up the sense of religion present through this book, religion can be defined as the quest for complex subjectivity, as a deeply human endeavor, a particular framing of human experience. Hence, *nontheistic humanism can be understood as a modality of religion in that it involves a quest for complex subjectivity, a push for greater life meaning both existential and ontological in nature, an orientation premised on a set of five guiding principles* and housed in a variety of patterns and structures:

1. There is recognition that humanity is fully and solely accountable and responsible for the human condition and the correction of humanity's plight.
2. There is a general suspicion toward or rejection of supernatural explanations and claims, combined with an understanding of humanity as an evolving part

of the natural environment as opposed to being a created being. This can involve disbelief in God(s).

3. There is an appreciation for African American cultural production and a perception of traditional forms of black religiosity as having cultural importance as opposed to any type of "cosmic" authority.
4. There is a commitment to individual and societal transformation.
5. There is a controlled optimism that recognizes both human potential and human destructive activities.[31]

As I have argued elsewhere, some enslaved Africans sang spirituals celebrating the ontological and existential synergy between the divine and the human, best represented through the immanence of the divine in Christ; others signified this perspective and gave their full attention to humanity through the language of the blues, in which metaphysical assertions are met with suspicion and immanence is of primary concern.

> I used to ask God questions,
> then answer that question my self.

Even the basic mode of communication between the transcendent realm and the immanent space known as human history is held suspect, and it is signified—giving priority to the demands and troubles of the existential condition of humanity:

> Our father, who is in heaven,
> White man owe me eleven and pay me seven,
> They kingdom come, they will be done,
> And if I hadn't took that, I wouldn't had none.

The blues provide a language of meaning that jettisons traditional metaphysical formulations dependent on notions of the divine, and in their place, these tunes advocate concern with human interaction(s) in the world.

Enslaved African Americans who embraced nontheistic humanism were not always shy about their stance. This was certainly Bishop Alexander Payne's experience when confronting a runaway slave who questioned the existence of God: "I asked him if he was a Christian; 'no, sir,' said he, 'white men treat us so bad in Mississippi that we can't be Christians.'... In a word, slavery tramples the laws of the living God under its unhallowed feet; weakens and destroys the influence which those laws are calculated to exert over the mind of man; and constrains the oppressed to blaspheme the name of the Almighty."[32] Marked as it is with a triumphant sense of immanent experience as the judge of metaphysical claims, the runaway's rejection of a theistic orientation involves of necessity a reliance on human ingenuity and skills for the fulfillment of life. Similar sentiments are expressed in folk wisdom present within African American culture. For instance, a chimney sweep named John Junior rejects the supposed comfort of the Christian faith and replaces this with intense devotion to human progress and achievement based strictly on the work of human hands:

> I strictly have my fun. No, I ain't tendin' been' no Christian.
> That's the trouble with niggers now. They pray too damn
> Much. Evertyine you look around you se some nigger on
> His knees and the white man figurin' at his desk. What in
> The world is they prayin' fo'? Tryin' to get to heaven?
> They is goin' to get there anyhow. There ain't no other
> Hell but this one down here. Look at me. I'm catchin'
> Hell right now.[33]

I suggest that the shadow, if not overt presence, of nontheistic humanism in early African American communities is replaced during the twentieth century with a much firmer presentation of this perspective.[34] For example, the early twentieth century witnessed the explicit articulation of principles and platforms consistent with nontheistic humanism through the participation of African Americans in the Communist Party and other organizations critical of traditional Christian perspectives. Late-twentieth-century political activities (i.e., civil rights activism) also housed this perspective. While members of the civil rights movement as orchestrated by figures like Martin Luther King Jr. by and large embraced traditional theism or theistic humanism, members of the Student Nonviolent Coordinating Committee (SNCC) and the Black Panther Party held a preference for the liberative possibilities of naturalistic humanism, when religion was mentioned at all.

The Harlem Renaissance, within the realm of artistic production, offered nontheistic humanism in various forms, most notably in the writings of Richard Wright, whose characters, such as Cross Damon (*The Outsider*), limited reach to the existential realities of a troubled and troubling world.[35] What we have here is not simply a fantastic presentation of fictional perspectives. To the contrary, African American literary figures such as Richard Wright and James Weldon Johnson personally embraced nontheistic humanism with great thoughtfulness. In the words of Johnson:

> My glance forward reaches no farther than this world. I admit that
> I throughout my life have lacked religiosity. I do not know if there is a
> personal God; I do not see how I can know; and I do not see how my

knowing can matter. As far as I am able to peer into the inscrutable, I do not see that there is any evidence to refute those scientists and philosophers who hold that the universe is purposeless: that man, instead of being the special care of a Divine Providence, is dependent upon fortuity and his own wits for survival in the midst of blind and insensate forces.[36]

The passion with which nontheistic humanism is expressed by these figures is also found in the words of African American women. Take, for instance, the rugged and human-centered approach offered by Zora Neale Hurston:

> So I do not pray. I accept the means at my disposal for working out my destiny. It seems to me that I have been given a mind and will-power for that very purpose.... Prayer is for those who need it. Prayer seems to me a cry of weakness, and an attempt to avoid, by trickery, the rules of the game as laid down. I do not choose to admit weakness. I accept the challenge of responsibility.[37]

Or consider Alice Walker's words:

> I seem to have spent all of my life rebelling against the church or other peoples interpretations of what religion is – the truth is probably that I don't believe there is a God, although I would like to believe it. Certainly I don't believe there is a God beyond nature. The world is God. Man is God. So is a leaf or a snake.[38]

Albeit important, nontheistic humanism as presented in African American political rhetoric and literature is a loose arrangement of a particular life orientation that does not hold the same communal weight as churches housing the alternate perspective of theistic humanism. Yet, this loose configuration is only one of the styles of presentation for nontheistic humanism. The Unitarian Universalist Association (UUA) has for decades served as an institutional home for some African American nontheistic humanists because of its commitment to a nondoctrinal community and its resulting comfort with congregations of varying theological orientations. While the relationship between African Americans and the UUA has involved significant rough patches, primarily revolving around issues of race relations within the church, it has also maintained both mixed and primarily black congregations in which metaphysical assertions take a back seat. One reason some African Americans have remained in the UUA in spite of cultural difficulties revolves around the manner in which the appeal to social justice, the framework of liberative activism, is expressed in terms of human accountability and responsibility without the implicit and explicit links to notions of the transcendent and biblical notions of divine intervention that undergird the sense of liberation found in most black churches.[39]

Theologizing Nontheistic Humanism

It is not until the writings of William R. Jones that nontheistic humanism challenges theistic humanism within the context of African American religious studies.[40] Jones, writing in 1973, critiqued theistic humanism vis-à-vis black theology for its failure to adequately address the paradox created when one considers positive statements concerning God's involvement with the oppressed in spite of the continuing presence of human suffering disproportionately experienced by people of color. In response to this theological quagmire, Jones offers a polemic that has shaped for the past several decades conversation regarding Jones: "Is God a white racist?"[41] Is the black theological formulation of divine character the most logical explanation of continued suffering of people of color? To continue to use the term God and all that it implies must entail for black liberationists both recognition of death and life. The latter is present in vibrant ways in their theology, and death, too—but only as the precursor to a continuing transcendence as it entails the removal of God in order for God to reappear (in "black" and as "ontologically black"). This, however, has done little to address the fundamental problems pointed out by Jones and later in some of my work. The corresponding discussions have not gone well. Typical responses to both—beyond the dominant silence—entail talk of God in louder terms, as if volume and passion can substitute for substance and historically situated presence. But would one expect challenges to the basic infrastructure of black and womanist theologies to go well, when I have suggested death of God as a human accomplishment in that humans rework their language, and God is only one of the symbols associated with humanity's religious language?

The assumption has been that my efforts point in the direction of Death of God theology, which, as I indicated earlier, J. Deotis Roberts and Charles Long addressed in less than flattering terms. Yet, there are distinctions to be made between Death of God theology and what I propose. Thomas J. J. Altizer claimed that God is dead. By this attention-grabbing statement, he intended to say in the Christ Event, God completely empties God's self into the world, and the spirit of God is not resurrected but defused through the world. Altizer gives us a hint, a theological nudge for further investigation: This proposition that God kills god-self in the Christ Event is a work of theodicy by humans to explain an apparent silence in the face of moral evil. It, I would argue, is a form of abandonment that does not theologically satisfy. In short, in killing God's self, God has done the work for us, saving us from the task but offering us nothing substantive in terms of our moral evil dilemma.

While many black and womanist theologians find such a pronouncement unacceptable—God is Dead?—they, consistent with the tension I noted, would agree with the notion that God allows God's self to be absorbed into the world. It seems this is one plausible way of interpreting the idea of God's preferential option for the oppressed or the notion of God being black—ontologically black. What offends, then, is not the process of God's emptying into the world; rather, it's the language used to describe this event. "God is Dead," as defined by Altizer, allows for a humanization of theological discourse and its subsequent agendas. And perhaps there is a way of linking this to Cone's pronouncement, also noted earlier, that gods not concerned with liberation must be killed or the need to reject the oppressors' God because it is a meaningless symbol.[42] The difference is God, in recognizing the need to be completely for and with humanity, "kills" God-self. What Cone suggests, then, is recognition of this death and the call for new life it promotes: "The oppressors' God is a God of slavery and must be destroyed along wit the oppressors. The question then, as black theology sees it, is not whether blacks believe in God, but whose God?"[43] Black and womanist theologies of the twentieth century wrestled with a development of language, and this was done to avoid a slide into nontheistic humanism. Kelly Brown Douglas gives some sense of the strength and depth of this wrestling as language shapes the meaning of faith:

> What is it about Christianity that has allowed it to be both a bane and a blessing for black people? Clearly it has played a significant role in the white assault on the black body. Christianity has conspired with white supremacy not simply in the horror of enslaving black people but also in the odious deed of lynching them. It has provided theological legitimation for the overall dehumanizing denigration of black bodies. Yet it has also sustained black people in their struggle against white dehumanization. It has provided them with the strength and courage to resist white assaults on their bodies.[44]

What nontheistic humanism recognizes is what African American theistic theologians hope to ignore: The development of doctrines and institutions is actually the failure of religion—its collapse into the familiar and a push away from its sharper challenge to life as it has been safely formulated. This failure entails a push away from the manner in which religion might expand our self-understanding (while also harming it) in relationship to others, the manner in which religion might recast difference by removing fear (while re-inscribing it in different ways).

There are dimensions and layers of African American embodied life that have been sacrificed for the sake of God-talk, and this process should end. To accomplish this outcome, however, requires the end of God-talk and the beginning of a theological discourse that does not lose sight of the humans at work in this world.

NOTES

Introduction

1. See, for example, "A Religious Portrait of African Americans," in the Pew Forum on Religion & Public Life at: http://pewforum.org/A-Religious-Portrait-of-African-Americans.aspx.

2. Readers will notice that in some cases the chapters build on previously published materials, and in other cases, the material is presented here for the first time. This is a natural outgrowth of my having thought about this project and developed small pieces of it over the course of the past fifteen years. In a very real way, this book brings together the various strands of my efforts to think theologically *as a nontheistic humanist*.

3. William Hamilton, "American Theology, Radicalism and the Death of God," in Thomas Altizer and William Hamilton, *Radical Theology and the Death of God* (Bobbs-Merrill, 1966).

4. William Hamilton, "The Death of God Theologies Today," in Altizer and Hamilton, *Radical Theology and the Death of God*, 40. Also see "Dietrich Bonhoeffer" in the same volume.

5. William Hamilton, "The Death of God Theologies Today," in Altizer and Hamilton, *Radical Theology and the Death of God*, 48–9.

6. Thomas Altizer, "The Sacred and the Profane: A Dialectical Understanding of Christianity," in *Radical Theology and the Death of God*, 154.

7. This is not a full deconstructive theology in that there is attention to the subject, for example, that does not fit deconstruction. While I am not certain subjectivity can be obtained, I think it is still a worthy pursuit. The outcome matters little. It is possible that my thinking will eventually move further in the direction of deconstructive theology in full. Or perhaps not. I am less certain of the death of self than of the death of God. The latter has had no meaning for some time, but the self—in light of the nature of racialization and other modalities of dis/embodied oppression—requires more thought. Perhaps the announcements of the death of the self as people of color are gaining greater sense of their occupation of time and space point to a deception. For work on deconstructive theology, see, for example, Mark C. Taylor, *Deconstructing Theology* (New York: Crossroads; Chico, CA: Scholars Press, 1982); Taylor, *After God* (Chicago: University of Chicago Press, 2007); Taylor, *Erring: A Postmodern A/theology* (Chicago: University of Chicago Press, 1987); and Don Cupitt, *After God: The Future of Religion* (New York: Basic Books, 1997).

8. Anthony B. Pinn, *Terror and Triumph: The Nature of Black Religion* (Minneapolis: Fortress, 2003).

Chapter 1

1. Some of the material in this chapter dealing with photographs is drawn from "Embodied Meaning: The 'Look' and 'Location' of Religion in the American Hemisphere," in Anthony B. Pinn, Caroline Levander, and Michael Emerson, eds., *Teaching and Studying the Americas: Cultural Influences from Colonialism to the Present* (New York: Palgrave Macmillan, 2010).

2. For an interesting discussion of the manner in which nonwritten materials become "texts" within the study of religion, see Lindsay Jones, *The Hermeneutics of Sacred Architecture: Experience, Interpretation, Comparison*, vol. 1 (Cambridge, MA: Harvard University Center for the Study of World Religions/Harvard University Press, 2000), 121–33.

3. Kaufman, Gordon. *An Essay on Theological Method*, 3rd ed. (New York: Oxford University Press, 2000).

4. In other texts, I have explored the value of body fluids and the visual and decorative arts as theological source materials. See, for example, "Blessed Irreverence: What Black Theology Can Learn from the Visual Arts," in *The Subjective Eye: Essays in Culture, Religion, and Gender* (Eugene, OR: PickWick, 2006), 310–20; "Sweaty Bodies in a Circle: Thoughts on the Subtle Dimensions of Black Religion as Protest," *Black Theology: An International Journal* 4, no. 1 (2006): 43–62. While these particular source materials are not explored in this book, my awareness of them and interest in them is evident in these publications.

5. My aim is not to provide a genealogy of the photographic image or offer discussion of the types of photography—documentary and so on. I am not concerned with the dynamics of photographic images—the types of materials used, the history of cameras, and so on. Rather, I am interested in a more general discussion of the meaning of the photographic image as a matter of theologizing. For information on other elements, readers should see texts such as Susan Sontag, *On Photography* (New York: Picador, 1977); Miles Orvell, *American Photography* (New York: Oxford University Press, 2003); Graham Clarke, *The Photograph* (New York: Oxford University Press, 1997); and Ian Jeffrey, *The Photograph: A Concise History* (New York: Oxford University Press, 1981).

6. Susan Sontag, *On Photography*, 8.

7. James Guimond offers an interesting analysis of photography in relationship to social crisis. See Guimond, *American Photography and the American Dream* (Chapel Hill: University of North Carolina Press, 1991).

8. In terms of the preparation of the body for public notice, Anne McClintock provides an interesting take on the significance of soap. See Anne McClintock, "Soft-Soaping Empire: Commodity Racism and Imperial Advertising," in Mariam Fraser and Monica Greco, eds., *The Body: A Reader* (New York: Routledge, 2005), chapter 37. Readers may want to consider McClintock's essay in connection to sensory history, such as Mark M. Smith's *How Race Is Made: Slavery, Segregation, and the Senses* (Chapel Hill: University of North Carolina, 2008).

9. Shawn Michelle Smith, *Photography on the Color Line: W. E. B. DuBois, Race, and Visual Culture* (Durham, NC: Duke University Press, 2004), 6.

10. Smith, *Photography on the Color Line*, 7–9.

11. Kathryn Linn Geurts, "Is There a Sixth Sense?" in Geurts, *Culture and the Senses: Bodily Ways of Knowing in an African Community* (Berkeley: University of California Press, 2002), 3. Also see chapter 10.

12. bell hooks, "In Our Glory: Photography and Black Life," in Deborah Willis, *Picturing Us: African American Identity in Photography* (New York: New Press, 1994), 44.

13. Readers will be interested in Deborah Willis, ed., *Picturing Us*; and Shawn Michelle Smith, *American Archives* (Princeton, NJ: Princeton University Press, 1999), chapter 6.

14. Mitchell Stephens, *The Rise of the Image and the Fall of the Word* (New York: Oxford University Press, 1998), 58–69.

15. Graham Clarke, *The Photograph* (New York: Oxford University Press, 1997), 11; Alan Trachtenberg, *Reading American Photographs: Images as History, Mathew Brady to Walker Evans* (New York: Hill and Wang, 1989), 4. I agree with Clarke that photographs are read, suggesting through this language an active process. See Clarke, *The Photograph*, 27.
16. Miles Orvell, *American Photography* (New York: Oxford University Press, 2003), 141–61.
17. Andrew Quick, "The Space Between: Photography and the Time of Forgetting in the Work of Willie Doherty," in Annette Kuhn and Kirsten McAllister, eds., *Locating Memory: Photographic Acts* (New York: Berghahn, 2006), 162–71.
18. Landscapes and other images that do not privilege the human presence can also serve to enhance black theological thought by forcing analysis of a complex range of relationships and notions of subjectivity that bring human bodies into contact with a wide ranger of other modes of life.
19. Shawn Michelle Smith, *American Archives: Gender, Race, and Class in Visual Culture* (Princeton, NJ: Princeton University Press, 1999), 161. The mere fact that a black family (or individual) could afford to make use of photography spoke to economic standing and social positioning unavailable to many.
20. "Introduction," in Linda B. Arthur, ed., *Religion, Dress and the Body* (New York: Berg, 1999), 3, 6.
21. Clarke, *The Photograph*, 33.
22. Susan Sontag, *On Photography*, 28.
23. Some of this was made clear to me in graduate courses with Dr. Richard R. Niebuhr, whose interest in works such as *Let Us Now Praise Famous Men* (James Agee and Walker Evans [New York: Mariner, 2001]) exposed me to the rich religious/theological significance found in the chronicling of the ordinary.
24. See Earl Riggins, *Dark Symbols, and Obscure Signs: God, Self, and Community in the Slave Mind* (Knoxville: University of Tennessee Press, 2003).
25. See Anthony Pinn, *Why, Lord? Suffering and Evil in Black Theology* (New York: Continuum, 1995), 142–4.
26. Alan Trachtenberg, *Reading American Photographs*, 8. The cultural function of museums is addressed in Ivan Karp and Steven D. Lavine, eds., *Exhibiting Cultures: The Poetics and Politics of Museum Display* (Washington, DC: Smithsonian Institution Press, 1991).
27. Trachtenberg, *Reading American Photographs*, 43.
28. Arthur C. Danto, *Philosophizing Art: Selected Essays* (Berkeley: University of California Press, 1999), 132.
29. See, for example, Jeanne Kilde, *Sacred Power, Sacred Space: An Introduction to Christian Architecture and Worship* (New York: Oxford University Press, 2008); Kilde, *When Church Became Theater: Transformation of Evangelical Architecture and Worship in Nineteenth Century America* (New York: Oxford University Press, 2002); Sigurd Bergmann, ed., *Architecture, Aesth/ethics and Religion* (Frankfurt: IKO-Verlag für Interkulturelle Kommunikation, 2005); Mary N. MacDonald, ed., *Experiences of Place* (Cambridge, MA: Center for the Study of World Religions, Harvard Divinity School/Harvard University Press, 2003); Lindsay Jones, *The Hermeneutics of Sacred Architecture: Experience, Interpretation, Comparison* (Cambridge, MA: Harvard University Center for the Study of World Religions/Harvard University Press, 2000); and Sigurd Bergmann, ed., *Theology in Built Environments: Exploring Religion, Architecture, and Design* (New Brunswick, NJ: Transaction, 2009). Examples of this produced for a more popular audience include Anthony Lawlor, *The Temple in the House: Finding the Sacred in Everyday Architecture* (Los Angeles: Jeremy P. Tarcher/Putnam, 1994).
30. Hazel Conway and Rowan Roenisch, *Understanding Architecture: An Introduction to Architecture and Architectural History* (New York: Routledge, 1994), 1–3.
31. For an early example of my understanding of theology as archaeology, see Anthony B. Pinn, *Varieties of African American Religious Experience* (Minneapolis, MN: Fortress, 1998), chapter 5.

32. Gordon Kaufman, *An Essay on Theological Method*, 3rd ed. (New York: Oxford University Press, 2000).

33. Arnold Berleant, "The Aesthetic in Place," in Sarah Menin, ed., *Constructing Place: Mind and Matter* (New York: Routledge, 2003), 42.

34. My purpose in what remains of this chapter is simply to begin outlining the theological implications of this theory. In subsequent work, however, it will be necessary to more fully articulate and theorize the nature and meaning of the two prime components: space and time.

35. Mary N. MacDonald, "Introduction: Place and the Study of Religions," in MacDonald, ed., *Experiences of Place*, 2, 3.

36. Arnold Berleant, "The Aesthetic in Place," 49.

37. Sarah Menin, "Introduction," in Menin, ed., *Constructing Place*, 1.

38. Heidi J. Nast and Steve Pile, "EverydayPlacesBodies," in Nast and Pile, eds., *Places through the Body* (New York: Routledge, 1998), 405, 406.

39. D. Canter, *The Psychology of Place* (London: Architectural Press, 1977), quoted in Birgit Cold, "Beautiful, True and Good Architecture: An Introduction," in Bergmann, ed., *Architecture, Aesth/ethics and Religion*, 13.

40. Anthony B. Pinn, *Terror and Triumph: The Nature of Black Religion* (Minneapolis, MN: Fortress, 2003), 179.

41. This might also include thoughts and perspectives on Starbucks found through online blogs and elsewhere.

42. For instance, see Mark Smith, *Sensory History* (Oxford: Berg, 2007); Smith, *Sensing the Past: Seeing, Hearing, Smelling, Tasting, Touching in History* (Berkeley: University of California Press, 2007).

43. Useful sources might include Dell Upton, *Another City: Urban Life and Urban Spaces in the New American Republic* (New Haven, CT: Yale University Press, 2008); Leon Krier, *The Architecture of Community* (Washington, DC: Island, 2009); Fred Rush, *On Architecture* (New York: Routledge, 2009); and Arthur Danto, *The Abuse of Beauty* (Chicago: Open Court, 2003).

44. Sources might include Nast and Pile, eds., *Places through the Body*; Panu Lehtouvuori, *Experience and Conflict: The Production of Urban Space* (Burlington, VT: Ashgate, 2010); Menin, *Constructing Place*; Wendy Schissel, ed., *Home/Bodies: Geographies of Self, Place, and Space* (Calgary, AB: University of Calgary Press, 2006); and Alan Read, ed., *Architecturally Speaking: Practices of Art, Architecture and the Everyday* (New York: Routledge, 2000).

45. This development is referenced and sourced in Jon Binnie, Robyn Longhurst, and Robin Peace, "Upstairs/Downstairs: Place Matters, Bodies Matter," in David Bell, Jon Binnie, Ruth Holliday, Robyn Longhurst, and Robin Peace, eds., *Pleasure Zones: Bodies, Cities, Spaces* (Syracuse, NY: Syracuse University Press, 2001), vii–xiv.

46. Michael Gates Gill, *How Starbucks Saved My Life: A Son of Privilege Learns to Live Like Everyone Else* (New York: Gotham, 2007), 1.

47. Gill, *How Starbucks Saved My Life*.

48. Delores Williams, *Sisters in the Wilderness* (Maryknoll, NY: Orbis, 1993).

49. This chapter does not provide a history of the coffee house, but rather focuses on a particular coffee house and its purpose. For more general information on the development of the coffee house, see, for example, Markman Ellis, *The Coffee House: A Cultural History* (Beverly Hills, CA: Phoenix, 2005); or the novel David Liss, *The Coffee Trader* (New York: Random House, 2003).

50. PRWeb at www.prweb.com/releases/Coffee/Reviews/prweb2466324.htm. The Coffee Review: www.coffeereview.com/.

51. Taylor Clark, *Starbucked: A Double Tall Tale of Caffeine, Commerce, and Culture* (New York: Little, Brown, 2007), 41.

52. Elsewhere in the world, coffeehouses play a social role. However, there is something I would label unique about the environment consciously fostered by Starbucks.

53. Bryant Simon records the following comment from Starbucks representative Frank Kern: "Five years ago,' he explained in 2007, 'about 3 percent of starbuck's [sic] customers were between the ages of 18 and 24, 16 percent were people of color, 78 percent had college degrees, and overall they had an average annual income of $81K. Today however about 13 percent of the company's customers are between 18 and 24, 37 percent are people of color, 56 percent are college graduates and they earn on avg. $55K a year.'" Bryant Simon, *Everything but the Coffee: Learning about America from Starbucks* (Berkeley: University of California Press, 2009), 8.

    Concerning diversity, the Starbucks Web site says: "Aside from extraordinary coffee, Starbucks has made a business out of human connections, community involvement and the celebration of cultures. We're committed to upholding a culture where diversity is valued and respected. So it's only natural that as a guiding principle, diversity is integral to everything we do" (www.starbucks.com/about-us/company-information/diversity-at-starbucks). This statement, however, must be read in conjunction with the following comment: "…a Starbucks store sits on just about every Midtown corner and along every Village square, but there is only one or two Starbucks in the overwhelmingly African American and Latino areas of the city [New York] above 125th Street, and there is not one in East Harlem or in the Bedford-Stuyvesant section of Brooklyn" (Simon, *Everything but the Coffee*, 92).

54. It remains the case that Starbucks expansion strategy involves three markers of store success: the income within a particular area, the size of the population in that community, and high levels of educational attainment (Clark, *Starbucked*, 119). It seems reasonable, then, to suggest the expansion into places like Harlem corresponded to its growing gentrification.

55. See www.starbucks.com/about-us/company-information/mission-statement.

56. Simon, *Everything but the Coffee*, 82–121.

57. This does not rule out the new strategy as also an economic opportunity in the same way the collection of offerings at a church does not rule out an understanding of church ritual and thought as being of spiritual significance. Nor does the fact that not all experience Starbucks as place take away from a theorizing of Starbucks along those lines, just as attendance of church for a variety of reasons (e.g., cultural enrichment, dating opportunities, spiritual renewal) does not, for Christians, reduce the spiritual authority and religious integrity of churches.

    Post-2007 Starbucks encountered the economic hardships that would grip the United States, and its economic power and presence would suffer some. See Simon, *Everything but the Coffee*.

58. Clark, *Starbucked*, 43.

59. Clark, *Starbucked*, 51.

60. Clark, *Starbucked*, 49.

61. Clark, *Starbucked*, 78–9. Clark mentions the work of sociologist Ray Oldenburg, who spoke of the "third place"—a public sphere of connection. This sense of place is charged in a different way than my notion of architecture as place. Yet, Oldenburg disagreed with the referencing of Starbucks as a "third place."

62. www.starbucks.com/about-us/company-information/mission-statement. This must have some appeal in that the Starbucks Facebook page had more than 9 million "fans" or "people who like this" as of July 9, 2010.

63. Simon, *Everything but the Coffee*, 86.

64. Clark, *Starbucked*, 111–13.

65. Clark, *Starbucked*, 75, 91–2. Simon, *Everything but the Coffee*, dissects the economic motivations for this development and raises questions concerning the Starbucks ongoing capacity for this function.

66. The idea this quest could be entertained at Starbucks by individuals or groups is discernible in the furniture: "There was even a rationale for the shape of the tables: they were small and round, ostensibly to preserve the self-esteem of customers drinking alone, since a circular table has no 'empty' seats" (Clark, *Starbucked*, 103). "Noses and ears received consideration as well: a heady coffee aroma saturated the air, as did the carefully chosen music, which changed in mood throughout the day to reflect the needs of customers in each 'day part'" (Clark, *Starbucked*, 104).

67. Robert A. Orsi, *Between Heaven and Earth: The Religious Worlds People Make and the Scholars Who Study Them* (Princeton, NY: Princeton University Press, 2005). I would disagree, however, with Orsi's assumption that theological analysis by its very nature is confessional: "Theology," he writes, "is the reflection upon the thought and practice of a religious tradition by its adherents..." (192). This is certainly one type of theology, the type presented in this book. However, it is not the only way in which theological discourse takes place.

68. The idea of measured realism as I have employed it is developed in Pinn, *Terror and Triumph*.

69. www.starbucks.com/about-us/company-information/mission-statement; Orsi, *Between Heaven and Earth*, 177–204.

70. Noted in Bryant Simon, *Everything but the Coffee*, 96.

71. A form of street dance marked by strong movements of the body. See Monica Miller, "Anti-Proper in the Popular: The Risky Religiosity of Hip-Hop Culture," PhD Dissertation (Chicago Theological Seminary, 2010).

72. I begin with an exploration of the theological significance of the barbershop, understanding fully that future work will need to include beauty salons so as to capture this notion of p(l)ace beyond a predominantly male context.

73. Douglas Walter Bristol Jr., *Kings of the Razor: Black Barbers in Slavery and Freedom* (Baltimore: Johns Hopkins University Press, 2009), 10–12.

74. Bristol, *Kings of the Razor*, 22–3.

75. Bristol, *Kings of the Razor*, 10, 2.

76. Bristol, Jr., *Knights of the Razor*, 33–7.

77. Bristol, *Knights of the Razor*, 75.

78. While beyond the scope of this discussion, Bristol's "guide to further reading" provides materials helpful for those interested in the development of the African American barbershop as economic reality, social concern, and historical marker of African American identity formation. In addition, for more general information on African American hairstyling and care, see, for example, Julia Kirk Blackwelder, *Styling Jim Crow: African American Beauty Training during Segregation* (College Station: Texas A & M University Press, 2003); Althea Prince, *The Politics of Black Women's Hair* (London, ON: Insomniac, 2009); Lanita Jacobs-Huey, *From the Kitchen to the Parlor: Language and Becoming in African American Women's Hair Care* (New York: Oxford University Press, 2006); Ayana Byrd, *Hairstory: Untangling the Roots of Black Hair in America* (New York: St. Martin's, 2001); and Ingrid Banks, *Hair Matters: Beauty, Power, and Black Women's Consciousness* (New York: New York University Press, 2000).

79. Melissa Victoria Harris-Lacewll, *Barbershops, Bibles, and BET: Everyday Talk and Black Political Thought* (Princeton, NJ: Princeton University Press, 2004), 163. One also sees, for example, the significance of barbershops as spaces of education and exchange on difficult issues with the "Black Barbershop Health Outreach Program." See www.blackbarbershop.org/.

80. The significance of barbershops as sociocultural and political institutions has caught the attention of various modes of cultural production, with perhaps none more influential than the Hollywood movie industry. See, for example, *Barbershop*, directed by Tim Story and produced by State Street Production (2002); and *Barbershop 2: Back in Business*, directed by Kevin Rodney Sullivan (2004).

Chapter 2

1. A small portion of material in this chapter is drawn from "God of Restraint: An African American Humanist Interpretation of Nimrod and the Tower of Babel," in Anthony B. Pinn and Allen Callahan, eds., *African American Religious Life and the Story of Nimrod* (New York: Palgrave Macmillan, 2008), 27–34.
2. www.americanreligionsurvey-aris.org/2009/09/american_nones_the_profile_of_the_no_religion_population.html.
3. Genesis 3:22–4; 9:25; 11:4–6 (King James Version). I would not argue that the serpent who plays a role in "original sin" was "good." No, whereas God as restraint seeks to prevent human freedom to safeguard certain relationships we assume good, the serpent seeks to open them for their problematic possibilities: radical good versus radical evil. Neither is beneficial.
4. This discussion is not meant to suggest the "reality" of God in any guise, a "reality" that must be "killed." Rather, the aim is to present the God concept as cultural construction, to critique and dismantle the mythology of the necessity of a God concept, and to offer a more historically driven humanist alternative.
5. Frank Burch Brown, *Religious Aesthetics: A Theological Study of Making and Meaning* (Princeton, NJ: Princeton University Press, 2004), 131–2.
6. While African American nontheistic humanism has little use for the notion of God, my focus here is on the impact of this concept, the language of God regardless of whether this concept points to a substantive cosmic reality. This conception of God, as a matter of language, focuses attention, defines epistemological and ethical boundaries, and shapes life.
7. For an interesting interpretation of the story of Babel that takes up this question of God's intent but offers an alternate, one that justifies God's actions, see: Leon R. Kass, "What's Wrong with Babel?" in George Wolfe, ed., *The New Religious Humanists: A Reader* (New York: Free Press, 1997), 60–83.
8. A similar argument is made in "The Hypostasis of the Archons," found in the Nag Hammadi Library. In this account, an effort is made to keep "Adam" in ignorance. The "rulers" are presented as acting against the interest of humans by attempting to restrict knowledge. I am grateful to Allen Callahan for bringing this account to my attention.
9. Genesis 11:6–8 (King James Version).
10. Much of my earlier work attempted to create an intellectual space for the discussion of African American humanism as religious orientation by dismantling the basic framework of African American theism—God. However, this more systematic effort presented in these pages does not operate simply through negation. It provides critique, to be sure, but it is more concerned with a construction of a theological alternative. In terms of my earlier work, see, for example: Pinn, *Why, Lord? Suffering and Evil in Black Theology* (New York: Continuum, 1995); Pinn, ed., *By These Hands: A Documentary History of African American Humanism* (New York: New York University Press, 2001); Pinn, *African American Humanist Principles: Living and Thinking Like the Children of Nimrod* (New York: Palgrave MacMillan, 2004).
11. Vered Amit, "Reconceptualizing Community," in Amit, ed., *Realizing Community: Concepts, Social Relationships and Sentiment* (New York: Routledge, 2002), 2; Colin Bell and Howard Newby, *Community Studies* (New York: Praeger, 1972); Ferdinand Tönnies, *Community and Society*, trans. Charles P. Loomis (New York: Harper, 1963); Alibert Reiss, ed., *Louis Wirth on Cities and Social Life* (Chicago: University of Chicago, 1964); William Vitek and Wes Jackson, eds., *Rooted in the Land: Essays on Community and Place* (New Haven, CT: Yale University Press, 1996). Andrew Mason argues that community is actually ambiguous—not reducible to any one formulation. See Mason, *Community, Solidarity and Belonging: Levels of Community and Their Normative Significance* (New York: Cambridge University Press, 2000), 17–41. Also of interest is John Dewey's *The Public and Its Problems* (New York: Holt, 1927).

12. See, for example, Seymour J. Mandelbaum, *Open Moral Communities* (Cambridge, MA: MIT Press, 2000); David Studdert, *Conceptualising Community: Beyond the State and Individual* (New York: Palgrave Macmillan, 2005).

13. Adrian Little, *The Politics of Community: Theory and Practice* (Edinburgh, Scotland: Edinburgh University Press, 2002), 2–3.

14. Derek Edyvane, *Community and Conflict: The Sources of Liberal Solidarity* (New York: Palgrave Macmillan, 2007), 4–11. Edyvane's sense of connection and comfort with conflict is in part based on his reading of and response to Alasdair MacIntyre's *After Virtue: A Study in Moral Theory*, 2nd ed. (Notre Dame, IN: University of Notre Dame, 1984).

15. Quoted in Anthony P. Cohen, "Epilogue," in Vered Amit, ed., *Realizing Community: Concepts, Social Relationships and Sentiment* (New York: Routledge, 2002), 168.

16. For a view on this perspective in religious studies, see Sharon D. Welch, *Sweet Dreams in America: Making Ethics and Spirituality Work* (New York: Routledge, 1999).

17. Cohen, "Epilogue," 169. The italics are in the original. Cohen raises questions concerning the ability to theorize community; however, I hope to suggest in the last portion of this chapter the continued value in theologizing community.

18. Studdert, *Conceptualising Community*, 2–3. Studdert seeks to rethink the nature and meaning of community in ways that privilege sociality: "community is co-operative being-ness—a 'who' created by disclosive action. This being-ness is a configuration of the objective-and subjective-in-betweens as they are created endlessly by the action-ed space and linked and re-linked back and forth between the space of appearance and the web of relations" (169). This is not simply a matter of scholarly research. There is evidence to suggest students often are encouraged to think in terms of relationships and interactions: see Tony Blackshaw, *Key Concepts in Community Studies* (Washington, DC: Sage, 2010); George S. Wood Jr. and Juan C. Judikis, *Conversations on Community Theory* (West Lafayette, IN: Purdue University Press, 2002).

19. Mason, *Community, Solidarity and Belonging*, 20–1. Mason's formulation of community can be interrogated in interesting ways in light of twenty-first-century crises such as the devastating earthquake in Haiti. How would this take on theory of community respond to the collectives of humans within the various geographies of shock and need marking the capital of Haiti? And how does one categorize those from outside that context who have made a commitment to "be with" the people of Haiti? Furthermore, in the realm of liberation ethics, are Latin American "base communities" misnamed?

20. Mason, *Community, Solidarity and Belonging*, 27.

21. Thomas Bender, *Community and Social Change in America* (New Brunswick, NJ: Rutgers University Press, 1978), 17, 20. Bender provides an interesting historiography of community in the United States.

22. Bender, *Community and Social Change in America*, 43.

23. Of interest is Talcott Parsons, *American Society: A Theory of the Societal Community*, ed. Giuseppe Sciortino (Boulder, CO: Paradigm, 2007).

24. Readers will come to discover the assumption of physicality, of material realness assumed by Mason and many others. Attention to Benedict Anderson later in this chapter will point out this out and offer an alternate way of framing community.

25. Studdert, *Conceptualising Community*, 4.

26. Studdert, *Conceptualising Community*, 4. In light of this, Studdert wants to understand community as "the ongoing part of ourselves which we have relinquished" (5).

27. Edyvane, *Community and Conflict*, 36–40. It might be interesting to also read this sense of community and how it functions in light of the sense of "association" in Alexis de Tocqueville's *Democracy in America* (New York: Signet, 2001).

28. Charlie Cooper, *Community, Conflict and the State: Rethinking Notions of "Safety," "Cohesion" and "Wellbeing"* (New York: Palgrave Macmillan, 2008), 97. Also see Bender, *Community and Social Change in America*, for an earlier stating of a similar perspective.

29. See Josiah Royce, *The Problem of Christianity* (New York: Macmillan, 1913).

30. Julius Seelye Bixler, "Josiah Royce: Twenty Years After," *Harvard Theological Review* 29, no. 3 (1936): 197–224 [200].

31. Bixler, "Josiah Royce," 208, 220–2.

32. Dwayne A. Tunstall, *Yes, But Not Quite: Encountering Josiah Royce's Ethico-Religious Insight* (New York: Fordham University Press, 2009), 96–7. Sharon Welch provides an interesting, and humanism influenced, understanding of the beloved community. See Sharon D. Welch, *A Feminist Ethic of Risk* (Minneapolis, MN: Fortress, 1990).

33. Martin Luther King Jr., *Stride toward Freedom: The Montgomery Story* (New York: Harper & Row, 1958), 197, 196.

34. Tunstall, *Yes, But Not Quite*, 101; Martin Luther King Jr., *Where Do We Go From Here: Chaos or Community?* (Boston: Beacon, 1967).

35. Martin L. King Jr., "The Ethical Demands for Integration," in James Melvin Washington, ed., *A Testament of Hope: The Essential Writings of Martin Luther King, Jr.* (San Francisco: Harper & Row, 1986), 118.

36. James H. Cone, *Martin & Malcolm & America: A Dream or a Nightmare* (Maryknoll, NY: Orbis, 1991), 80.

37. King, "The Ethical Demands for Integration," 118.

37. Cone, *Martin & Malcolm & America*, 121.

38. King, *Stride toward Freedom*, 106.

39. Martin L. King Jr., "Remaining Awake through a Great Revolution," in James Melvin Washington, ed., *A Testament of Hope: The Essential Writings of Martin Luther King, Jr.* (San Francisco: Harper & Row, 1986), 269.

40. King, *Stride toward Freedom*, 206. Also see: "The task of conquering segregation is an inescapable must confronting the church today" (205).

41. See King, *Where Do We Go from Here*, 167–91.

42. King, *Stride toward Freedom*, 102.

43. Martin L. King Jr., "Unfulfilled Dreams," in Clayborne Carson, ed., *The Autobiography of Martin Luther King, Jr.* (New York: Warner, 1998), 358; Martin L. King Jr., "The Drum Major Instinct," in James M. Washington, ed., *A Testament of Hope: The Essential Writings of Martin Luther King, Jr.* (San Francisco: Harper & Row, 1986), 259–67.

44. King, *Stride toward Freedom*, 105.

45. Luther E. Smith Jr., *Howard Thurman: Essential Writings* (Maryknoll, NY: Orbis, 2006), 14.

46. Smith, *Howard Thurman*, 88.

47. "Whether we call it an unconscious process, an impersonal Brahman, or a Personal Being of matchless power and infinite love, there is a creative force in this universe that works to bring the disconnected aspects of reality into a harmonious whole" (King, *Stride toward Freedom*, 107).

48. See, for example, King, "Remaining Awake through a Great Revolution," 270.

49. Mason, *Community, Solidarity and Belonging*, 17.

50. I am grateful to Caroline Levander for bringing Benedict Anderson to my attention: Benedict Anderson, *Imagined Communities: Reflections on the Origin and Spread of Nationalism* (London: Verso, 1983). While Anderson's book has been extremely influential, it has met with some strong critique. See, for example, Sara Castro-Klarén and John Charles Chasteen, eds., *Beyond Imagined Communities: Reading and Writing the Nation in Nineteenth-Century Latin America* (Baltimore: Johns Hopkins University Press, 2003); Anthony Smith, *Nationalism and Modernism: A Critical Survey of Recent Theories of Nations and Nationalism* (New York: Routledge, 1998). Also see Michiel Baud's review, "Beyond Benedict Anderson: Nation-Building and Popular Democracy in Latin America," *International Review of Social History* 50, no. 3 (2005): 485–98.

51. Bender, *Community and Social Change in America*, 6, 7.

52. Anderson, *Imagined Communities*, 15–16, 20, 28.

53. Anderson, *Imagined Communities*, 40, 41.

54. Anderson, *Imagined Communities*, 129.

55. Amit, "Reconceptualizing Community," 3.
56. Neil Davidson, "Review of Benedict Anderson, *Imagined Communities: Reflections on the Origin and Spread of Nationalism*," International Socialism, issue 17, posted December 18, 1997: www.isj.org.uk/index.php4?id=401&issue=117.
57. My thinking on community here has evolved since it was introduced several years ago. At that point, I thought of community as still extending beyond humanity but with a much higher degree of fixedness than is currently the case. It was more consistent with a Tillichian sense of "Ultimate Concern" and framed by human relationships than I am now uncomfortable with. In fact, I named it "Community as Ultimate Concern." I defined it as: "Religious experience as outlined here is religious in that it addressed the search for ultimate meaning also called complex subjectivity. It is humanistic in that this ultimate meaning does not entail transcendence beyond this world and it is African American because it is shaped by and within the context of African American historical realities and cultural creations. Ultimacy here is understood as a certain quality of finite relationship called 'community.'...My concern with community as a mediating factor, the way in which the individual is 'humbled' and connected to a larger existence held accountable, keeps my perspective from being mere religious solipsism" (Pinn, *African American Humanist Principles*, 104–5).
58. Bo Weavil Jackson, "You Can't Keep No Brown," in Eric Sackheim, compiler. *The Blues Line: A Collection of Blues Lyrics from Leadbelly to Muddy Waters* (Hopewell, NJ: Ecco, 1969), 185.
59. Booker White, "Sleepy Man Blues," in Eric Sackheim, compiler. *The Blues Line: A Collection of Blues Lyrics from Leadbelly to Muddy Waters* (Hopewell, NJ: Ecco, 1969), 238.
60. Outkast, "Bowtie," *Speakerboxxx/Love Below* (Arista Records, 2003).
61. While *The End of God-Talk* seeks to think about the ordinary dimensions of life form within the context of theological thinking, readers will find Michel de Certeau's philosophical work interesting: *Practices of the Everyday* (Berkeley: University of California Press, 2002). I am less interested in the ways in which individuals seek to safeguard autonomy from the intrusions of the political and the like. I am more concerned with the manner in which ordinariness actually promotes opportunity for humanism-based engagement with the fundamental questions of life meaning as represented by the quest for complex subjectivity. I am not seeking to suggest that the ordinary elements of life point toward the religious. Rather, in a humanist turn, this book suggests the ordinary is the religious.

Chapter 3

1. See, for example, Dwight Hopkins, *Being Human: Race, Culture, and Religion* (Minneapolis, MN: Fortress, 2005).
2. James H. Cone, *A Black Theology of Liberation*, 2nd ed. (Maryknoll, NY: Orbis, 1986), chapter 4.
3. Luther H. Martin, Huck Gutman, and Patrick H. Hutton, eds., *Technologies of the Self: A Seminar with Michel Foucault* (Amherst: University of Massachusetts Press, 1988), 17.
4. Hayes Carll, "She Left Me for Jesus," *Trouble in Mind* (Lost Highway Records, 2008).
5. Martin et al., *Technologies of the Self*, 17–18.
6. While my thought on this subject has advanced over time and I have presented pieces of this thought in a variety of locations, my most substantive discussion of this theory of the body is: Pinn, *Embodiment and the New Shape of Black Theological Thought* (New York: New York University Press, 2010). This chapter draws some ideas from that text, while extending that discussion by reframing it as a body theology of sorts and with a focus on humanism.
7. Monica L. Miller, *Slaves to Fashion: Black Dandyism and the Styling of Black Diasporic Identity* (Durham, NC: Duke University Press, 2009), 3.

8. This manipulation of time and space here should not be confused with the formation of p(l)ace discussed later in this book. P(l)ace is discussed in relationship to the awareness constituted by community. This manipulation of time and space related to play does not have this additional dimension in full, although it does relate to the nature of the human as subject within the framework of the quest for complex subjectivity.

9. This chapter builds on my thinking related to anthropology and theological discourse as outlined, for example, in *Embodiment and the New Shape of Black Theological Thought*.

10. Thomas J. J. Altizer, "Foreword," in Mark C. Taylor, *Deconstructing Theology* (New York: Crossroad; Chico, CA: Scholars Press, 1982), xi.

11. Altizer, "Foreword," xii.

12. It is interesting to note that Mark C. Taylor and I both studied at Harvard University, with the late Gordon Kaufman, and in our own ways have taken his theorizing of the god concept to more atheistic conclusions. This, in some sense, and while Kaufman might disagree, is an effort to address Kaufman's concern with god as problem.

13. Taylor, *Deconstructing Theology*, 94.

14. Altizer, "Foreword," xiv.

15. Taylor, *Deconstructing Theology*, 89. Readers should also be aware of Taylor's *Erring: A Postmodern A/Theology* (Chicago: University of Chicago Press, 1984); and *After God* (Chicago: University of Chicago Press, 2007).

16. For an interesting and concise exploration of key ideas and concepts related to subjectivity, see, for example, Donald E. Hall, *Subjectivity* (New York: Routledge, 2004).

17. Jeremy R. Carrette, *Foucault and Religion: Spiritual Corporality and Political Spirituality* (New York: Routledge, 2000), 112–3. Carrette's sense of multiple theologies must be connected to a theory of religion as well, a framing and interrogation of religious experience in that theology responds to and forms something. The plurality of religions is already present, as is the plurality of theologies. Carrette speaks of multiple theologies but from the vantage point of what seem fixed religious categories of experience. He speaks really of Christianity but yet suggest multiple realities, plurality.

18. Ann Laura Stoler, *Race and the Education of Desire: Foucault's History of Sexuality and the Colonial Order of Things* (Durham, NC: Duke University Press, 1995), 119–30; 163–207.

19. Paul Gilroy, *The Black Atlantic: Modernity and Double Consciousness* (Cambridge, MA: Harvard University Press, 1993), 30–1.

20. Edward O. Wilson, *Consilience: The Unity of Knowledge* (New York: Vintage, 1998), 130, 132.

21. Black and womanist theologies imply a rehabilitation of the individual within community— an effort to redeem blackness and gender, for example, from the degradation once used to demonize these social constructs attached to certain bodies, all couched on the assumption of biblical authority (when properly interpreted).

22. Foucalt, *Language, Counter-Memory, Practice* (Ithaca, NY: Cornell University Press, 1977) 148. Quoted in Nikki Sullivan, *Tattooed Bodies: Subjectivity, Textuality, Ethics, and Pleasure* (Westport, CT: Praeger, 2001), 2.

23. Wilson, *Consilience*, 178–96.

24. It is common within liberation theologies to find critiques of essentialism and the reification of identity. In this way, liberation theologies' use of a hermeneutic of suspicion makes possible adherence to at least some principles of postmodern thought.

25. Calvin O. Schrag, *The Self after Postmodernity* (New Haven, CT: Yale University Press, 1997), 1.

26. Robert Pete Williams, "I Got So Old," in Eric Sackheim, ed., *The Blues Line: A Collection of Blues Lyrics from Leadbelly to Muddy Waters* (Hopewell, NJ: Ecco, 1993), 445.

27. Schrag, *The Self after Postmodernity*, 8–9. I would want to understand the self as an "aware" subject. At times I will use either of these terms, and the difference is marked by context.

28. Schrag, *The Self after Postmodernity*, 8–9, 16–41. Should this disappearance of the author have consequences for, or at least require alteration with respect to, mundane considerations such as intellectual property and copyrights? Should the question of intentionality also open to discussion issues related to the claiming of ideas as one's own—the particular

expression of ideas through a particular arrangement of words and concepts as proprietary? Perhaps not, but interesting questions nonetheless.

29. Schrag, *The Self after Postmodernity*, 26.
30. Schrag, *The Self after Postmodernity*, 42–74.
31. Schrag, *The Self after Postmodernity*, 42–74.
32. Connections between the subject and space are worked out in Kathleen M. Kirby, *Indifferent Boundaries: Spatial Concepts of Human Subjectivity* (New York: Guilford, 1996). I find chapters 2, 4, and the conclusion to be particularly helpful. Readers might find it informative to read Kirby's theorizing of geography in light of the lived life orientation of texts such as Carolyn Ellis and Michael G. Flaherty, eds., *Investigating Subjectivity: Research on Lived Experience* (Newbury Park, CA: Sage, 1992).
33. Kathleen M. Kirby, *Indifferent Boundaries*, 96–121.
34. Big Bill Broonzy, "I'm Gonna Move to the Outskirts of Town," in Eric Sackheim, ed., *The Blues Line*, 404.
35. Richard Wright, *Black Boy (American Hunger)* (New York: Perennial Classics, 1998); Nella Larsen, *The Complete Fiction of Nella Larsen*, ed. Charles Larson (New York: Anchor, 2001).
36. I give more sustained attention to geography and space in chapters 1, 4, 5, and 6.
37. I would argue this challenge to the subject involves the tragic nature of life, as Cornel West describes it. That is to say, it recognizes the uncertainty of advancement, the give-and-take of life that involves both promise and pitfall. See Cornel West, *The Cornel West Reader* (New York: Basic Civitas, 2000), section 2; West, *Prophesy Deliverance* (Louisville, KY: Westminster John Knox, 2002); West, *Keeping Faith* (New York: Routledge, 2008), section 2; Mark Wood, *Cornel West and the Politics of Prophetic Pragmatism* (Urbana: University of Illinois Press, 2000); Keith Gilyard, *Composition and Cornel West: Notes toward a Deep Democracy* (Carbondale: Southern Illinois University Press, 2008), chapter 4. Yet, this sense of the tragic is not fully captured by the sense of "tragic subjectivity" (and accompanying responses to "victimization," for instance) as articulated by Gabriela Basterra, *Seductions of Fate: Tragic Subjectivity, Ethics, Politics* (New York: Palgrave Macmillan, 2004).
38. See Jupiter Hammon, *America's First Negro Poet: The Complete Works of Jupiter Hammon of Long Island* (Port Washington, NY: Kennikat, 1970); Frederick Douglass, *Narrative of the Life of Frederick Douglass: An American Slave, Written by Himself* (New York: St. Martin's, 2002); Harriet Jacobs, *Incidents in the Life of a Slave Girl* (Cambridge, MA: Harvard University Press, 2009); Olaudah Equiano (Gustavus Vassa), *The Interesting Narrative of the Life of Oluadah Equinao, or Gustavus Vassa, the African, Written by Himself* (London: 1794; New York: Penguin Putnam, 1995); Vincent Carretta *Equiano, The African: Biography of a Self-Made Man* (Athens: University of Georgia Press, 2005).
39. Susan Bordo, *Unbearable Weight: Feminism, Western Culture, and the Body*, 10th ed. (Berkeley: University of California Press, 2003), 73–4; Schrag also pushes this point. See *The Self after Postmodernity*, 46–59. My concern is more focused, however, than that offered by Bordo and Schrag in that I discuss embodiment with focused attention on the nature and meaning of African American embodiment, in light of the particular history of African Americans in the New World.
40. Paul Gilroy, *The Black Atlantic: Modernity and Double Consciousness* (Cambridge, MA: Harvard University Press, 1993).
41. Stephen Jay Gould, *The Mismeasure of Man* (New York: W. W., 1983), 21.
42. Kenneth R. Manning, "Race, Science, and Identity," in Gerald Early, ed., *Lure and Loathing: Essays on Race, Identity, and the Ambivalence of Assimilation* (New York: Allen Lane/Penguin, 1993), 319. Also see Keith Wailoo, "Inventing the Heterozygote: Molecular Biology, Racial Identity, and the Narratives of Sickle-Cell Disease, Tay-Sachs, and Cystic Fibrosis," in Margaret Lock and Judith Farquhar, eds., *Beyond the Body Proper: Reading the Anthropology of Material Life* (Durham, NC: Duke University Press, 2007), 658–71.
43. Wilson, *Consilience*, 180.
44. Gould, *The Mismeasure of Man*, 21.

45. Vicent Berdayes, Luigi Esposito, and John W. Murphy, eds., "Introduction," in *The Body in Human Inquiry: Interdisciplinary Explorations of Embodiment* (Cresskill, NJ: Hampton, 2004), 14.

46. See Erving Goffman, *Stigma: Notes on the Management of Spoiled Identity* (New York: Touchstone, 2009).

47. Contrary to the opinion of some, Ann Laura Stoler insightfully points out Foucault's interest in race, even wanting to present a genealogy of the discourse of race (*Race and the Education of Desire*). Yet it appears to me that Foucault's analysis removes some of the sting of racism by making it a matter of power relationships and social discourse meant to preserve the nation first, not focused first on the destruction of others. Stoler seems to agree with this assessment: "Because Foucault's account of racial discourse is so endemically detached from the patterned shifts in world-wide imperial labor regimes of which those discourses were a part," she writes, "we are diverted from the gritty historical specificities of what racial discourse did both to confirm the efficacy of slavery and to capture new populations in the transition to wage labor. Our task then would not be to follow his genealogy of racism...but rather to explore how his insights might inform our own" (91).

48. I give attention to this framing of the body in *Embodiment and the New Shape of Black Theological Thought*, introduction and chapters 1–2.

49. Linda B. Arthur, ed., *Religion, Dress and the Body* (New York: Berg, 1999), 6.

50. There are deep connections between the body and religion—influencing and informing each other. For example: Carrette, *Foucault and Religion*; Bryan Turner, *Religion and Social Theory: A Materialist Perspective* (London: Heinemann, 1983); and Turner, *The Body and Society: Explorations in Social Theory* (Oxford: Basil Blackwell, 1984).

51. Simon J. Williams and Gillian Bendelow, *The Lived Body: Sociological Themes, Embodied Issues* (New York: Routledge, 1998), 4.

52. Susan Bordo, "Bringing Body to Theory," in Donn Welton, ed., *Body and Flesh: A Philosophical Reader* (Malden, MA: Blackwell, 1998), 91.

53. Williams and Bendelow, *The Lived Body*, 54.

54. Wilson, *Consilience*, 6. I would like to thank Humanist Institute "Class 15" for the wonderful conversation regarding this book and others from a humanist perspective. The variety of perspectives and commitments represented by that small group (Ann, Anne, Bob, and Maggie) has been of great benefit. Readers may find some of the other texts discussed during those meetings of interest: Robert Wright, *The Moral Animal: Why We are the Way We Are: The New Science of Evolutionary Psychology* (New York: Vintage, 1994).

55. Wilson, *Consilience*, 106–7.

56. One need only think, for example, about organ transplants for what this says about the significance of embodiment and individuality. The significance of brain activity as connected to transplants—mobile markers of embodiment—is also an interesting consideration in light of this discussion of the brain in this chapter. In addition, neurological problems such as *asomatognosia*—the inability to recognize a portion of the body as being a part of that body—say something about brain-body connections. See, for example, Kenneth M. Heilman, *Matter of Mind: A Neurologist's View of Brain-Behavior Relationships* (New York: Oxford University Press, 2002), 117–40.

57. Heilman, *Matter of Mind*, vii, viii.

58. William B. Hurlbut, "The Meaning of Embodiment: Neuroscience, Cognitive Psychology, and Spiritual Anthropology," in Paul C. Vitz and Susan M. Felch, eds., *The Self: Beyond the Postmodern Crisis* (Wilmington, DE: Intercollegiate Studies Institute Books, 2006), 105.

59. Referencing A. Damasio, *The Feeling of What Happens: Body and Emotion in the Making of Consciousness* (San Diego, CA: Harcourt, 1999) in William B. Hurlbut, "The Meaning of Embodiment: Neuroscience, Cognitive Psychology, and Spiritual Anthropology," in Vitz and Felch, eds., *The Self*, 107. Readers may also find of interest João Biehl, Bryon Good, and Arthur Kleinman, eds., *Subjectivity: Ethnographic Investigations* (Berkeley: University of California Press, 2007).

60. Paul C. Vitz, "The Embodied Self: Evidence from Cognitive Psychology and Neuro-psychology," in Vitz and Felch, eds., *The Self*, 113–15.
61. Wilson, *Consilience*, 179.
62. Gould, *The Mismeasure of Man*, 325.
63. Gould, *The Mismeasure of Man*, 328.
64. See Pinn, *Embodiment and the New Shape of Theological Thought*, section 1; Pinn, "Charting DuBois' Souls: Thoughts on 'Veiled' Bodies, Celebratory Skepticism, and the Study of Religion," in Edward Blum and Jason Young, eds., *The Souls of W. E. B. DuBois: New Essays and Reflections* (Macon, GA: Mercer University Press, 2009), 69–84.
65. Williams and Bendelow, *The Lived Body*, 28.
66. "Patrick H. Hutton, "Foucault, Freud, and the Technologies of the Self," in Martin, Gutman, and Hutton, eds., *Technologies of the Self*, 140.
67. Antonio Damasio, *The Feeling of What Happens: Body and Emotion in the Making of Consciousness* (New York: Harvest Books, 1999), 137.
68. Sharon D. Welch, *A Feminist Ethic of Risk* (Minneapolis, MN: Fortress, 1990), 2.
69. The humanist can think of the human self as verb, and in a somewhat related manner and as an earlier theological formulation, Mary Daly described God as Verb. See *Beyond God the Father: Toward a Philosophy of Women's Liberation* (Boston: Beacon, 1973).
70. Luther E. Smith Jr., *Howard Thurman: Essential Writings* (Maryknoll, NY: Orbis, 2006), 137.
71. Amelia Jones, *Self/Image: Technology, Representation, and the Contemporary Subject* (New York: Routledge, 2006), xiii-xiv.
72. www.nytimes.com/2010/03/12/arts/design/12abromovic.html; also see www.moma .org/visit/calendar/exhibitions/965. Also of interest: Marsha Meskimmon, *Women Marking Art: History, Subjectivity, Aesthetics* (New York: Routledge, 2003).
73. My initial interest in Basquiat's work as source for theologizing and a mode of religio-theological reflection was amplified after I saw the retrospective of his work during its time at the Museum of Fine Arts in Houston.
74. Phoebe Hoban, *Basquiat: A Quick Killing in Art* (New York: Penguin, 2004), 12.
75. For examples of Cy Twombly's work: www.cytwombly.info/. See Marc Mayer, "Basquiat in History," in Marc Mayer, ed., *Basquiat* (New York: Merrell, 2005), 41–57. For information on the collaboration between Basquiat and Andy Warhol, see Jonathan Weinberg, *Ambition & Love in Modern American Art* (New Haven, CT: Yale University Press, 2001), 211–41.
76. Robert Farris Thompson notes this blending of blues and Jazz. See his "Royalty, Heroism, and the Streets: The Art of Jean-Michel Basquiat," in Richard Marshall, ed., *Jean-Michel Basquiat* (New York: Whitney Museum of American Art/Harry N. Abrams, 1992), 28–42.
77. These images are available in a variety of texts, including Gianni Mercurio, ed., *The Jean-Michel Basquiat Show* (Milan: Skira Editore, 2006); Marshall, ed., *Jean-Michel Basquiat*; Mayer, "Basquiat in History."
78. Rene Ricard, "World Crown©: Bodhisattva with Clenched Mudra," in Marshall, ed., *Jean-Michel Basquiat*, 47. Also see Rene Ricard, "The Radiant Child," ARTFORM 20, no. 4 (1981): 35–43.
79. Hoban, *Basquiat*, 89.
80. Jean-Michel Basquiat, *King for a Decade* (Tokyo, Japan: Korinsha, 1997), 97.
81. For another take on his use of the written word, see Mayer, "Basquiat in History," 41–57.
82. Leonhard Emmerling, *Jean-Michel Basquiat, 1960–1988* (Los Angeles: Taschen, 2003), 11. Also see Basquiat, *King for a Decade*, 64. Other sources of information on the depiction of the body included Leonardo da Vinci (*Leonardo da Vinci* [New York: Reynal, 1966) and Paul Richer (*Artistic Anatomy* [New York: Watson-Guptill, 1986]). See Richard Marshall, "Repelling Ghosts," in Marshall, editor. *Jean-Michel Basquiat*, 23.
83. See, for example, Jonathan Harris, ed., *Dead History, Live Art? Spectacle, Subjectivity and Subversion in Visual Culture Since the 1960s* (Liverpool, England: Liverpool University Press, 2007), 165–86; Kobena Mercer, ed., *Exiles, Diasporas & Strangers* (Cambridge, MA: MIT Press, 2008).

84. Jonathan Weinberg, *Ambition and Love in Modern American Art* (New Haven, CT: Yale University Press, 2001), 222.

85. Interview of Basquiat by Miller quoted in Hoban, *Basquiat*, 169.

86. Emmerling, *Jean-Michel Basquiat*, 79.

87. Marshall, "Repelling Ghosts," 15. Gianni Mercurio argues that these images from the first phase of his work speak to a deep fascination with death: Mercurio, "The Moon King," in Mercurio, ed., *The Jean-Michel Basquiat Show*, 26.

88. Fred Hoffman, "The Defining Years: Notes on Five Key Works," in Mayer, ed., *Basquiat*, 130.

89. Dick Hebdige, "Welcome to the Terrordome: Jean-Michel Basquiat and the 'Dark' Side of Hybridity," in Marshall, ed., *Jean-Michel Basquiat*, 61.

90. Mercurio, "The Moon King," 31; Cathleen McGuigan, "Jean Michel Basquiat," *New York Times Magazine*, February 10, 1985.

91. Hoban, *Basquiat*, 338. Romare Bearden's collage work also provides opportunities for a somewhat similar discussion. For examples, see Mary Schmidt Campbell and Sharon F. Patton, editors. *Memory and Metaphor: The Art of Romare Bearden, 1940–1987* (New York: Oxford University Press, 1991). Images of the collages are available at www.beardenfoundation.org/artlife/beardensart/collage/collage.shtml.

Chapter 4

1. Howard Thurman, *The Luminous Darkness: A Personal Interpretation of the Anatomy of Segregation and the Ground of Hope* (Richmond, IN: Friends United Press, 1989), 4.

2. Toni Morrison, *Beloved* (New York: Knopf, 1987), 88.

3. Howard Thurman, "Mysticism and Social Change," in *A Strange Freedom: The Best of Howard Thurman on Religious Experience and Public Life*, ed. Walker Earl Fluker and Catherine Tumber (Boston: Beacon, 1998), 111, 113.

4. Thurman, *The Luminous Darkness*, 112.

5. Howard Thurman, "Religion in a Time of Crisis," in *A Strange Freedom*, 127, 129.

6. See, for example, Howard Thurman, "Jesus—An Interpretation," in *A Strange Freedom*, 131–4. For a full explication of Thurman's perspective on the Christ Event: *Jesus and the Disinherited* (Nashville, TN: Abingdon, 1949).

7. This chapter contains some material from "A Beautiful Be-ing: Humanist Thought and the Aesthetics of a New Salvation," in Pinn, ed., *Black Religion and Aesthetics: Religious Thought and Life in Africa and the African Diaspora* (New York: Palgrave Macmillan, 2009), 19–35. It also draws some elements from "Watch the Body with New Eyes: Womanist Thought's Contribution to a Humanist Notion of Ritual," *CrossCurrents* 57, no. 3 (2007): 404–11.

8. Readers may be interested in connecting this discussion to my thinking on embodiment and sexuality as outlined in *Embodiment and the New Shape of Black Theological Thought* (New York: New York University Press, 2010).

9. James H. Cone, "Preface to the 1989 Edition," in *Black Theology & Black Power* (San Francisco: Harper & Row, 1989), vii. While Cone's work represents the first generation of academic black theology, it is appropriate to frame this discussion in terms of the categories established in his work because his students, with almost no exceptions, have maintained his theological sensibilities with regard to major categories such as soteriology and Christology. Hence, some thirty years after first published, Cone's work remains highly representative of black theological discourse.

10. See Katie G. Cannon, *Black Womanist Ethics* (Eugene, OR: Wipf & Stock, 1988), chapter 6.

11. See, for example, Delores S. Williams, *Sisters in the Wilderness: The Challenge of Womanist God-Talk* (Maryknoll, NY: Orbis, 1993).

12. Cone, *Black Theology & Black Power*, 120.

13. Kelly Brown Douglas, *The Black Christ* (Maryknoll, NY: Orbis, 1994), 116.

14. Cone, *Black Theology & Black Power*, 121.

15. James H. Cone, *God of the Oppressed* (New York: Harper & Row, 1975), 138.

16. Cone, *God of the Oppressed*, 152, 153.

17. Douglas, *The Black Christ*, 110.

18. Cone, *Black Theology & Black Power*, 125–6.

19. James H. Cone, *A Black Theology of Liberation*, (Maryknoll, NY: Orbis, 1990), 141.

20. Cone, *God of the Oppressed*, 141.

21. Douglas, *The Black Christ*, 106–13. It is important to note that Douglas's use of community differs from what I proposed in chapter 1. In addition, her sense of wholeness is also inconsistent with what I propose in this book. By wholeness, she implies the basic sociopolitical and economic advancement of the African American community. However, what I mean by wholeness and fullness has more to do with a form of symmetry—a sense of elegance of life that is not sufficiently captured through the traditional markers of liberation.

22. Williams, *Sisters in the Wilderness*, 164. See Joanne Terrell for another womanist discussion on atonement: *Power in the Blood? The Cross in the African American Experience* (Maryknoll, NY: Orbis, 1998).

23. Williams, *Sisters in the Wilderness*, 165.

24. James H. Evans Jr., *We Have Been Believers: An African American Systematic Theology* (Minneapolis, MN: Fortress, 1992), 142.

25. Douglas, *The Black Christ*, 117.

26. Anthony B. Pinn, "Embracing Nimrod's Legacy: The Erotic, the Irreverence of Fantasy, and the Redemption of Black Theology," in Anthony Pinn and Dwight Hopkins, eds., *Loving the Body: Black Religious Studies and the Erotic* (New York: Palgrave Macmillan, 2004), 164.

27. Anthony B. Pinn, "Introduction," in Pinn and Hopkins, eds., *Loving the Body*, 3.

28. See Kelly Brown Douglas, *The Black Church and Sexuality* (Maryknoll, NY: Orbis, 2003) and Douglas, *What's Love Got to Do with It?* (Maryknoll, NY: Orbis, 2005).

29. Michael Eric Dyson, "When You Divide Body and Soul, Problems Multiply: The Black Church and Sexuality," in *The Michael Eric Dyson Reader* (New York: Basic Civitas, 2004), 221.

30. This chapter is not concerned with a full presentation of beauty within the sciences. Rather, I am concerned with the application of the notion of beauty as symmetry one finds in the sciences for the purpose of building African American humanist theology. Hence, the presentation of symmetry and beauty in the sciences is limited.

31. As readers will note, my references are popular depictions of this dimension of physics. This discussion of symmetry is rather loose (and limited) and entails theologized use of a few conceptual framings from physics and mathematics to the extent they offer an alternate way of capturing and articulating humanist perceptions of beauty as life objective.

32. Lisa Randall, *Warped Passages: Unraveling the Mysteries of the Universe's Hidden Dimensions* (New York: Ecco/HarperCollins, 2005); Hermann Weyl, *Symmetry* (Princeton, NJ: Princeton University Press, 1952); Ian Stewart and Martin Golubitsky, *Fearful Symmetry: Is God a Geometer?* (Cambridge, MA; Blackwell, 1992); Brian Greene, *The Elegant Universe: Superstrings, Hidden Dimensions, and the Quest for the Ultimate Theory* (New York: W. W. Norton, 1999).

33. As a graduate student taking courses prior to qualifying examinations, I first read *Religion in an Age of Science* and had occasion to think about the potentiality of religionist embracing the challenge of scientific thought, vocabulary, and grammar. However, my commitment to a certain brand of constructive—liberation—theology entailed limited follow-through on that possibility. See Ian Barbour, *Issues in Science and Religion* (Upper Saddle River, NJ: Prentice Hall, 1966); Barbour, *Religion in an Age of Science*, rev. ed. (New York: HarperOne, 1997).

34. The history of string theory's development and reception also suggests a parallel for nontheistic humanist theology: Dominant perspectives and assumptions do not necessarily preclude the need for additional creative thinking and insights. There is something of value in a willingness to develop ideas and possibilities that run against the grain. That is to say, the dominance of black and womanist theologies and their perceptions of the issues addressed in this book does not suggest the end of conversation and the need for alternate perspectives.

35. World involves the full range of materiality, interactions, relationships, and encounters that shape us. Yet, world is not simply a matter of known substance; it is also defined in terms of absence—of lack—of uncertainty.

36. I should also note that while I give attention to Richard Wright in this chapter, I am aware of Hazel Carby's important critique, and I am not attempting to caste symmetry in terms of a male-centered approach to the world. My ongoing work must also include attention to the development of this symmetry within the context of authors such as Toni Morrison and Nella Larsen. I begin, however, with Richard Wright because of his explicit humanism and his explicit efforts to wrestle with the types of issues at the core of this chapter.

37. Edward Farley, *Faith and Beauty: A Theological Aesthetic* (Burlington, VT: Ashgate, 2001), 11.

38. Farley, *Faith and Beauty*, 11.

39. Farley, *Faith and Beauty*, 110.

40. In Richard Wright, *Eight Men* (New York: HarperPerennial, 1996), 19–84; Wright, *The Outsider*, Library of America ed. (New York: HarperPerennial, 1991). Readers will find it enlightening to read Richard Wright in light of other authors such as Ralph Ellison: Ellison, *Invisible Man* (New York: Vintage, 1972); Ellison, *Going to the Territory* (New York: Vintage International, 1995), particularly, 104–12, 198–216, 308–20; Ellison, *Shadow and Act* (New York: Vintage International, 1995), particularly 24–44, 77–94.

41. Alain Locke "The New Negro," in Alain Locke, ed., *The New Negro* (New York: Atheneum, 1986), 8.

42. Wright, *The Outsider*, 585.

43. Wright, *The Outsider*, 585.

44. Richard Wright, "The Man Who Lived Underground," in Richard Wright, *Eight Men* (New York: HarperPerennial, 1996), 81.

45. Wright, "The Man Who Lived Underground," 60.

46. Lewis R. Gordon, "Existential Dynamics of Theorizing Black Invisibility," in Lewis Gordon, ed., *Existence in Black: An Anthology of Black Existential Philosophy* (New York: Routledge, 1997), 72.

47. Gordon, "Existential Dynamics of Theorizing Black Invisibility," 72–5.

48. Robert Birt, "Existence, Identity, and Liberation," in Gordon, ed., *Existence in Black*, 206.

49. Birt, "Existence, Identity, and Liberation," 212.

50. Katherine Fishburn, *Richard Wright's Hero: The Faces of a Rebel-Victim* (Metuchen, NJ: Scarecrow, 1977), 148.

51. See, for example, Arnold Rampersad, "Introduction," in Rampersad, ed., *Richard Wright: A Collection of Critical Essays* (Englewood Cliffs, NJ: Prentice Hall, 1995).

52. I am grateful to James Cone for the generous sharing of his time and insights. My thinking on this aspect of nontheistic humanist theology was refined and sharpened in light of several conversations we had in New York concerning the posture of second- and third-generation black theologians toward "the work."

53. Fishburn, *Richard Wright's Hero*, 160.

54. Wright, "The Man Who Lived Underground," 30.

55. Rampersad, "Introduction," 4.

56. Michael F. Lynch, *Creative Revolt: A Study of Wright, Ellison, and Dostoevsky* (New York: Peter Lang, 1990), 94.

57. Wright, "The Man Who Lived Underground," 60.

58. Patricia Watkins, "The Paradoxical Structure of Richard Wright's 'The Man Who Lived Underground,'" in Arnold Rampersad, ed., *Richard Wright: A Collection of Critical Essays* (Englewood Cliffs, NJ: Prentice Hall, 1995), 157.

59. Brian Greene, *The Elegant Universe*, 169. Readers may also find Steven S. Gubser's *The Little Book of String Theory* (Princeton, NJ: Princeton University Press, 2010) of interest. According to Lisa Randall: "In colloquial usage people often equate symmetry with beauty, and certainly some of the fascination with symmetry arises from the regularity and neatness that it guarantees" (*Warped Passages*, 193).

60. Special relativity: The laws of physics always apply and the speed of light is consistent. General relativity: Theory dealing with gravity.

61. Greene, *The Elegant Universe*, 169.

62. Randall, *Warped Passages*, 191.

63. Weyl, *Symmetry*, 5.

64. See Charles Long, *Significations* (Philadelphia: Fortress, 1986), introduction; A. Zee, *Fearful Symmetry: The Search for Beauty in Modern Physics* (Princeton, NJ: Princeton University Press, 1999), 17. Symmetry is not only of concern to physicists, for example, but is also an area of interest to those in the social sciences. For example, anthropologists will make use of symmetry to address expressive cultural forms. My concern in this chapter, however, is with the description of symmetry offered in the sciences, primarily physics. Furthermore, chaos appears the opposite of this interest in patterns. However, according to Stewart and Golubitsky, "Chaos, of course, is really part of that enterprise too: it extracts new regularities from apparent disorder" (*Fearful Symmetry*, xvii).

65. Stewart and Golubitsky, *Fearful Symmetry*, 149. Readers interested in symmetry—bilateral, translatory, rotational, ornamental, and crystallographic—should also see Weyl, *Symmetry*.

66. Ian Stewart, when reflecting on superstring theory and the idea that "mathematical beauty" comes before "physical truth," says: "It is important not to lose sight of the physical world, and whatever theory finally emerges from today's deliberations cannot be exempt from comparison with experiments and observations, however strong its mathematical pedigree" (*Why Beauty Is Truth*, xiii).

67. Matthew E. May provides an interesting discussion of Jackson Pollock's work with respect to symmetries, noting the appeal of symmetries on the level of aesthetics. See his *In Pursuit of Elegance: Why the Best Ideas Have Something Missing* (New York: Broadway, 2009), 29–52. What I purpose is similar to the question asked by Rollo May, although I would connect symmetry to community as opposed to his notion of ultimate concern (which for me is too singular): "Suppose that 'elegance'—as the word is used by physicists to describe their discoveries—is a key to ultimate reality?" (May, *The Courage to Create* [New York: W. W. Norton, 1975], 7). I am grateful to Dr. Margarita Simon Guillory, one of my former graduate students, for introducing me to this book.

68. Zee, *Fearful Symmetry*, 255.

69. Ian Stewart, *Why Beauty Is Truth: A History of Symmetry* (New York: Basic Books, 2007), ix. "Symmetry also plays a central role at the frontiers of physics, in the quantum world of the very small and the relativistic world of the very large. It may even provide a route to the long-sought 'Theory of Everything,' a mathematical unification of those two key branches of modern physics" (ix). In addition, Stewart says the idea behind this theory is a hope that "the whole of physics could be boiled down to a set of equations simple enough to be printed on a T-shirt" (222).

70. Stewart and Golubitsky, *Fearful Symmetry*, 28; Stewart, *Why Beauty Is Truth*, ix; Greene, *The Elegant Universe*.

71. Zee, *Fearful Symmetry*, 3, 9, 13.

72. David Oliver, *The Shaggy Steed of Physics: Mathematical Beauty in the Physical World* (New York: Springer-Verlag, 1994), ix.

73. I am added here by my reading of Brian Greene, *The Elegant Universe*, 23–52.

74. Zee, *Fearful Symmetry*, 97.

75. Wright, *The Outsider*, 585.

76. I am grateful to Dr. Heather Sullivan for taking time from her own work to help me think about the implications of symmetry (various types) for reading fiction. Her suggestions have been extremely useful here and will also play into to my subsequent work on this topic. Dr. Torin Alexander, one of my former graduate students, also provides key insights and suggestions. In future work, I plan to give attention to the development of this sense of theological symmetry in science fiction. However, for this book, I felt it important to dem-

onstrate through the same materials both primary and secondary symmetry as a way to more graphically outline its role in humanist theology.

77. Wright, "The Man Who Lived Underground," 21.
78. One might also note that Daniels's encounter with animals does not have the effect on him that Thoreau's encounters in Walden entail. With Daniels, there is a better sense of the look of nature with "fangs."
79. Wright, "The Man Who Lived Underground," 23.
80. Weyl, *Symmetry*, 13.
81. Stewart and Golubitsky, *Fearful Symmetry*, 28.
82. Stewart and Golubitsky, *Fearful Symmetry*, 30, 51–72.
83. Wright, "The Man Who Lived Underground," 25.
84. Wright, "The Man Who Lived Underground," 37. (Italics in the original.)
85. Wright toys with this premise: "His dreaming made him feel that he was standing in a room watching over his own nude body lying stiff and cold upon a white table. At the far end of the room he saw a crowd of people huddled in a corner, afraid of his body. Though lying dead upon the table, he was standing in some mysterious way at his side, warding off the people, guarding his body, and laughing to himself as he observed the situation. They're scared of me, he thought" (58).
86. Wright, "The Man Who Lived Underground," 30.
87. Wright, "The Man Who Lived Underground," 40.
88. Wright, "The Man Who Lived Underground," 47.
89. Wright, "The Man Who Lived Underground," 51.
90. Wright, "The Man Who Lived Underground," 52.
91. Wright, "The Man Who Lived Underground," 53.
92. Readers will find the following texts of interest: Peter Tallybrass and Allon White, "The City: The Sewer, The Gaze, and the Contaminating Touch," in Margaret Lock and Judith Farquhar, eds., *Beyond the Body Proper: Reading the Anthropology of Material Life* (Durham, NC: Duke University Press, 2007), 266–85; Mary Douglas, *Purity and Danger: An Analysis of Concepts of Pollution and Taboo* (New York: Routledge, 1966).
93. Wright, "The Man Who Lived Underground," 61.
94. Wright, "The Man Who Lived Underground," 58.
95. Wright, "The Man Who Lived Underground," 69, 72.
96. Wright, "The Man Who Lived Underground," 81.
97. Wright, "The Man Who Lived Underground," 78.
98. Wright, "The Man Who Lived Underground," 80.
99. Even black and womanist theologies of the late twentieth and early twenty-first centuries run this risk to the extent they continue to suffer from a Cartesian dualism regarding the physical body, as evident in the unsatisfying response to issues of homophobia, for example. See, for example, Dyson, *The Michael Dyson Reader*, 219–57; Douglas, *Sexuality and the Black Church*.
100. Zee, *Fearful Symmetry*, 98.

Chapter 5

1. While there are various accounts of Concord, the particular intent of this chapter requires a more focused description of the town. For that type of description, see, for example, Shannon L. Mariotti, *Thoreau's Democratic Withdrawal: Alienation, Participation, and Modernity* (Madison: University of Wisconsin Press, 2010), 86–116; Elise Lemire, *Black Walden: Slavery and Its Aftermath in Concord, Massachusetts* (Philadelphia: University of Pennsylvania Press, 2009).
2. Henry D. Thoreau, *Walden* (Princeton, NJ: Princeton University Press, 1973), 3.
3. Thoreau, *Walden*, 90.
4. Thoreau, *Walden*, 187–8.

5. I am a theologian and not an ethicist. And while I see the value in understanding the distinctions between those two projects—theology and ethics—I also admit a need for the theologian to say something about values and behavior embedded in theological discourse. I see the need to provide a rudimentary outline of the ethical implications of African American humanism and humanist theology, while I acknowledge the need for those trained in ethics to provide the more substantive discussion of these points. With this said, a turn to Walden over against some of Thoreau's other writings is reasonable. I agree with Philip Cafaro, who writes: "Because Walden is a work in virtue ethics, it is hard for some readers—and most contemporary philosophers—to see it as a work of ethics at all. For we tend to define ethics as the discipline that specifies proper interpersonal relations, or even more narrowly, our strict obligations toward one another.... To call something an ethical question, though, says that it involves value judgments and asserts its importance. It is precisely the sense that these personal decisions are important—that they help make us who we are and that it matters—which Thoreau works so hard to instill in his readers" (Philip Cafaro, *Thoreau's Living Ethics: Walden and the Pursuit of Virtue* [Athens: University of Georgia Press, 2004], 28–9).

6. Lemire, *Black Walden*, 9.

7. Lemire, *Black Walden*, 112–27.

8. Alfred I. Tauber, *Henry David Thoreau and the Moral Agency of Knowing* (Berkeley: University of California Press, 2001), 169.

9. George Shulman, *American Prophecy: Race and Redemption in American Political Culture* (Minneapolis: University of Minnesota Press, 2008), 40.

10. George Shulman, *American Prophecy: Race and Redemption in American Political Culture* (Minneapolis: University of Minnesota Press, 2008), 41; Philip Cafaro, *Thoreau's Living Ethics: Walden and the Pursuit of Virtue* (Athens: The University of Georgia Press, 2004), 44.

11. Shulman, *American Prophecy*, 42.

12. Thoreau, *Walden*, 7.

13. Thoreau, *Walden*, 8.

14. Thoreau, *Walden*, 34.

15. Cafaro, *Thoreau's Living Ethics*, 18, 19, 21.

16. Shulman, *American Prophecy*, 53.

17. Thoreau, *Walden*, 8.

18. Thoreau, *Walden*, 74.

19. Thoreau, *Walden*, 75–6.

20. Thoreau, *Walden*, 73.

21. Thoreau, *Walden*, 91.

22. Thoreau, *Walden*, 97.

23. Thoreau, *Walden*, 217.

24. Thoreau, *Walden*, 326.

25. Delores Williams, *Sisters in the Wilderness* (Maryknoll, NY: Orbis, 1995).

26. "Every man is the builder of a temple, called his body, to the god he worships, after a style purely his own, nor can he get off by hammering marble instead. We are all sculptors and painters, and our material is our own flesh and blood and bones. Any nobleness beings at once to refine a man's features, any meanness or sensuality to imbrute them." *Walden*, 221. Also see pp. 307–8.

27. Thoreau, *Walden*, 78.

28. Thoreau, *Walden*, 90.

29. Thoreau, *Walden*, 77.

30. Thoreau, *Walden*, 77.

31. Robert D. Richardson Jr., "The Social Ethics of *Walden*," in Joel Myerson, ed., *Critical Essays on Henry David Thoreau's* Walden (Boston: G. K. Hall, 1988), 235–48; Mariotti, *Thoreau's Democratic Withdrawal*, 85.

32. Cafaro, *Thoreau's Living Ethics*, 106–7.

33. Black and womanist theologies should recognize this need in that their critique, for example, of homophobia and sexism in black churches is premised on Christians who speak of social injustices such as racism while failing to recognize that they as individuals practice discrimination. In this way, Christians who speak of oppression as wrong and work to combat it on the social level should first make certain they as individuals are "being good." This being good comes before one has the ability to do good in ways that matter.

34. A similar tension is noted in black theology. For example, one can read Victor Anderson's critique of ontological blackness in *Beyond Ontological Blackness* and his theory of cultural fulfillment and exchange in *Creative Exchange* as tied to this tension between individual need and communal want. See Anderson, *Beyond Ontological Blackness: An Essay in African American Religious and Cultural Criticism* (New York: Continuum, 1995) and *Creative Exchange: A Constructive Theology of African American Religious Experience* (Minneapolis, MN: Fortress, 2009).

35. Tauber, *Henry David Thoreau and the Moral Agency of Knowing*, 1–5.

36. There are interesting points of convergence between Thoreau's *Walden* and the work of Alice Walker. This is particularly the case with texts such as Walker, *Living by the Word* (New York: Mariner, 1989) and Walker, *Anything You Love Can Be Saved* (New York: Ballantine, 1998). Some of the epistemological and praxis-related connections between Thoreau and Walker are explored in this book with respect to humanist celebration as an extension of ethics considered, although future work will give greater attention to the ethical implications of Walker's work for African American humanism.

37. Richardson, "The Social Ethics of *Walden*," 238.

38. Richardson, "The Social Ethics of *Walden*," 245.

39. Richardson, "The Social Ethics of *Walden*," 244.

40. Thoreau, *Walden*, 323; Mariotti, *Thoreau's Democratic Withdrawal*, 118, 120, 153; Jane Bennett, *Thoreau's Nature: Ethics, Politics, and the Wild* (Thousand Oaks, CA: Sage, 1994), 16–46, 105–38. There is no sense in African American humanism or African American humanist theology that "God is on the throne and all is well." There is no sense of certainty based on cosmic assistance or prehistorical framings of life in either of the two. Such metaphysical assumptions and epistemological certainties are left to theistic theological discourses, again like black and womanist theologies.

41. Mary Elkins Moller, *Thoreau in the Human Community* (Amherst: University of Massachusetts Press, 1980), 131. Also see 101–21 of the same book ("Thoreau's Humanism").

42. Thoreau, *Walden*, 22.

43. Thoreau often uses *world* as a negative label, as a way of describing the overlay of human stultifying practices and structures onto life. I do not mean it in this sense. My use is more neutral, simply meaning the "real" location of time and space without value judgments regarding the former. S see Moller, *Thoreau in the Human Community*, 123–36.

44. Thoreau, *Walden*, 31.

45. There is also something mundane about his turn to the woods. A long-term career path eluded Thoreau: "As I did not teach for the good of my fellow-men, but simply for a livelihood, this was a failure" (69). At Walden Pond, he saw opportunity to complete writing projects—to advance his vocational possibilities.

46. Mariotti, *Thoreau's Democratic Withdrawal*, 93.

47. Thoreau, *Walden*, chapter 18.

48. Shulman, *American Prophecy*, 51.

49. Moller, *Thoreau in the Human Community*, 155–86.

50. Lemire, *Black Walden*, 10–11, 119–27.

51. See, for example, Henry D. Thoreau, *Walden, Civil Disobedience and Other Writings*, ed. William Rossi (New York: W. W. Norton, 2008).

52. After more than forty years of African American religious studies, there should be little ground for such resource xenophobia. The detrimental nature of this myopic approach to theoretical and methodological tools should be obvious.

53. Frederick Douglass, *Narrative of the Life of Frederick Douglass, An American Slave Written by Himself* (Boston: Anti-Slavery Office, 1845).

54. Reginald F. Davis, *Frederick Douglass: A Precursor of Liberation Theology* (Macon, GA: Mercer University Press, 2005). Also see John Ernest, "Crisis and Faith in Douglass's Work," in Maurice S. Lee, *The Cambridge Companion to Frederick Douglass* (New York: Cambridge University Press, 2009), 67–71.

55. Eddie Glaude provides an important discussion of this process in his recent work, arguing that efforts to copy strategies and paradigms from the civil rights movement fails to recognize essential differences between periods of history and does not require creative strategies that meet the tragic nature of life with appropriate force and form. See Glaude, *In a Shade of Blue: Pragmatism and the Politics of Black America* (Chicago: University of Chicago Press, 2008).

56. For a concise but historically expansive set of examples of this redemptive suffering paradigm, see Anthony Pinn, *Moral Evil and Redemptive Suffering: A History of Theodicy in African American Religious Thought* (Gainesville: The University Press of Florida, 2002); Lewis R. Gordon, "Douglass as an Existentialist," in Bill E. Lawson and Frank M. Kirkland, editors., *Frederick Douglass: A Critical Reader* (Malden, MA: Blackwell Publishers, 1999), 210, 212.

57. Some might argue that my earlier effort to articulate the history of African American humanism through attention to early writings by figures such as Douglass contains the same flaw. However, I would argue my work did not entail making Douglass and others humanists. I suggest that much of their thought and activity is consistent with what we have come to refer to as humanist principles. And, African American humanists might gain from attention to these figures. See Anthony B. Pinn, *By These Hands: A Documentary History of African American Humanism* (New York: New York University Press, 2003); Pinn, *African American Humanist Principles: Living and Thinking Like the Children of Nimrod* (New York: Palgrave Macmillan, 2004).

58. Frederick Douglass, *Frederick Douglass: The Narrative and Selected Writings* (New York: Modern Library College Editions, 1984), 47.

59. Douglass, *Frederick Douglass*, 53.

60. Douglass, *Frederick Douglass*, 45.

61. Douglass, *Frederick Douglass*, 68.

62. Douglass, *Frederick Douglass*, 70.

63. Douglass, *Frederick Douglass*, 73.

64. Douglass, *Frederick Douglass*, 353.

65. Douglass, *Frederick Douglass*, 376.

66. Douglass, *Frederick Douglass*, 376.

67. It is not certain Douglass viewed keeping this root as anything more than a pragmatic move, a gesture of communal obligation in that Sandy Jenkins insisted that he take it, and gratitude for Jenkins's assistance in spite of the danger involved. (As Jenkins remarked, Douglass's "book learning had not kept Covey off [him].... If it [the root] did no good, it could do no harm" [144].) The following note in the *Narrative* raises questions regarding Douglass holding a fundamental belief in the power of root work: He and Jenkins were in the habit of talking "about the fight with Covey, and as often as we did so, he would claim my success as the result of the roots which he gave me. This superstition is very common among the more ignorant slaves" (Douglass, *Frederick Douglass*, 88).

68. While I would argue, and have in other texts, Douglass's thinking is in line with humanist principles, I am not suggesting that Douglass is a humanist in line with my late-twentieth-century and early-twenty-first-century formulations of this orientation. However, readers should not assume Douglass's measured critique of Christianity's application (slaveholder Christianity), particularly in the appendix to the *Narrative*, entails he is a Christian who rejects the "religion-ness" that has come to define the practice of the Christian faith. There are pragmatic reasons for that apology. He may not be a humanist in the tradition of

Reverend Ethelred Brown or James Forman, but he is also not a Christian. See Pinn, *By These Hands* and *African American Humanist Principles*; Juan Floyd-Thomas, *The Origins of Black Humanism in America: Reverend Ethelred Brown and the Unitarian Church* (New York: Palgrave Macmillan, 2008).

69. Douglass, *Frederick Douglass*, 81; Scott C. Williamson, *The Narrative Life: The Moral and Religious Thought of Frederick Douglass* (Macon, GA: Mercer University Press, 2002), 29–102.

70. Douglass, *Frederick Douglass*, 81.

71. Douglass, *Frederick Douglass*, 103–4.

72. Stephen L. Thompson, "The Grammar of Civilization: Douglass and Crummell on Doing Things with Words," in Lawson and Kirkland, eds., *Frederick Douglass*, 188.

73. Gail Weiss, *Body Images: Embodiment as Intercorporeality* (New York: Routledge, 1999), 3.

74. Judith Farquhar and Margaret Lock, "Introduction," in Farquhar and Lock, *Beyond the Body Proper: Reading the Anthropology of Material Life* (Durham, NC: Duke University Press, 2007), 1–3.

75. This is a not so veiled play on the episode presented by Fanon in which the young boy speaks Fanon's body as the embodiment of terror. See Franz Fanon, *Black Skin, White Masks* (1952; New York: Grove, 1994).

76. Lewis R. Gordon, "Douglass as an Existentialist," in Lawson and Kirkland, eds., *Frederick Douglass*, 222.

77. David Walker, *David Walker's Appeal* (1829; Baltimore: Black Classic, 1997).

78. Frank Kirkland offers an interesting take on moral suasion and struggle related to Douglass and Covey. See his "Enslavement, Moral Suasion, and Struggles for Recognition: Frederick Douglass's Answer to the Question—'What Is Enlightenment,'" in Lawson and Kirkland, eds., *Frederick Douglass*, 243–310.

79. Liz Eckermann, "Foucault, Embodiment and Gendered Subjectivities: The Case of Voluntary Self-Starvation," in Alan Petersen and Robin Bunton, eds., *Foucault: Health and Medicine* (New York: Routledge, 1997), 155.

80. Douglass, *Frederick Douglass*, 135–8.

81. Douglass, *Life and Times of Frederick Douglass*, 913, quoted in John Ernest, "Crisis and Faith in Douglass's Work," in Lee, ed. *The Cambridge Companion to Frederick Douglass*, 60.

82. Thompson, "The Grammar of Civilization," 180.

83. The written interviews with Tubman can be problematic due to issues of context and interpretation—the degree to which they reflect the interviewer over against Tubman. But this is a problem with much of the material we make use of in our scholarship. The WPA materials contain this cultural-social flaw as well. Jean A. Humez, *Harriet Tubman: The Life and the Life Stories* (Madison: University of Wisconsin Press, 2003), 139. For information on the benefits and shortcomings of the Tubman materials, see Humez, *Harriet Tubman*, 133–72.

84. For readers interested in general discussions of the underground railroad, relevant works include Fergus M. Bordewich, *Bound for Canaan: The Underground Railroad and the War for the Soul of America* (New York: Amistad, 2005); Jacqueline Tobin, *From Midnight to Dawn: The Last Tracks of the Underground Railroad* (New York: Doubleday, 2007); David Blight, *Passages to Freedom: The Underground Railroad in History and Memory* (Washington, DC: Smithsonian, 2004). Kate Clifford Larson argues that the phrase "underground railroad" has an etymology related to the emergence of the train system in the United States, but that framework for the movement of enslaved Africans north predates the terminology. See Larson, *Bound for the Promised Land: Harriet Tubman, Portrait of an American Hero* (New York: Ballantine, 2004), 87.

85. Beverly Lowry, *Harriet Tubman: Imagining a Life* (New York: Doubleday, 2000, 204.

86. Douglass, in describing his escape from slavery, cast certain aspersions on "the underground railroad" when in fact some involved in this process, through their words, have really made it so very visible that it is really the "upperground" railroad. Douglass has his story to tell and the merit of his story—his approach to redeeming despised bodies—does

not negate the value of other approaches. And while he objected to some, there is clear evidence (including his housing of fugitive slaves during numerous trips) that he knew of and appreciated the work of transporters and, in particular, knew of and had great admiration for Tubman's attitude and actions. See Douglass, *Frederick Douglass*, 105–6. Some argue that the relationship between Douglass and Tubman is not clear and that neither was willing to explicate the depth of their contact, although they certainly knew each other and encountered each other during Tubman's work as one of the most significant conductors of enslaved Africans to the North. See Larson, *Bound for the Promised Land*, 94–6.

87. The lack of critical attention given to Tubman over against male heroes of American culture warrants more attention. See Hazel Carby, *Race Men* (Cambridge, MA: Harvard University Press, 2000) for some indicators of why this privileging on the male perspective takes place in more general terms. Regarding Tubman in particular, Larson says: "The 1960s brought renewed attention to black history and historical figures, and by the 1980s Tubman's life story became a staple of mainstream juvenile literature. Still, racial and gender proscriptions have muted and reconfigured Tubman's place in the collective memory, making her suitable for children's biographies but not as a subject of serious historical inquiry [although I would argue this is changing]. Though the myth has served the varied cultural needs of black and white Americans over time, the obscurity in which the details of her life have remained until now is a deeply troubling reflection of the racial, class, and gender dynamics of our nation" (*Bound for the Promised Land*, 295).

88. From my perspective, Tubman's limited abilities with respect to the written word is not the point. Vital are the strategies she implements regarding an ethical stance against enslavement as opposed to how she later recounts those activities.

89. Bordewich, *Bound for Canaan*, 350.

90. See Carby, *Race Men*; Bordewich, *Bound for Canaan*, 347.

91. Humez, *Harriet Tubman*, 192.

92. For an examination of how and why Harriet Tubman holds such a mythic status in American political and cultural history, see Milton C. Sernett, *Harriet Tubman: Myth, Memory, and History* (Durham, NC: Duke University Press, 2007).

93. This take on Tubman's spiritual awareness is not meant to suggest she was a humanist in spite of the clear indications that her sense of history is teleological in nature due to her sense of the Divine.

94. Some might suggest that the head trauma experienced during her youth resulted in a medical condition of which a part involved fantastic dreams—and perhaps the underlying rationale for her spiritual orientation. For instance, as Lowry notes in passing: "The head wound released her from restrictive, rational thinking and put her in touch with a deeper source, a native intuition something like the experience some have during a migraine aura, or after ingesting a hallucinogenic drug" (Lowry, *Harriet Tubman*, 205).

95. Larson, *Bound for the Promised* Land, 73.

96. Douglass, *Narrative of the Life of Frederick Douglass* (1845).

97. It is interesting to note that nonwritten texts, such as photographs, played a significant role in Tubman's work. Already presented in this book as a resource for theological thinking, photographs were used by Tubman to identify those who were known to assist in the effort to move enslaved Africans to spaces of greater liberty. For example, "when she made contact with persons she had never met before, Tubman's treasured pack of cartes-de-visite [small portrait cards] became her insurance policy. She showed these persons her images and asked them to name the people in the pictures to test their credentials. If they could identify the images of her antislavery friends, she felt secure, knowing she was dealing with some-one who had a personal relationship with her comrades." See Catherine Clinton, *Harriet Tubman: The Road to Freedom* (New York: Little, Brown, 2004), 88–9.

98. For additional discussion of Thoreau's relationship to John Brown, see, for example, Thoreau, "A Plea for Captain John Brown" (1859), in James Redpath, *Echoes of Harper's Ferry* (Boston: Thayer and Eldridge, 1860); Andrew Taylor, "Consenting to Violence: Henry David Thoreau, John Brown, and the Transcendent Intellectual," in Andrew Taylor

and Eldrid Herrington, eds., *The Afterlife of John Brown* (New York: Palgrave Macmillan, 2005), 89–105. For the connection between Douglass, Tubman, and Brown, see Lowry, *Harriet Tubman*, 228–56; Frederick Douglass, "John Brown" (Dover, NH: Morning Star, 1881) and at www.archive.org/stream/johnbrownaddress00doug#page/n1/mode/2up.

99. Larson, *Bound for the Promised Land*, 99.

100. Clinton, *Harriet Tubman*, 62.

101. Humez, *Harriet Tubman*, 233.

102. Charles L. Blockson, *The Underground Railroad* (New York: Prentice Hall Press, 1987), 121.

103. The reasoning behind Tubman's public presentation of her life and activities was pragmatic in nature but also deeply religious. According to Jean Humez, "Her public testimony certainly had economic value, and from the moment she arrived in the North she began to struggle with the problem she would face for the rest of her life—how to feed, clothe, and shelter those who depended on her. Recognition that her telling her life story could help her raise funds did not imply a cynical perspective on the project—as perhaps it might for the celebrity today.... To make sure that at least some of the facts of her experience as a former slave would become part of the public record was a political act, even if it also helped her support herself and her family.... Like other spiritual autobiographers who have been confident of divine guidance in their lives, Tubman believed that telling her life story could be a way of making God's active participation in antislavery work more widely known" (Humez, *Harriet Tubman*, 133–4).

104. Lowry, *Harriet Tubman*, 200.

105. Toni Morrison, *Beloved* (New York: Everyman's Library, 2006), 103.

106. Anita Durkin, "Object Written, Written Object: Slavery, Scarring, and Complications of Authorship in *Beloved*," *African American Review* (Fall 2007), 11.

107. Bryan S. Turner, *The Body and Society: Explorations in Social Theory* (New York: Basil Blackwell, 1984), 205.

108. Gail Weiss, *Body Images: Embodiment as Intercorporeality* (New York: Routledge, 1999), 5.

109. "Introduction," in Sarah Nettleton and Jonathan Watson, eds., *The Body in Everyday Life* (New York: Routledge, 1998), 2.

110. Cresddia J. Heyes, *Self-Transformations: Foucault, Ethics, and Normalized Bodies* (New York: Oxford University Press, 2007), 9, 11.

111. Alec McHoul and Wendy Grace, *A Foucault Primer: Discourse, Power, and the Subject* (New York: New York University Press, 1993), 46.

112. Michel Foucault, *Ethics: Subjectivity and Truth*, ed. Paul Rabinow (New York: New Press, 1997), 282.

113. Foucault, *Ethics*, 282.

114. Foucault, *Ethics*, 282.

115. Foucault, *Ethics*, 283.

116. Susan Hekman, "Material Bodies," in Donn Welton, ed., *Body and Flesh: A Philosophical Reader* (Malden, MA: Blackwell, 1998), 68–9.

117. This section draws from the discussion of perpetual rebellion in my *Terror and Triumph: The Nature of Black Religion* (Minneapolis, MN: Fortress Press, 2003), 153–4.

118. Sharon Welch, *A Feminist Ethic of Risk* (Minneapolis, MN: Fortress, 2000).

119. Foucault, *Ethics*, 319.

120. Edward Casey, "The Ghost of Embodiment: On Bodily Habitudes and Schemata," in Welton, ed., *Body and Flesh*, 207.

121. Susan Bordo, "Bringing Body to Theory," in Welton, ed., *Body and Flesh*, 91.

122. Bordo, "Bringing Body to Theory," 92.

123. Some of the debate and disagreement between African American humanists and non-humanists involves possibilities of shared concern and commitment. That is, can humanists do more than critique? Can they, in fact, see the potential for shared engagement on common issues? I suggest a strong yes. Cooperation where possible is a necessity for African American humanists who understand human ingenuity and creative as our last best—but deeply flawed—hope. I give a fuller explication of this affirmative

response to the question in "Atheists Gather in Burbank: A Humanist Response," *Religion Dispatches,* October 27, 2009 at www.religiondispatches.org/archive/atheologies/1894/atheists_gather_in_burbank%3A_a_humanist%E2%80%99s_response/.

Chapter 6

1. This chapter builds on ideas and concepts expressed in the last several paragraphs of "Watch the Body with New Eyes: Womanist Thought's Contribution to a Humanist Notion of Ritual," *CrossCurrents* 57, no. 3 (2007): 404–11. It also is an expansion of the Alexander Lincoln Lecture given in 2006.

2. Harold Bloom, *The American Religion: The Emergence of the Post-Christian Nation* (New York: Touchstone, 1992), 243.

3. Algernon D. Black, *Without Burnt Offerings: Ceremonies of Humanism* (New York: Viking, 1974), xiii. This need for celebration and rituals appropriate for nontheists had been addressed by a variety of writers. Beyond Black's work, another popular offering is Sarah York's *Remembering Well: Rituals for Celebrating Life and Mourning Death* (San Francisco: Jossey-Bass, 2000). She writes, "For centuries, religious traditions have provided a safe place for the expression of feelings through ritual. In the decades leading up to the twenty-first century, however, we have witnessed, particularly among individuals born after World War II, an alienation and exodus from traditional religion. This has given rise to an increasing number of people for whom traditional religious ritual has become empty, awkward, or irrelevant" (xiv).

   Into this mix, there have also been a good number of texts exploring and explaining "spirituality" through frameworks of humanism, skepticism, or secularism. These include Robert C. Solomon, *Spirituality for the Skeptic: The Thoughtful Love of Life* (New York: Oxford University Press, 2002).

4. Black, *Without Burnt Offerings,* xiv.

5. Presentation of the history of these two is beyond the scope of this chapter. Readers interested in this material should consult, for example: Warren Ross, *The Premise and the Promise: The Story of the Unitarian Universalist Association* (Boston: Unitarian Universalist Association, 2001); *A Chosen Faith: An Introduction to Unitarian Universalism* (Boston: Beacon, 1998); David Robinson, *The Unitarians and the Universalists* (Santa Barbara, CA: ABC-CLIO/Greenwood, 1985); Mark D. Morrison-Reed, *Black Pioneers in a White Denomination,* 3rd ed. (Boston: Skinner House, 1994); Juan Floyd-Thomas, *The Origins of Black Humanism in America: Reverend Ethelred Brown and the Unitarian Church* (New York: Palgrave Macmillan, 2008); Howard Radest, *Toward Common Ground: The Story of the Ethical Societies in the United States* (New York: Ungar, 1969); Felix Adler, *Society for Ethical Culture* (Whitefish, MT: Kessinger, 2009). Also see their Web sites for information on activities, beliefs, and so on: Unitarian Universalist Association at www.uua.org/ and American Ethical Union at www.aeu.org/.

6. www.uua.org/visitors/worship/index.shtml.

7. Christopher Gist Raible et al., "Leading Congregations in Worship: A Guide" at www.uua.org/spirituallife/worshipweb/theory/leadingcongregations/index.shtml.

8. Christopher Gist Raible et al., "Leading Congregations in Worship: A Guide," in the "Validity of Worship" section of the document at www.uua.org/spirituallife/worshipweb/theory/leadingcongregations/120344.shtml.

9. Christopher Gist Raible et al., "Leading Congregations in Worship: A Guide," in "The Contribution of Von Ogden Vogt" section of the document at www.uua.org/spirituallife/worshipweb/theory/leadingcongregations/120345.shtml.

10. Christopher Gist Raible et al., "The Contribution of Von Ogden Vogt."

11. "Welcome to the American Ethical Union," www.aeu.org/.

12. New York Society for Ethical Culture, "Sundays at the Society," www.nysec.org/Sundays.

13. According to a recent study, "The 2008 American Religious Identification Survey found that those who claimed 'no religion'—popularly known as the 'nones'—were the only demographic group that grew in every state within the last 18 years, according to researchers at Trinity College. Between 1990 and 2009, the number of nonreligious Americans nearly doubled, from 8 percent to 15 percent, according to the ARIS study. Among African Americans, the increase was also nearly double, from 6 to 11 percent." Quoted at Chika Oduah and Laren E. Bohn/Religion News Service, "Black Non-Believers Come out of the Closet, Fight Stigma," *District Chronicles*, July 4, 2010: http://media.www.districtchronicles.com/media/storage/paper263/news/2010/06/06/DivineIntervention/Black.NonBelievers.Come.Out.Of.The.Closet.Fight.Stigma-3921604.shtml. For the "2008 American Religious Identification Survey," see www.americanreligionsurvey-aris.org/.

14. See, for example, Joseph Murphy, *Working the Spirit: Ceremonies of the African Diaspora* (Boston: Beacon, 1995); Karen McCarthy Brown, *Mama Lola: A Vodou Priestess in Brooklyn*, expanded ed. (Berkeley: University of California Press, 2001).

15. In discussing what I hoped to demonstrate through use of Walker, Thoreau, and Thurman, I mentioned to my colleague Caroline Levander my interest in developing humanist theologizing in a way that challenged the dominance of the written word and highlighted the nature and meaning of embodiment through other modalities of knowledge arrangement. At that point, she suggested I take a look at a little book that proved to be very intriguing through its somewhat subtle interrogation of the materiality of the written word—the book as embodiment—and the ways in which the symbol and content of the "book" affects our sense of be-ing and our cartographies and housings of life/life meaning. I am grateful to Caroline for introducing me to this book. It provided a great deal to think about, and I hope to come back to it in a more substantial way. Carlos María Domínguez, *the house of paper*, trans. Nick Caistor (New York: Harcourt, 2004).

16. Howard Thurman, *The Inward Journey* (Richmond, IN: Friends United Press, 1971), 110.

17. Delores Williams, *Sisters in the Wilderness: The Challenge of Womanist God-Talk* (Maryknoll, NY: Orbis, 1993), 119–20.

18. Alice Walker, "The Only Reason You Want to Go to Heaven Is That You Have Been Driven Out of Your Mind (Off Your Land and Out of Your Lover's Arms)," in *Anything We Love Can Be Saved: A Writer's Activism* (New York: Ballantine, 1997), 14.

19. Walker, "The Only Reason You Want to Go to Heaven," 17.

20. Walker, "The Only Reason You Want to Go to Heaven," 26.

21. Howard Thurman, *Deep Is the Hunger* (Richmond, IN: Friends United Press, 2000), 105. Thurman, in addition, finds intriguing the notion of solitariness as connected to the religious (169–70).

22. Howard Thurman, *The Centering Moment* (Richmond, IN: Friends United Press, 2000), 77.

23. Thurman, *The Centering Moment*, 87.

24. I am grateful to Luther Smith for his insights during a brief conversation at the Society for the Study of Black Religion meeting in Atlanta in March 2009. He is an important scholar of Howard Thurman's thought and praxis, and I have learned a great deal from his writings and conversations. Readers interested in Smith's work should see: Luther Smith, *Howard Thurman: The Mystic as Prophet* (Richmond, IN: Friends United Press, 2007). Also, attention should be given to the work of Walter Fluker, Alton Pollard, and Mozella Mitchell: Walter Fluker, *They Looked for a City: A Comparative Analysis of the Ideal of Community in the Thought of Howard Thurman and Martin Luther King, Jr.* (Washington, DC: University Press of America, 1989); Alton Pollard, *Mysticism and Social Change: The Social Witness of Howard Thurman* (New York: Peter Lang, 1992); Alton Pollard and Mozella G. Mitchell, *Mysticism and Social Change: The Social Witness of Howard Thurman*, vol. 2 (New York: Peter Lang, 1992); Mozella Mitchell, ed., *Human Search: Howard Thurman and the Quest for Freedom* (New York: Peter Lang, 1992); Mozella Mitchell, *Spiritual Dynamics of Howard Thurman's Theology* (Lima, OH: Wyndham Hall, 1985). Also see Henry James Young, ed., *God and Human*

Freedom: A Festschrift in Honor of Howard Thurman (Richmond, IN: Friends United Press, 1982).

25. Thurman, *The Centering Moment*, 20.
26. Thurman, *Deep Is the Hunger*, 94.
27. Shannon L. Mariotti, *Thoreau's Democratic Withdrawal: Alienation, Participation, and Modernity* (Madison: University of Wisconsin Press, 2010), 120–44.
28. Although something along these lines is not out of the question. For example, Alice Walker tells the story of a horse named Blue whose sadness and "disgust with human beings" had a particularly strong effect on her. When recounting the visit of a friend to her home, she ends the story of Blue and this visit with these words: "As we talked of freedom and justice one day for all, we sat down to steaks. I am eating misery, I thought, as I took the first bite. And spit it out" (Alice Walker, *Living by the Word: Selected Writings, 1973–1987* [New York: Harcourt Brace Jovanovich, 1988], 8).
29. Robert C. Solomon, *Spirituality for the Skeptic: The Thoughtful Love of Life* (New York: Oxford University Press, 2002), xvi. A similarly interesting volume is Walter Sinnott-Armstrong, *Morality Without God?* (New York: Oxford University Press, 2009).
30. Certain works of fiction provide an interesting counterpoint to this type of development that presents the underbelly of these efforts. See, for example, Toni Morrison, *Paradise* (New York: Alfred A. Knopf, 1998); Sutton Griggs, *Imperium in Imperio: A Study of the Negro Race Problem, A Novel* (Sioux Falls, SD: NuVision, 2008); Nella Larsen, *Quicksand and Passing*, ed. Deborah E. McDowell (New Brunswick, NJ: Rutgers University Press, 1986).
31. Philip Cafaro, *Thoreau's Living Ethics: Walden and the Pursuit of Virtue* (Athens: University of Georgia Press, 2004), 106–7, 118–30.
32. Walker, *Living by the Word*, xix.
33. Alice Walker, "Not Only Will Your Teachers Appear, They Will Cook New Foods for You," in Walker, *Living by the Word*, 138.
34. Arrested Development, "Children Play with Earth" on *3 Years, 5 Months and 2 Days in the Life of…* (Chrysalis/EMI Records, 1992). Lyrics from www.lyricsdepot.com/arrested-development/children-play-with-earth.html.
35. Much of what I say in the following paragraphs is in response to Melvin Dixon, *Ride Out the Wilderness: Geography and Identity in Afro-American Literature* (Urbana: University of Illinois Press, 1987), 1–7, 11–28.
36. Dixon, *Ride Out the Wilderness*, 17.
37. Williams, *Sisters in the Wilderness*, 113, 117.
38. Melvin Dixon, in his literary analysis of wilderness, argues that enslaved Africans made use of religio-theological vocabulary in their literature (including songs and narratives) not because of metaphysical assumptions but rather of the effectiveness of this vocabulary for communication. (See Dixon, *Ride Out the Wilderness*, 12.) Whereas James Cone renders the blues "secular spirituals" and attempts to divest them of their naturalistic leanings, Dixon seeks to "secularize" the spirituals. (See James Cone, *The Spirituals and the Blues: An Interpretation* [Maryknoll, NY: Orbis, 1992]. This, however, is not a claim that can be substantiated with satisfaction when one considers the fact that the blues developed during the same period and without strong theological assumptions. That is to say, enslaved and free Africans who did not "believe" the metaphysical claims had another options. Hence, one could just as easily argue that the spirituals by and large are based on Christian belief and the blues represent a more naturalistic perspective. Furthermore, Delores Williams holds, in a somewhat unconvincing manner, that "wilderness experience" connotes both secular and sacred encounter, marking "the unity of the sacred and the secular in African-American reality." However, the singular nature of her theological assumptions (i.e., God and Christ) raise questions concerning how expansive her sense of "wilderness experience" can be in reality. See Williams, *Sisters in the Wilderness*, 160.
39. Williams, *Sisters in the Wilderness*, 119–22.

40. Kelly Brown Douglas gives attention to this troubling dualism still present in much African American religious thought in *What's Faith Got to Do with It? Black Bodies/Christian Souls* (Maryknoll, NY: Orbis, 2005).

41. Williams, *Sisters in the Wilderness*, 60–83, 161–77.

42. See Anthony Pinn, *Why, Lord? Suffering and Evil in Black Theology* (New York: Continuum, 1995). My text seeks to build on the tremendously important work of philosopher of religion William R. Jones, reprinted from the 1973 original: *Is God a White Racist? A Preamble to Black Theology* (Boston: Beacon, 1997).

43. I think there are ways in which the African American theistic imaginary of transformative struggle conceptualized with respect to wilderness reflects some of the thinking guiding other texts, such as *The Pilgrim's Progress*. See John Bunyan, *The Pilgrim's Progress* (Westwood, NJ: Barbour, 1985). One gets a sense of "wilderness" as spiritually damaging in the Yokub Mythology guiding the Nation of Islam during its early phases. See Elijah Muhammad, *Message to the Black Man in America* (Chicago: Muhammad's Temple No. 2, 1965); Elijah Muhammad, *The True History of Master Fard Muhammad*, ed. Nasir Makr Hakim (Atlanta: Messenger Elikjah Muhammad Propagation Society, 1996).

44. As mentioned elsewhere in this book, see Williams, *Sisters in the Wilderness*.

45. Mariotti, *Thoreau's Democratic Withdrawal*, 135.

46. Alice Walker, "Everything Is a Human Being," in Walker, *Living by the Word*, 143.

47. bell hooks, "Touching the Earth," in *At Home on the Earth: Becoming Native to Our Place, a Multicultural Anthology* (Berkeley: University of California Press, 1999), 55. Cited and discussed in Sylvia Mayer, "Introduction," *Restoring the Connection to the Natural World: Essays on African American Environmental Imagination* (Münster: Lit Verlag; New Brunswick, NJ: Transaction, 2003), 2.

48. Lorraine Hansberry, *A Raisin in the Sun: A Drama in Three Acts* (New York: Random House, 1959).

49. Hansberry, *A Raisin in the Sun*, 15.

50. Hansberry, *A Raisin in the Sun*, 35.

51. Hansberry, *A Raisin in the Sun*, 36.

52. Hansberry, *A Raisin in the Sun*, 60.

53. Hansberry, *A Raisin in the Sun*, 61.

54. Hansberry, *A Raisin in the Sun*, 84.

55. Hansberry, *A Raisin in the Sun*, 126.

56. Hansberry, *A Raisin in the Sun*, 131.

57. This attention to Bigger Thomas within the context of imprisonment should not be read as even a subtle statement concerning the pedagogical utility of the prison system. Furthermore, there is no theodical intent in this depiction. Such is far from the case.

58. See Michel Foucault, *Discipline and Punish: The Birth of the Prison* (New York: Vintage, 1979).

59. Richard Wright, *Native Son* (New York: Harper & Brothers, 1940), 233.

60. Wright, *Native Son*, 305.

61. Wright, *Native Son*, 302.

62. Wright, *Native Son*, 306.

63. Wright, *Native Son*, 306.

64. Joyce Ann Joyce, *Richard Wright's Art of Tragedy* (Iowa City: University of Iowa Press, 1986), 46.

65. Wright, *Native Son*, 309, 354. The following words offered during the trial by his attorney are very telling over against Bigger's shift in self-perception and perspective: "'We are dealing here with an impulse stemming from deep down. We are dealing here not with how man acts toward man, but with how a man acts when he feels that he must defend himself against, or adapt himself to, the total natural world in which he lives. The central fact to be understood here is not who wronged this boy, but what kind of a vision of the world did he have before his eyes, and where did he get such a vision as to make him, without premeditation, snatch the life of another person so quickly and instinctively that even though there

was an element of accident in it, he was willing after the crime to say: 'Yes' I did it. I had to … Your Honor, remember that men can starve from a lack of self-realization as much as they can from a lack of bread! And they can murder for it, too!'" (333, 335). Also see the attorney's depiction of prison and its benefits for Bigger (338).

Conculsion

1. This introduction includes some material from "African American Humanism in Practice and Thought," in Miguel De La Torre, ed., *The Hope of Liberation in the World Religions* (Waco, TX: Baylor University Press, 2008), 51–64; William R. Jones, *Is God a White Racist? A Preamble to Black Theology* (Boston: Beacon, 1996).
2. Karl Rahner, "Christian Humanism," *Journal of Ecumenical Studies*, vol. 4: No. 3, 1967 369–84. Quoted in Roger L. Shinn, "Christianity and the New Humanism: Second Thoughts," *Review and Expositor*, 1970 67(3) 315–27.
3. William R. Jones, *Is God a White Racist? A Preamble to Black Theology* (Boston: Beacon, 1996). For more information on weak humanism, see Anthony B. Pinn, *Why, Lord? Suffering and Evil in Black Theology* (New York: Continuum, 1995), chapter 6. I have presented my thinking on the history of African American humanism in a variety of other locations, including *The African American Religious Experience in America* (Westport, CT: Greenwood, 2006); *African American Humanist Principles: Living and Thinking Like the Children of Nimrod* (New York: Palgrave Macmillan, 2004); and *African American Religious Cultures*, vol. 1 (Santa Barbara, CA: ABC-CLIO, 2009). What is contained in this conclusion involves a restating of some of that history and expansion of particular points related to that history.
4. "Ride on King Jesus" from John W. Work, *American Negro Songs* (New York: Howell, Soskin, 1940): www.negrospirituals.com/news-song/ride_on_king_jesus.htm.
5. "Didn't My Lord Deliver Daniel" from Work, *American Negro Songs* (New Ork: Howell, Soskin: www.negrospirituals.com/news-song/didn_t_my_lord_delier_daniel.htm.
6. Alice M. Dunbar, "What Has the Church to Offer the Men of Today?" *AME Church Review* 30 (1913), in Stephen Angell and Anthony Pinn, eds., *Social Protest Thought in the African Methodist Episcopal Church, 1862–1939* (Knoxville: University of Tennessee Press, 2000), 176, 177.
7. Robert L. Pope, "The Tendency of Modern Theology," *AME Church Review* 27 (April 11, 1911) in Angell and Pinn, eds., *Social Protest Thought in the African Methodist Episcopal Church*, 133.
8. Pope, "The Tendency of Modern Theology," 133.
9. Norman W. Brown, "What the Negro Thinks of God," *AME Church Review* 51 (April–June 1935), in Angell and Pinn, eds., *Social Protest Thought in the African Methodist Episcopal Church*, 137.
10. Brown, "What the Negro Thinks of God," 138.
11. See Edwin S. Redkey, ed., *Respect Black: The Writings and Speeches of Henry McNeal Turner* (New York: Arno, 1971).
12. Anthony B. Pinn, *The Black Church in the Post–Civil Rights Era* (Maryknoll, NY: Orbis, 2002), 17–18.
13. Quoted in "Introduction," *A Strange Freedom: The Best of Howard Thurman on Religious Experience and Public Life*, ed. Walter Earl Fluker and Catherine Tumber (Boston: Beacon, 1998), 15.
14. See Howard Thurman, *The Luminous Darkness: A Personal Interpretation of the Anatomy of Segregation and the Ground of Hope* (New York: Harper and Row, 1965).
15. Howard Thurman, "Jesus—An Interpretation," in *A Strange Freedom*, 143.
16. Thurman, "Jesus–An Interpretation," 135.

17. J. Deotis Roberts, "Black Theology and the Theological Revolution," in J. Deotis Roberts, *Black Religion, Black Theology: The Collected Essays of J. Deotis Roberts*, ed. David Emmanuel Goatley (Harrisburg, PA: Trinity Press International, 2003), 37.

18. Charles Long, "Interpretations of Black Religion in America," in *Significations* (Philadelphia: Fortress, 1986), 137.

19. Roberts, "Black Theology and the Theological Revolution," 38, 49.

20. Roberts, "Black Theology and the Theological Revolution," 41–2.

21. James H. Cone, *A Black Theology of Liberation*, 2nd ed. (Maryknoll, NY: Orbis, 1986), 59.

22. J. Deotis Roberts, "Black Theology and the Theological Revolution," 42.

23. Readers may find interesting the conversation on the "Death of God" during the 2009 American Academy of Religion meeting. See "Whither the 'Death of God': A Continuing Currency?" at http://vimeo.com/12744096.

24. Cone, *A Black Theology of Liberation*, 60.

25. Cone, *A Black Theology of Liberation*, 70.

26. Cone, *A Black Theology of Liberation*, 77.

27. Cone, *A Black Theology of Liberation*, 63.

28. Readers will be interested in Sharon Welch's take on liberal theology in *A Feminist Ethic of Risk* (Minneapolis, MN: Fortress, 1990).

29. Peter C. Hodgson, "Liberal Theology and Transformative Pedagogy," in Mark D. Chapman, ed., *The Future of Liberal Theology* (Burlington, VT: Ashgate, 2002), 103.

30. William Hamilton, "In Piam Memoriam: The Death of God after Ten Years," *Christian Century* 92, no. 32 (October 8, 1975): 872. Also see Emerson W. Shideler, "Taking the Death-of-God Seriously," *Theology Today* v. 23, no. 2 (July 1966) 183–99.

31. I have given attention to this understanding of humanism as religion elsewhere and will not cover that topic again here in any detail. See *Varieties of African American Religious Experience* (Minneapolis, MN: Fortress, 1998) and *African American Humanist Principles*.

32. Daniel Payne, "Daniel Payne's Protestation of Slavery," *Lutheran Herald and Journal of the Franckean Synod* (Fort Plain, NY: Committee of Publication of the Franckean Synod, 1839), 115.

33. "Experiences of a Chimney Sweeper," in J. Mason Brewer, editor., *America's Negro Folklore* (Chicago: Quadrangle Books, 1968), 268.

34. Here and elsewhere, I understand religion to mean the quest for complex subjectivity, and theology is the exploration (celebration and critique) of this quest. For more information on this theory of religion, see Anthony B. Pinn, *Terror and Triumph: The Nature of Black Religion* (Minneapolis,MN: Fortress, 2003).

35. See Pinn, *African American Humanist Principles*; Pinn, *By These Hands: A Documentary History of African American Humanism* (New York: New York University Press, 2001); Norm Allen Jr., *African American Humanism: An Anthology* (Buffalo, NY: Prometheus, 1991).

36. Quoted in Anthony B. Pinn, *African American Humanist Principles*, 19.

37. From Zora Neale Hurston, "Religion," in *Dust Tracks on Road* (1942). Excerpt here is from Norm R. Allen Jr., *African American Humanism: An Anthology* (Buffalo: Prometheus, 1991), 154.

38. Trudier Harris, "Three Black Women Writers and Humanism: A Folk Perspective," in R. Baxter Miller, ed., *African American Literature and Humanism* (Lexington: University Press of Kentucky), 72.

39. See *Empowerment: One Denomination's Quest for Racial Justice, 1967–1982* (Boston: Unitarian Universalist Association, 1993).

40. Jones did not articulate in this text a clear humanist theology. He provides, instead, a descriptive genealogy of African American humanism as a way of critiquing theodical developments in black theology. Developed in response to Jones, in *African American Humanist Principles*, I gave attention to the practice of African American humanism as a type of religious orientation, framed in terms of a rethinking of the biblical account of Nimrod and the Tower of Babel. I concluded that text with a call for the development of African American humanist

studies, with the first move in this direction the articulation of an African American humanist theology. This proposed humanist theology is what Gordon Kaufman might label a second-order theology, one that recognizes the significance and vitality of other theological approaches but holds firm to the exploration and explication of a particular religious trajectory.

41. In light of their strong critique of sexism within black churches and black theology, womanist might ask, Is God a black sexist?
42. See Cone, *A Black Theology of Liberation*, 57–8.
43. Cone, *A Black Theology of Liberation*, 58.
44. Kelly Brown Douglas, *What's Faith Got to Do with It? Black Bodies/Christian Souls* (Maryknoll, NY: Orbis, 2005), xiii.

BIBLIOGRAPHY

Allen, Norm, Jr. *African American Humanism: An Anthology* (Buffalo, NY: Prometheus, 1991).

Altizer, Thomas, and William Hamilton. *Radical Theology and the Death of God* (Bobbs-Merrill, 1966).

Amit, Vered, ed. *Realizing Community: Concepts, Social Relationships and Sentiment* (New York: Routledge, 2002).

Anderson, Benedict. *Imagined Communities: Reflections on the Origin and Spread of Nationalism* (London: Verso, 1983).

Anderson, Victor. *Creative Exchange: A Constructive Theology of African American Religious Experience* (Minneapolis, MN: Fortress, 2009).

Anderson, Victor. *Beyond Ontological Blackness: An Essay in African American Religious and Cultural Criticism* (New York: Continuum, 1995).

Angell, Stephen, and Anthony Pinn, eds. *Social Protest Thought in the African Methodist Episcopal Church, 1862–1939* (Knoxville: University of Tennessee Press, 2000).

Arthur, Linda B., ed. *Religion, Dress and the Body* (New York: Berg, 1999).

Banks, Ingrid. *Hair Matters: Beauty, Power, and Black Women's Consciousness* (New York: New York University Press, 2000).

Barbour, Ian. *Religion in an Age of Science*, rev. ed. (New York: HarperOne, 1997).

Barbour, Ian. *Issues in Science and Religion* (Upper Saddle River, NJ: Prentice Hall, 1966).

Basquiat, Jean-Michel. *King for a Decade* (Tokyo, Japan: Korinsha, 1997).

Basterra, Gabriela. *Seductions of Fate: Tragic Subjectivity, Ethics, Politics* (New York: Palgrave Macmillan, 2004).

Baud, Michiel. "Beyond Benedict Anderson: Nation-Building and Popular Democracy in Latin America," *International Review of Social History* 50, no. 3 (2005): 485–98.

Bell, Colin, and Howard Newby. *Community Studies* (New York: Praeger, 1972).

Bell, David, Jon Binnie, Ruth Holliday, Robyn Longhurst, and Robin Peace, eds. *Pleasure Zones: Bodies, Cities, Spaces* (Syracuse, NY: Syracuse University Press, 2001).

Bender, Thomas. *Community and Social Change in America* (New Brunswick, NJ: Rutgers University Press, 1978).

Bennett, Jane. *Thoreau's Nature: Ethics, Politics, and the Wild* (Thousand Oaks, CA: Sage, 1994).

Berdayes, Vicent, Luigi Esposito, and John W. Murphy, eds. "Introduction," in *The Body in Human Inquiry: Interdisciplinary Explorations of Embodiment* (Cresskill, NJ: Hampton, 2004).

Bergmann, Sigurd, ed. *Theology in Built Environments: Exploring Religion, Architecture, and Design* (New Brunswick, NJ: Transaction, 2009).

Bergmann, Sigurd, ed. *Architecture, Aesth/ethics and Religion* (Frankfurt, Germany: IKO-Verlag für Interkulturelle Kommunikation, 2005).

Biehl, João, Bryon Good, and Arthur Kleinman, eds. *Subjectivity: Ethnographic Investigations* (Berkeley: University of California Press, 2007).

Bixler, Julius Seelye. "Josiah Royce: Twenty Year After," *Harvard Theological Review* 29, no. 3 (1936): 197–224.

Black, Algernon D. *Without Burnt Offerings: Ceremonies of Humanism* (New York: Viking, 1974).

Blackshaw, Tony. *Key Concepts in Community Studies* (Washington, DC: Sage, 2010).

Blackwelder, Julia Kirk. *Styling Jim Crow: African American Beauty Training during Segregation* (College Station: Texas A & M University Press, 2003).

Blight, David. *Passages to Freedom: The Underground Railroad in History and Memory* (Washington, DC: Smithsonian, 2004).

Blockson, Charles L. *The Underground Railroad* (New York: Prentice Hall, 1987).

Bloom, Harold. *The American Religion: The Emergence of the Post-Christian Nation* (New York: Simon & Schuster, 1992).

Blum, Edward, and Jason Young, eds. *The Souls of W. E. B. DuBois: New Essays and Reflections* (Macon, GA: Mercer University Press, 2009).

Bordewich, Fergus M. *Bound for Canaan: The Underground Railroad and the War for the Soul of America* (New York: Amistad, 2005).

Bordo, Susan. *Unbearable Weight: Feminism, Western Culture, and the Body* (Berkeley: University of California Press, 2003).

Brewer, J. Mason, ed. *America's Negro Folklore* (Chicago: Quadrangle, 1968).

Bristol, Douglas Walter, Jr. *Kings of the Razor: Black Barbers in Slavery and Freedom* (Baltimore: Johns Hopkins University Press, 2009).

Brown, Frank Burch. *Religious Aesthetics: A Theological Study of Making and Meaning* (Princeton, NJ: Princeton University Press, 2004).

Byrd, Ayana. *Hairstory: Untangling the Roots of Black Hair in America* (New York: St. Martin's, 2001).

Cafaro, Philip. *Thoreau's Living Ethics: Walden and the Pursuit of Virtue* (Athens: University of Georgia Press, 2004).

Campbell, Mary Schmidt, and Sharon F. Patton, eds. *Memory and Metaphor: The Art of Romare Bearden, 1940–1987* (New York: Oxford University Press, 1991).

Carby, Hazel. *Race Men* (Cambridge, MA: Harvard University Press, 2000).

Carrette, Jeremy R. *Foucault and Religion: Spiritual Corporality and Political Spirituality* (New York: Routledge, 2000).

Carson, Clayborne, ed. *The Autobiography of Martin Luther King, Jr.* (New York: Warner, 1998).

Castro-Klarén, Sara, and John Charles Chasteen, eds. *Beyond Imagined Communities: Reading and Writing the Nation in Nineteenth-Century Latin America* (Baltimore: Johns Hopkins University Press, 2003).

Chapman, Mark D., ed. *The Future of Liberal Theology* (Burlington, VT: Ashgate, 2002).

Clark, Taylor. *Starbucked: A Double Tall Tale of Caffeine, Commerce, and Culture* (New York: Little, Brown, 2007).

Clarke, Graham. *The Photograph* (New York: Oxford University Press, 1997).

Clinton, Catherine. *Harriet Tubman: The Road to Freedom* (New York: Little, Brown, 2004).

Cone, James H. *Martin & Malcolm & America: A Dream or a Nightmare* (Maryknoll, NY: Orbis, 1991).

Cone, James H. *Black Theology & Black Power* (San Francisco: Harper & Row, 1989).

Cone, James H. *A Black Theology of Liberation*, 2nd ed. (Maryknoll, NY: Orbis, 1986).

Cone, James H. *God of the Oppressed* (New York: Harper & Row, 1975).

Conway, Hazel, and Rowan Roenisch. *Understanding Architecture: An Introduction to Architecture and Architectural History* (New York: Routledge, 1994).

Cooper, Charlie. *Community, Conflict and the State: Rethinking Notions of "Safety," "Cohesion" and "Wellbeing"* (New York: Palgrave Macmillan, 2008).

Cupitt, Don. *After God: The Future of Religion* (New York: Basic Books, 1997).

Damasio, Antonio. *The Feeling of What Happens: Body and Emotion in the Making of Consciousness* (New York: Harvest, 1999).

Danto, Arthur C. *The Abuse of Beauty* (Chicago: Open Court, 2003).

Danto, Arthur C. *Philosophizing Art: Selected Essays* (Berkeley: University of California Press, 1999).

Davis, Reginald F. *Frederick Douglass: A Precursor of Liberation Theology* (Macon, GA: Mercer University Press, 2005).

De La Torre, Miguel, editor. *The Hope of Liberation in the World Religions* (Waco, TX: Baylor University Press, 2008).

Dewey, John. *The Public and Its Problems* (New York: Holt, 1927).

Dixon, Melvin. *Ride Out the Wilderness: Geography and Identity in Afro-American Literature* (Urbana: University of Illinois Press, 1987).

Douglas, Kelly Brown. *What's Love Got to Do with It?* (Maryknoll, NY: Orbis, 2005).

Douglas, Kelly Brown. *The Black Church and Sexuality* (Maryknoll, NY: Orbis, 2003).

Douglas, Kelly Brown. *The Black Christ* (Maryknoll, NY: Orbis, 1994).

Douglass, Frederick. *Narrative of the Life of Frederick Douglass: An American Slave, Written by Himself* (New York: St. Martin's, 2002).

Douglass, Frederick. *Frederick Douglass: The Narrative and Selected Writings* (New York: Modern Library College Editions, 1984).

Durkin, Anita. "Object Written, Written Object: Slavery, Scarring, and Complications of Authorship in *Beloved*," *African American Review* (Fall 2007), 11.

Dyson, Michael Eric. *The Michael Eric Dyson Reader* (New York: Basic Civitas, 2004).

Early, Gerald, ed. *Lure and Loathing: Essays on Race, Identity, and the Ambivalence of Assimilation* (New York: Allen Lane/Penguin, 1993).

Edyvane, Derek. *Community and Conflict: The Sources of Liberal Solidarity* (New York: Palgrave Macmillan, 2007).

Ellis, Carolyn, and Michael G. Flaherty, eds. *Investigating Subjectivity: Research on Lived Experience* (Newbury Park, CA: Sage, 1992).

Emmerling, Leonhard. *Jean-Michel Basquiat, 1960–1988* (Los Angeles: Taschen, 2003).

Evans, James H., Jr. *We Have Been Believers: An African American Systematic Theology* (Minneapolis, MN: Fortress, 1992).

Fanon, Franz. *Black Skin, White Masks* (1952; New York: Grove, 1994).

Farley, Edward. *Faith and Beauty: A Theological Aesthetic* (Burlington, VT: Ashgate, 2001).

Farquhar, Judith, and Margaret Lock. *Beyond the Body Proper: Reading the Anthropology of Material Life* (Durham, NC : Duke University Press, 2007).

Fishburn, Katherine. *Richard Wright's Hero: The Faces of a Rebel-Victim* (Metuchen, NJ: Scarecrow, 1977).

Floyd-Thomas, Juan. *The Origins of Black Humanism in America: Reverend Ethelred Brown and the Unitarian Church* (New York: Palgrave Macmillan, 2008).

Fluker, Walter. *They Looked for a City: A Comparative Analysis of the Ideal of Community in the Thought of Howard Thurman and Martin Luther King, Jr.* (Washington, DC: University Press of America, 1989).

Foucault, Michel. *Ethics: Subjectivity and Truth*, ed. Paul Rabinow (New York: New Press, 1997).

Foucault, Michel. *Discipline and Punish: The Birth of the Prison* (New York: Vintage, 1979).

Fraser, Mariam, and Monica Greco, eds. *The Body: A Reader* (New York: Routledge, 2005).

Geurts, Kathryn Linn. *Culture and the Senses: Bodily Ways of Knowing in an African Community* (Berkeley: University of California Press, 2002).

Gill, Michael Gates. *How Starbucks Saved My Life: A Son of Privilege Learns to Live Like Everyone Else* (New York: Gotham, 2007).

Gilroy, Paul. *The Black Atlantic: Modernity and Double Consciousness* (Cambridge, MA: Harvard University Press, 1993).

Gilyard, Keith. *Composition and Cornel West: Notes toward a Deep Democracy* (Carbondale: Southern Illinois University Press, 2008),

Glaude, Eddie. *In a Shade of Blue: Pragmatism and the Politics of Black America* (Chicago: University of Chicago Press, 2008).

Goatley, David Emmanuel. *Black Religion, Black Theology: The Collected Essays of J. Deotis Roberts* (Harrisburg, PA: Trinity Press International, 2003).

Goffman, Erving. *Stigma: Notes on the Management of Spoiled Identity* (New York: Touchstone, 2009).

Gordon, Lewis R., ed. *Existence in Black: An Anthology of Black Existential Philosophy* (New York: Routledge, 1997).

Gould, Stephen Jay. *The Mismeasure of Man* (New York: W. W. Norton, 1983).

Greene, Brian. *The Elegant Universe: Superstrings, Hidden Dimensions, and the Quest for the Ultimate Theory* (New York: W. W. Norton, 1999).

Gubser, Steven S. *The Little Book of String Theory* (Princeton, NJ: Princeton University Press, 2010).

Hall, Donald E. *Subjectivity* (New York: Routledge, 2004).

Hamilton, William. "In Piam Memoriam: The Death of God after Ten Years," *Christian Century* 92, no. 32 (1975): 872.

Hansberry, Lorraine. *A Raisin in the Sun: A Drama in Three Acts* (New York: Random House, 1959).

Harris, Jonathan, ed. *Dead History, Live Art? Spectacle, Subjectivity and Subversion in Visual Culture since the 1960s* (Liverpool, England: Liverpool University Press, 2007).

Harris-Lacewell, Melissa Victoria. *Barbershops, Bibles, and BET: Everyday Talk and Black Political Thought* (Princeton, NJ: Princeton University Press, 2004).

Heilman, Kenneth M. *Matter of Mind: A Neurologist's View of Brain-Behavior Relationships* (New York: Oxford University Press, 2002).

Heyes, Cresddia J. *Self-Transformations: Foucault, Ethics, and Normalized Bodies* (New York: Oxford University Press, 2007).

Hoban, Phoebe. *Basquiat: A Quick Killing in Art* (New York: Penguin, 2004).

Hopkins, Dwight. *Being Human: Race, Culture, and Religion* (Minneapolis, MN: Fortress, 2005).

Humez, Jean A. *Harriet Tubman: The Life and the Life Stories* (Madison, WI: University of Wisconsin Press, 2003).

Jacobs-Huey, Lanita. *From the Kitchen to the Parlor: Language and Becoming in African American Women's Hair Care* (New York: Oxford University Press, 2006).

Jeffrey, Ian. *The Photograph: A Concise History* (New York: Oxford University Press, 1981).

Jones, Amelia. *Self/Image: Technology, Representation, and the Contemporary Subject* (New York: Routledge, 2006).

Jones, Lindsay. *The Hermeneutics of Sacred Architecture: Experience, Interpretation, Comparison*, vol. 1 (Cambridge, MA: Harvard University Center for the Study of World Religions/ Harvard University Press, 2000).

Jones, William R. *Is God a White Racist? A Preamble to Black Theology* (Boston: Beacon, 1996).

Joyce, Joyce Ann. *Richard Wright's Art of Tragedy* (Iowa City: University of Iowa Press, 1986).

Karp, Ivan, and Steven D. Lavine, ed. *Exhibiting Cultures: The Poetics and Politics of Museum Display* (Washington, DC: Smithsonian Institution, 1991).

Kaufman, Gordon. *An Essay on Theological Method*, 3rd ed. (New York: Oxford University Press, 2000).

Kilde, Jeanne. *Sacred Power, Sacred Space: An Introduction to Christian Architecture and Worship* (New York: Oxford University Press, 2008).

Kilde, Jeanne. *When Church Became Theater: Transformation of Evangelical Architecture and Worship in Nineteenth Century America* (New York: Oxford University Press, 2002).

King, Martin Luther, Jr. *Where Do We Go from Here: Chaos or Community?* (Boston: Beacon, 1967).

King, Martin Luther, Jr. *Stride toward Freedom: The Montgomery Story* (New York: Harper & Row, 1958).

Kirby, Kathleen M. *Indifferent Boundaries: Spatial Concepts of Human Subjectivity* (New York: Guilford, 1996).

Krier, Leon. *The Architecture of Community* (Washington, DC: Island, 2009).

Kuhn, Annette, and Kirsten McAllister, eds. *Locating Memory: Photographic Acts* (New York: Berghahn, 2006).

Larsen, Nella. *The Complete Fiction of Nella Larsen*, ed. Charles Larson (New York: Anchor, 2001).

Larsen, Nella. *Quicksand and Passing*, ed. Deborah E. McDowell (New Brunswick, NJ: Rutgers University Press, 1986).

Larson, Kate Clifford. *Bound for the Promised Land: Harriet Tubman, Portrait of an American Hero* (New York: Ballantine, 2004).

Lawlor, Anthony. *The Temple in the House: Finding the Sacred in Everyday Architecture* (Los Angeles: Jeremy P. Tracher/Putnam, 1994).

Lawson, Bill E., and Frank M. Kirkland, eds. *Frederick Douglass: A Critical Reader* (Malden, MA: Blackwell, 1999).

Lee, Maurice S. *The Cambridge Companion to Frederick Douglass* (New York: Cambridge University Press, 2009).

Lehtouvuori, Panu. *Experience and Conflict: The Production of Urban Space* (Burlington, VT: Ashgate, 2010).

Lemire, Elise. *Black Walden: Slavery and Its Aftermath in Concord, Massachusetts* (Philadelphia: University of Pennsylvania Press, 2009).

Little, Adrian. *The Politics of Community: Theory and Practice* (Edinburgh, Scotland: Edinburgh University Press, 2002).

Lock, Margaret, and Judith Farquhar, eds. *Beyond the Body Proper: Reading the Anthropology of Material Life* (Durham, NC: Duke University Press, 2007).

Locke, Alain, ed. *The New Negro* (New York: Atheneum, 1986).

Long, Charles H. *Significations* (Philadelphia: Fortress, 1986).

Lowry, Beverly. *Harriet Tubman: Imagining a Life* (New York: Doubleday, 2007).

Lynch, Michael F. *Creative Revolt: A Study of Wright, Ellison, and Dostoevsky* (New York: Peter Lang, 1990).

MacDonald, Mary N., ed. *Experiences of Place* (Cambridge, MA: Center for the Study of World Religions, Harvard Divinity School/Harvard University Press, 2003).

Mandelbaum, Seymour J. *Open Moral Communities* (Cambridge, MA: MIT Press, 2000).

Mariotti, Shannon L. *Thoreau's Democratic Withdrawal: Alienation, Participation, and Modernity* (Madison: University of Wisconsin Press, 2010).

Marshall, Richard, ed. *Jean-Michel Basquiat* (New York: Whitney Museum of American Art/Harry N. Abrams, 1992).

Martin, Luther H., Huck Gutman, and Patrick H. Hutton, eds. *Technologies of the Self: A Seminar with Michel Foucault* (Amherst: University of Massachusetts Press, 1988).

Mason, Andrew. *Community, Solidarity and Belonging: Levels of Community and Their Normative Significance* (New York: Cambridge University Press, 2000).

May, Matthew E. *In Pursuit of Elegance: Why the Best Ideas Have Something Missing* (New York: Broadway, 2009).

Mayer, Marc, ed. *Basquiat* (New York: Merrell, 2005).

Mayer, Sylvia, ed. *Restoring the Connection to the Natural World: Essays on African American Environmental Imagination* (Münster, Germany: Lit Verlag; New Brunswick, NJ: Transaction, 2003).

McGuigan, Cathleen. "Jean Michel Basquiat," *New York Times Magazine*, February 10, 1985.

McHoul, Alec, and Wendy Grace. *A Foucault Primer: Discourse, Power, and the Subject* (New York: New York University Press, 1993).

Menin, Sarah, ed. *Constructing Place: Mind and Matter* (New York: Routledge, 2003).

Mercer, Kobena, ed. *Exiles, Diasporas & Strangers* (Cambridge, MA: MIT Press, 2008).

Mercurio, Gianni, ed. *The Jean-Michel Basquiat Show* (Milan, Italy: Skira Editore S.p.A, 2006).

Meskimmon, Marsha. *Women Marking Art: History, Subjectivity, Aesthetics* (New York: Routledge, 2003).

Miller, Monica. "Anti-Proper in the Popular: The Risky Religiosity of Hip-Hop Culture," PhD Dissertation (Chicago Theological Seminary, 2010).

Miller, Monica L. *Slaves to Fashion: Black Dandyism and the Styling of Black Diasporic Identity* (Durham, NC: Duke University Press, 2009).

Mitchell, Mozella, ed. *Human Search: Howard Thurman and the Quest for Freedom* (New York: Peter Lang, 1992).

Mitchell, Mozella. *Spiritual Dynamics of Howard Thurman's Theology* (Lima, OH: Wyndham Hall, 1985).

Moller, Mary Elkins. *Thoreau in the Human Community* (Amherst: University of Massachusetts Press, 1980).

Morrison, Toni. *Beloved* (New York: Knopf, 1987).

Myerson, Joel, ed. *Critical Essays on Henry David Thoreau's Walden* (Boston: G. K. Hall, 1988).

Nast, Heidi J., and Steve Pile, ed. *Places through the Body* (New York: Routledge, 1998).

Nettleton, Sarah, and Jonathan Watson, eds. *The Body in Everyday Life* (New York: Routledge, 1998).

Oliver, David. *The Shaggy Steed of Physics: Mathematical Beauty in the Physical World* (New York: Springer-Verlag, 1994).

Orsi, Robert A. *Between Heaven and Earth: The Religious Worlds People Make and the Scholars Who Study Them* (Princeton, NJ: Princeton University Press, 2005).

Orvell, Miles. *American Photography* (New York: Oxford University Press, 2003).

Parsons, Talcott. *American Society: A Theory of the Societal Community*, ed. Giuseppe Sciortino (Boulder, CO: Paradigm, 2007).

Payne, Daniel. "Daniel Payne's Protestation of Slavery," *Lutheran Herald and Journal of the Franckean Synod* (Fort Plain, NY: Committee of Publication of the Franckean Synod, 1839).

Petersen, Alan, and Robin Bunton, eds. *Foucault: Health and Medicine* (New York: Routledge, 1997).

Pinn, Anthony. *Embodiment and the New Shape of Black Theological Thought* (New York: New York University Press, 2010).

Pinn, Anthony, ed. *Black Religion and Aesthetics: Religious Thought and Life in Africa and the African Diaspora* (New York: Palgrave Macmillan, 2009).

Pinn, Anthony. "Watch the Body With New Eyes: Womanist Thought's Contribution to a Humanist Notion of Ritual," *CrossCurrents* 57, no. 3 (2007): 404–11.

Pinn, Anthony. *African American Humanist Principles: Living and Thinking Like the Children of Nimrod* (New York: Palgrave Macmillan, 2004).

Pinn, Anthony. *Terror and Triumph: The Nature of Black Religion* (Minneapolis, MN: Fortress, 2003).

Pinn, Anthony. *By These Hands: A Documentary History of African American Humanism* (New York: New York University Press, 2001).

Pinn, Anthony B. *The Black Church in the Post–Civil Rights Era* (Maryknoll, NY: Orbis, 2002).

Pinn, Anthony. *Moral Evil and Redemptive Suffering: A History of Theodicy in African American Religious Thought* (Gainesville: University Press of Florida, 2002).

Pinn, Anthony. *Varieties of African American Religious Experience* (Minneapolis, MN: Fortress, 1998).

Pinn, Anthony B. *Why, Lord? Suffering and Evil in Black Theology* (New York: Continuum, 1995).

Pinn, Anthony, and Allen Callahan, eds. *African American Religious Life and the Story of Nimrod* (New York: Palgrave Macmillan, 2008).

Pinn, Anthony, and Dwight Hopkins, eds. *Loving the Body: Black Religious Studies and the Erotic* (New York: Palgrave Macmillan, 2004).

Pollard, Alton. *Mysticism and Social Change: The Social Witness of Howard Thurman* (New York: Peter Lang, 1992).

Pollard, Alton, and Mozella G. Mitchell, *Mysticism and Social Change: The Social Witness of Howard Thurman*, vol. 2 (New York: Peter Lang, 1992).

Prince, Althea. *The Politics of Black Women's Hair* (London, ON: Insomniac, 2009).

Rahner, Karl. "Christian Humanism," *Journal of Ecumenical Studies*, Vol. 4: No. 3, (1967): 369–84.

Rampersad, Arnold, ed. *Richard Wright: A Collection of Critical Essays* (Englewood Cliffs, NJ: Prentice Hall, 1995).

Randall, Lisa. *Warped Passages: Unraveling the Mysteries of the Universe's Hidden Dimensions* (New York: Ecco/HarperCollins, 2005).

Read, Alan, ed. *Architecturally Speaking: Practices of Art, Architecture and the Everyday* (New York: Routledge, 2000).

Redkey, Edwin S., ed. *Respect Black: The Writings and Speeches of Henry McNeal Turner* (New York: Arno, 1971).

Reiss, Alibert, ed. *Louis Wirth on Cities and Social Life* (Chicago: University of Chicago, 1964).

Ricard, Rene. "The Radiant Child," ARTFORM Magazine 20, no. 4 (1981): 35–43.

Royce, Josiah. *The Problem of Christianity* (New York: Macmillan, 1913).

Rush, Fred. *On Architecture* (New York: Routledge, 2009).

Sackheim, Eric. *The Blues Line: A Collection of Blues Lyrics from Leadbelly to Muddy Waters* (Hopewell, NJ: Ecco, 1969).

Schissel, Wendy, ed. *Home/Bodies: Geographies of Self, Place, and Space* (Calgary, AB: University of Calgary Press, 2006).

Schrag, Calvin O. *The Self after Postmodernity* (New Haven, CT: Yale University Press, 1997).

Sernett, Milton C. *Harriet Tubman: Myth, Memory, and History* (Durham, NC: Duke University Press, 2007).

Shideler, Emerson W. "Taking the Death-of-God Seriously," *Theology Today* v. 23, no. 2 (July 1966): 183–99.

Shinn, Roger L. "Christianity and the New Humanism: Second Thoughts," *Review and Expositor* 1970 67(3): 315–27.

Shulman, George. *American Prophecy: Race and Redemption in American Political Culture* (Minneapolis: University of Minnesota Press, 2008).

Simon, Bryant. *Everything but the Coffee: Learning about America from Starbucks* (Berkeley: University of California Press, 2009).

Sinnott-Armstrong, Walter. *Morality without God?* (New York: Oxford University Press, 2009).

Smith, Anthony. *Nationalism and Modernism: A Critical Survey of Recent Theories of Nations and Nationalism* (New York: Routledge, 1998).

Smith, Luther E., Jr., *Howard Thurman: The Mystic as Prophet* (Richmond, IN: Friends United Press, 2007).

Smith, Luther E., Jr., *Howard Thurman: Essential Writings* (Maryknoll, NY: Orbis, 2006).

Smith, Mark M. *How Race Is Made: Slavery, Segregation, and the Senses* (Chapel Hill: University of North Carolina Press, 2008).

Smith, Shawn Michelle. *Photography on the Color Line: W. E. B. DuBois, Race, and Visual Culture* (Durham, NC: Duke University Press, 2004).

Smith, Shawn Michelle. *American Archives* (Princeton, NJ: Princeton University Press, 1999).

Solomon, Robert C. *Spirituality for the Skeptic: The Thoughtful Love of Life* (New York: Oxford University Press, 2002).

Sontag, Susan. *On Photography* (New York: Picador, 1977).

Stephens, Mitchell. *The Rise of the Image and the Fall of the Word* (New York: Oxford University Press, 1998).

Stewart, Ian. *Why Beauty Is Truth: A History of Symmetry* (New York: Basic Books, 2007).

Stewart, Ian, and Martin Golubitsky. *Fearful Symmetry: Is God a Geometer?* (Cambridge, MA: Blackwell, 1992).

Stoler, Ann Laura. *Race and the Education of Desire: Foucault's History of Sexuality and the Colonial Order of Things* (Durham, NC: Duke University Press, 1995).

Studdert, David. *Conceptualising Community: Beyond the State and Individual* (New York: Palgrave Macmillan, 2005).

Sullivan, Nikki. *Tattooed Bodies: Subjectivity, Textuality, Ethics, and Pleasure* (Westport, CT: Praeger, 2001).

Tauber, Alfred I. *Henry David Thoreau and the Moral Agency of Knowing* (Berkeley: University of California Press, 2001).

Taylor, Andrew, and Eldrid Herrington, eds. *The Afterlife of John Brown* (New York: Palgrave Macmillan, 2005).

Taylor, Mark C. *Deconstructing Theology* (New York: Crossroads; Chico, CA: Scholars Press, 1982).

Thoreau, Henry D. *Walden* (Princeton, NJ: Princeton University Press, 1973).

Thurman, Howard. *Deep Is the Hunger* (Richmond, IN: Friends United Press, 2000).

Thurman, Howard. *The Centering Moment* (Richmond, IN: Friends United Press, 2000).

Thurman, Howard. *The Inward Journey* (Richmond, IN: Friends United Press, 1971).

Thurman, Howard. *The Luminous Darkness: A Personal Interpretation of the Anatomy of Segregation and the Ground of Hope* (New York: Harper and Row, 1965).

Tobin, Jacqueline. *From Midnight to Dawn: The Last Tracks of the Underground Railroad* (New York: Doubleday, 2007).

Tönnies, Ferdinand. *Community and Society*, trans. Charles P. Loomis (New York: Harper, 1963).

Trachtenberg, Alan. *Reading American Photographs: Images as History Mathew Brady to Walker Evans* (New York: Hill and Wang, 1989).

Tunstall, Dwayne A. *Yes, but Not Quite: Encountering Josiah Royce's Ethico-Religious Insight* (New York: Fordham University Press, 2009).

Turner, Bryan. *The Body and Society: Explorations in Social Theory* (Oxford: Basil Blackwell, 1984).

Turner, Bryan. *Religion and Social Theory: A Materialist Perspective* (London: Heinemann, 1983).

Upton, Dell. *Another City: Urban Life and Urban Spaces in the New American Republic* (New Haven, CT: Yale University Press, 2008).

Vitek, William, and Wes Jackson, eds. *Rooted in the Land: Essays on Community and Place* (New Haven, CT: Yale University Press, 1996).

Vitz, Paul C., and Susan M. Felch, eds. *The Self: Beyond the Postmodern Crisis* (Wilmington, DE: Intercollegiate Studies Institute, 2006).

Walker, Alice. *Anything You Love Can Be Saved* (New York: Ballantine, 1998).

Walker, Alice. *Living by the Word: Selected Writings, 1973–1987* (New York: Harcourt Brace Jovanovich, 1988).

Walker, David. *David Walker's Appeal* (1829; Baltimore: Black Classic, 1997).

Washington, James Melvin, ed. *A Testament of Hope: The Essential Writings of Martin Luther King, Jr.* (San Francisco: Harper & Row, 1986).

Weinberg, Jonathan. *Ambition & Love in Modern American Art* (New Haven, CT: Yale University Press, 2001).

Weiss, Gail. *Body Images: Embodiment as Intercorporeality* (New York: Routledge, 1999).

Welch, Sharon D. *Sweet Dreams in America: Making Ethics and Spirituality Work* (New York: Routledge, 1999).

Welch, Sharon D. *A Feminist Ethic of Risk* (Minneapolis, MN: Fortress, 1990).

Welton, Donn, ed. *Body and Flesh: A Philosophical Reader* (Malden, MA: Blackwell, 1998).

West, Cornel. *Keeping Faith* (New York: Routledge, 2008).

West, Cornel. *Prophesy Deliverance* (Louisville, KY: Westminster John Knox, 2002).

West, Cornel. *The Cornel West Reader* (New York: Basic Civitas, 2000).

Weyl, Hermann. *Symmetry* (Princeton, NY: Princeton University Press, 1952).

Williams, Delores S. *Sisters in the Wilderness: The Challenge of Womanist God-Talk* (Maryknoll, NY: Orbis, 1993).

Williams, Simon J., and Gillian Bendelow, *The Lived Body: Sociological Themes, Embodied Issues* (New York: Routledge, 1998).

Willis, Deborah, ed. *Picturing Us: African American Identity in Photography* (New York: New Press, 1994).

Wilson, Edward O. *Consilience: The Unity of Knowledge* (New York: Vintage, 1998).

Wolfe, George, ed. *The New Religious Humanists: A Reader* (New York: Free Press, 1997).

Wood, George S., Jr., and Juan C. Judikis. *Conversations on Community Theory* (West Lafayette, IN: Purdue University Press, 2002).

Wood, Mark. *Cornel West and the Politics of Prophetic Pragmatism* (Urbana: University of Illinois Press, 2000).

Wright, Richard. *Black Boy (American Hunger)* (New York: Perennial Classics, 1998).

Wright, Richard. *Eight Men* (New York: HarperPerennial, 1996).

Wright, Richard. *The Outsider* (New York: HarperPerennial, 1993).

Wright, Richard. *Native Son* (New York: Harper & Brothers, 1940).

Wright, Robert. *The Moral Animal: Why We Are the Way We Are: The New Science of Evolutionary Psychology* (New York: Vintage, 1994).

York, Sarah. *Remembering Well: Rituals for Celebrating Life and Mourning Death* (San Francisco: Jossey-Bass, 2000).

Young, Henry James, ed. *God and Human Freedom: A Festschrift in Honor of Howard Thurman* (Richmond, IN: Friends United Press, 1982).

Zee, A. *Fearful Symmetry: The Search for Beauty in Modern Physics* (Princeton, NJ: Princeton University Press, 1999).

INDEX